Pathways to the Gods

Also by Erich von Däniken

Chariots of the Gods
Return to the Stars
Gold of the Gods
In Search of Ancient Gods
Miracles of the Gods
According to the Evidence
Signs of the Gods

PATHWAYS TO THE GODS

The Stones of Kiribati

Erich von Däniken

Translated by Michael Heron

G. P. Putnam's Sons
New York

First American Edition 1982

First published in Germany by Econ Verlag
under the title *Reise Nach Kiribati*
First published in Great Britain 1982 by Souvenir Press Ltd,
43 Great Russell Street, London WC1B 3PA,
and simultaneously in Canada

Library of Congress Cataloging in Publication Data

Däniken, Erich von, date.
Pathways to the Gods.

Bibliography: p.
Includes index.
1. Civilization, Ancient—Extraterrestrial influences.
I. Title.
CB156.D344 1982 930.1 82-11308
ISBN 0-399-12751-8

Printed in the United States of America

Contents

	Letter to My Readers	vii
1	Journey to the Kiribatis	11
2	For Some Reason or Other	69
3	Mind: The Fundamental Basis of All Matter	101
4	Chasing Little Green Men (and Canards)	117
5	In the Promised Land?	149
6	Twilight of the Gods	195
	Photographic Credits	257
	Bibliography	259
	Index	263
	Introduction to the Ancient Astronaut Society	268

Letter to My Readers

> 'You can't blow dust away without making a lot of people cough.'
>
> Prince Philip,
> Duke of Edinburgh

Dear Readers,

A brainy man, whose field is our reading habits—I think it was Professor Alphons Silbermann—discovered that a 'reading generation' lasts four years. Work it out for yourself and I think you'll find he's right. From the age of two to six, brightly coloured picture books form the first generation of readers. Then come fairytales and tiresome school books, until the age of ten (nowadays!) when children start to read comics and in the case of smart girls and boys adventure and travel books and stories about animals. Early developers, at the age of about 14, use interesting factual books and the whole spectrum of novels as reading material. At 18 begins the first predilection for specialised subjects, which may last a lifetime or alter the rhythm of the reading generations, depending on a person's profession, private life, hobbies or on special events.

If I reflect on this rhythm, three and a half generations of readers have grown up since the publication of my first book in 1967. Anyone who was 16 years old in 1967 is 30 today. Perhaps we have already met, dear reader, perhaps you are one of the great mass of my public who can be relied on to be there when a new book by me comes out nearly every two years.

But of course many of my new readers come up against it when I confirm my 'old' theories in a new book with brand new items of knowledge. That is the fate of all hypotheses, even the most scientific of them. They must be developed. And I admit that this puts me in a dilemma every time. My starting points are clear to my faithful readers, but what sort of basic data should I give my new readers, so that they have firm ground under their feet amid all the talk of heaven and earth? I don't want to bore my old readers, but neither do I want to send my new adherents into the forest without a compass.

So I shall simply state in 'telegrammese' what I have been claiming for 14 years.

The world was visited by alien beings from space in prehistoric times. They are known as extraterrestrials in the literature on the subject.

The extraterrestrials created human intelligence by altering the hereditary material of the still primitive inhabitants. Scientists would describe it as mutation, an artificially produced change in the hereditary process. In my view the origin of human intelligence is not a chance result, not a winning ticket in a lottery with milliards of possibilities, but a planned intervention by alien beings from space.

The aliens' visits to earth also produced the oldest religions and the creation of myths and legends at the heart of which the facts about real events that took place in the past are handed down.

If these briefly sketched hypotheses had not been highly explosive, they could not have set off a global controversy. In fact I was sawing unashamedly at the foundation pillars of the traditional mental edifice. Equipped with knowledge that I had acquired over 14 years I was constantly crossing the frontiers between the territories earmarked by archaeologists, ethnologists, space-travel specialists and, inevitably, theologians. I freely admit that I had to tread on a lot of toes during my wanderings. And also that I was led into error in some special cases. No doubt about that.

But, and I found that out on my travels, there is a lot in my hypotheses. Books attacking me were published in every language in the world. A whole phalanx of authors ganged up to assail my global success, sometimes hitting below the belt. Drowning people hit out in all directions. I am tolerant about this. On the other hand an increasing number of books are appearing that take my theories seriously and even welcome them. Some of them are by well-known scientists.

The subject had global reverberations almost unparalleled in our century. It was not only my films *Memories of the Future* and *Message of the Gods* which contributed to this, the American super-films *Star Wars* and *The Empire Strikes Back* were also fertilised by my ideas. My faithful readers met situations on the screen that were familiar to them.

The pop group Exiled (RCA PL 25297) has hit the bull's- eye with their latest hit.

> It was thousands of years ago when a mighty armada of spaceships crossed a sea of stars. They were searching for planets suitable to continue and develop their life. The discovery and settlement of the planet earth also served this goal. We are only just beginning to decipher the descriptions of that fantastic event . . . And from now on we shall have a better understanding of whatever may happen on earth and in heaven . . .

The author, who is definitely 'not guilty' of the text, is delighted that his theses are so popular that they have passed into pop music. It makes me confident that the younger generation is wide open to futuristic ideas.

Dear readers, let us listen to the prophet Ezekiel, who lived *c.* 592 BC 'Son of man, you dwell in the midst of a rebellious house, who have eyes to see, but see not, who have ears to hear, but hear not.'

As for me I shall keep on blowing the dust away, even if a lot of people start to cough.

I invite my readers, old and new, to accompany me on some of my travels. They will learn much that is new and also read about the hardships a 'Sunday research worker' encounters on his travels round the world.

Sincerely yours,
Erich von Däniken

1 Journey to the Kiribatis

'Surprise and wonder are the beginning of understanding.'

Ortega y Gasset.

If it had not been for this letter from Cape Town, South Africa, I should never have dreamed of going to the Kiribatis:

> Dear Mr von Däniken,
>
> I know that you are a man with a lot of commitments and therefore I will not waste your time but come to the point.
>
> I have been intending to write to you about some definite evidence of 'gods that came from the sky'. During my time as a missionary in the Pacific, I was shown the graves of two giants who, the locals told in their folk-tales, came from the skies. These are well-preserved graves and each is approximately 5 m long. There are also many footsteps fossilised in the rocks and these are so numerous as to make photography quite simple.
>
> There is also a 'stone compass' and a site where the folk-tales say that the 'gods' landed. This place is most interesting because it is completely devoid of plant life and is in a perfect circle.
>
> If you are interested I would be pleased to follow it up and give you more information; if, on the other hand, you know all the evidence already, I shall not be offended not to hear from you.
>
> With every good wish and again many thanks for hours of good reading.
>
> Yours sincerely,
> Reverend C. Scarborough

I received this letter at the end of May 1978. A Protestant parson who was receptive to my ideas?

I thanked him by return, asking for the information he offered and also whether there were any photographs of the mysterious places or literature about them. Naturally I offered to pay any expenses he might incur. A month passed before Reverend Scarborough answered:

Dear Mr von Däniken,

Thank you for the reply to my letter. Firstly let me explain that I have no need of remuneration. I am only too happy to help you in your quest for information.

You inquire as to available literature. Unfortunately it is almost non-existent, and on the subject about which we will be corresponding there is no literature whatsoever. More's the pity.

I appreciate that you must hear news from 'cranks' all over the world, so it might be a good idea to establish my credentials from the start.

I am a Congregational minister in Sea Point, South Africa. Before coming to take up this position my wife and I and two children were missionaries in the Kiribati Islands (formerly Gilbert Islands) South Pacific under the authority of the London Missionary Society. We spent a period of three and a half years there and could speak the native language fluently. We travelled extensively throughout the 16 islands and spent many months on each island. We became aware of the strange and inexplicable ancient history of the islands very soon after learning the language.

The first thing that struck me was the fact that the islanders had two names for people. They themselves they referred to as *aomata*, meaning simply man in the plural. Anyone with a white skin and tall was referred to as *te i-matang*, which is translated literally as 'man from the land of gods'. As we got to know the islanders better we found that this difference between them and foreigners existed on all the islands.

As you may wish to investigate the matter yourself at some point, I must tell you that the islanders can be very uncommunicative to strangers unless you adopt the right approach. They are very religious. They are ruled by the Protestant and Catholic native ministers to a great degree and unless you make your peace with the ministers you might as well stay at home.

Be seen to mix with the islanders themselves and not so

> much with the government and European community and you will make headway. I am sure that you are a past master of all this kind of diplomacy.

The letter contained instructions about where to find the giants' graves and a description of the compass stones in the south of 'an' island, which, the missionary discovered, had lines scratched on them giving the bearings of far distant goals. It was also interesting to hear that the stones must have been transported from elsewhere, because that kind of stone does not exist on the island. My correspondent had this to say about the 'landing site of the gods':

> On this point I must give you two possibilities as I confess to have forgotten on which island it was. It was either Tarawa North or Abaiang, both of which are close enough to see one island from the other.
>
> If my memory serves me correctly, it was Abaiang. There the local *tabunia* (witch-doctor) keeps watch over this strange site. It is known to the islanders and they will readily tell you where the open site is to be found. It is a part of the island with dense undergrowth. The islanders go there secretly when the ministers are not watching to make their offerings to the gods.
>
> In this case you will most certainly need the help of the local *tabunia*. He will lead you as he did me through the bush until you come to the circle. There nothing grows, not a weed or a tree, and there is no living thing to be seen. He will tell you that anyone who walks over the large open circle will soon die. Why? Radiation or what? It is interesting when you are there to note that trees that have begun to grow leaning towards the circle have turned in their growth and leaned away from this open area. Nothing grows in the centre of the circle. When the Resident Commissioner visited the spot in 1965, he said to me that it must be radioactive. But radioactivity on a coral island? Again it is referred to in folk-lore as the landing place of the gods.

This minister, miles away and unknown to me, had got me going. I was champing at the bit: where were the Kiribatis?

There are four big atlases on the shelves of my library, but none of them mentions the Kiribatis. Three famous reference works, the *Encyclopaedia Britannica*, Brockhaus and Larousse tell me that there are 1,200 kinds of flea, but they've never head of the Kiribatis. Well-informed books of the seventies still do not mention them, these Kiribati Isles floating in the Pacific. They do exist, for I was there, and they are interesting fleas in that infinite sea.

As my pious informant had lived on the Kiribatis, they must exist. I asked everyone I could think of: 'Have you heard of the Kiribatis?' The answer was always the same blank look, followed by 'Kiribatis?'. Finally I wrote to Cape Town and asked my clerical friend:

> Where are the Kiribatis? How does one get there? Are there any flights?
>
> Where can I stay? Are there any hotels?
>
> What is the currency used on the islands?
>
> What sort of presents should we take with us for the priests, magicians and other local inhabitants?
>
> Should we look out for any special dangers such as snakes, poisonous scorpions or spiders?
>
> Are you still in touch with friends or acquaintances there? Could you give me the names of people I could get in touch with and to whom I could mention your name as a reference?

Reverend Scarborough answered promptly and helpfully. The mist around the Kiribatis was cleared away.

They consisted of a group of sixteen islands forming part of the British Crown Colony of the Gilbert Islands until they obtained their independence in 1977 and the name was changed. They float in the Pacific Ocean, have an area of 973 sq km and a population of some 52,000 Micronesians.

One can fly to the main island of Tarawa, with a port and the seat of government, from Nauru, the island republic, or Suva, the capital of the biggest Fijian island.

As gifts the Reverend recommended modern multi-purpose pocket-knives for the community leaders, cheap sunglasses for the fishermen and aspirin for the priests and women.

Reverend Scarborough wrote comfortingly that there were

no snakes or spiders, and although there were scorpions their bite was no worse than a wasp sting. The letter warned:

> The real danger lies in the sea. Never bathe in the sea, even if the islanders tell you otherwise. Sharks are a real danger to every swimmer, as are other forms of submarine life. I can't warn you too strongly: never bathe in the sea!

When I look back, I know for certain that we should have gone swimming if it had not been for this emphatic warning.

My unknown well-wisher invited me to get in touch with his old friends, the ministers Kamoriki and Eritaia, and said they were nice men who would certainly help me. Likewise Captain Ward of the ship *Moana Roi*, with his deep knowledge of the islands, could be helpful, since Ward was familiar with local legend and the islanders' holy places.

Contrary to the popular belief that I am a rich man who can make such journeys simply by putting my hand in my pocket, I always plan to visit several places in a particular region so that expenditure on travel does not exceed the potential income. Only too often, advance information turns out to be false on arrival, the fantasies of cranks, as the Reverend wrote, and then time and money are wasted. However, in 1980 a useful combination came up. The Seventh World Congress of the Ancient Astronaut Society was to take place in the summer in New Zealand. The AAS is an international non-profit-making organisation which discusses the subjects of my books.

New Zealand! That was half the cost of reaching my goal, the Kiribati Islands.

I dictated a letter to Reverend Kamoriki on Tarawa. Early in 1980 I had an answer written in a shaky hand which indicated that the parson was quite an old man. I read that Captain Ward had been pensioned off some years ago and returned to England, but Kamoriki and his family would be glad to receive me and my friends, and naturally we must be his house guests. That sounded good. Feeling very grateful I deciphered the postscript in tiny spidery writing: 'Have you got an entry permit?'

My secretary Willi Dünnenberger and I set the telephone wires humming. Who would give us a visa? During the last ten years we have travelled to the ends of the earth, but there were always embassies and legations in Berne representing the goals of our daring journeys. The Kiribatis are a blank spot in the diplomatic landscape of Switzerland. An official in the Ministry for Foreign Affairs gave us a tip: 'Phone the Australians or the English.' The Australian Embassy told me that they did in fact trade with the group of islands and gave them development grants, but were not responsible for visas. In London the Office for Pacific Affairs was able to tell us that Swiss nationals could obtain an entry permit on their arrival at Tarawa, provided they undertook not to stay longer than three months and could produce a return air ticket. Three months! It wasn't as if we were going to build huts on the Kiribatis!

We got our kit ready: four cameras with cases for object lenses, films, a small Geiger counter, a first-aid case, pocket-knives, sunglasses and aspirins. As always we tried to cut down as much as possible, but there was still a mountain big enough to make two men weak at the knees. We were in despair when we were saved by a tall young friend, Rico Mercurio, one of those rare people for whom nothing is too much trouble and who does not watch the clock when something important needs doing. Rico cuts diamonds and even more valuable jewels for a well-known Zürich firm. They are used to adorn the watches which the oil sheikhs give to the women in their harems. Rico said that after two years without a holiday a break in the Kiribatis, wherever they were, would do him good. We told him it would.

On 3 July 1980 our fully laden trio flew to Singapore via Bombay on a Swiss Air DC 10, flight 176. There we changed to Air New Zealand flight 28 to Auckland. There are 25 long hours of flying time between Zürich and Auckland.

These long-distance flights are horrible. At first you read a pile of newspapers you haven't had time to catch up with. More out of boredom than hunger you gulp down the rich meals. You clamp the headphones over your ears, you try to sleep, but your time rhythm is out of step and you can't. We watch the film of Agatha Christie's *Death on the Nile*, but even that does not kill time. At a flying speed of 850 km per hour you don't really notice anything, you have no point of reference—below there is nothing but water, then the

Australian desert and water again. The crew has changed three times since Zürich. The passengers are still draped in their seats, fed at intervals and supplied with information from the cockpit. Time stands still. Why on earth do reactionaries run the supersonic Concorde down? Why is the American super aircraft SST, planned so long ago, not being built?

We play a little game on our own. We think up things that could be offered to the passengers. Electronic games like Space Invaders. Or maybe occupational therapy—like embroidery or sewing mailbags. That would be something. And with the proceeds from these in-flight labours air fares that have risen to astronomical heights under the OPEC dictatorship might gradually be reduced. At a height of 11,000 m we even thought of a casino. *Rien ne va plus.* And in fact after a long-distance flight like this, nothing does.

I love New Zealand. It resembles the green landscape of the Swiss Jura with its meadows and spotlessly clean villages; there are hills and real alps, mountain farms, climbing tours, ski-lifts, limpid mountain lakes—just like home. But New Zealand has something we cannot offer—the sea. If anyone wants Switzerland plus sea, they should emigrate to New Zealand. Owing to the constant breezes from the Pacific, the air here is purer and tangier than in Switzerland in spite of the 40 million sheep. Forty million sheep and only 4 million New Zealanders. Let us hope that one day the sheep will not take over the government, following the revolutionary motto 'Four legs good, two legs bad' in George Orwell's *Animal Farm.*

Our onward flight from Auckland to the island of Nauru with Air Nauru was planned for 13 July. The fact that the flight was delayed for 24 hours had nothing to do with the number 13. The oddest airline in the world does not stick to timetables. We waited. We were tired and often rather hungry, a state explained by the consumption in the airport restaurant of a gruesome speciality of the country—spaghetti sandwiches. White worms in sticky sweet tomato sauce coiled inside two slices of cottonwool toast. They don't taste any better if they're heated. We waited and at hourly intervals swallowed this frightful creation of the New Zealand cuisine,

New Zealand! Before leaving this beautiful country for Nauru we were delayed for a seemingly interminable day, for Air Nauru seldom sticks to its timetable.

which is outstandingly bad in general. Songs from *The White Horse Inn*, whose redoubtable landlady by the Wolfgangsee would have sent all the cooks in the country packing, streamed from the loudspeakers for the umpteenth time during our 24-hour wait.

On the flight from Auckland to Nauru there were three passengers on board the Air Nauru Boeing 737, Rico, Willi and I plus nine members of the crew. Air Nauru operates with two twin-jet Boeing 727 passenger aircraft and two triple-jet 737s. The President of the Republic of Nauru is reputed to have said that Air Nauru was needed to fly in phosphate contracts, cheques, engineers and repairmen, but if a 'normal' passenger wanted to go along, he would be allowed to. That is certainly a rare occurrence, for the rich island has no tourism.

With its 21 sq km Nauru is an islet that lies just below the Equator on longitude 167° east of Greenwich. Nauru is surrounded by a reef that descends steeply into the open sea and consists of coral containing phosphate deposits. The wealth of this tropical island is based on phosphate. All 6000 inhabitants make their living directly or indirectly from phosphate, which is claimed to be the best and purest in the world. Dusty conveyor belts rattle down to the harbour with the indispensable fertiliser which cranes load on to freighters bound for Australia and New Zealand. According to the Annual Report of the Nauru Phosphate Corporation for 1979, reserves will last for another 14 years, although in that year alone phosphate to the value of 79,444,463 Australian dollars was sold. Given the present volume of exports, the phosphate deposits could be exhausted in five years. Then the island's wealth would come to an end. The export of coconuts and vegetables brings in very little.

A few years ago the government had the only acceptable hotel, the Meneng, built for Air Nauru pilots, engineers and businessmen in the Phosphate Corporation so that travellers used to better accommodation would at least have somewhere cool to stay. So the first thing that hits your sweaty face at the entrance is a blast from the air-conditioning.

The waitresses in the dining-room look serious and dignified. They bring you a menu, the front page of which offers rather simple fare: baked fish with sweet potatoes and corn on the cob with melted butter. But on the back there is something sensational: three Australian and two New Zealand wines, the Château Mouton Rothschild, 1970 vintage, for 35 Australian dollars, about £22.

We thought it was a joke or a misprint. This 1970 vintage from Bordeaux was the wine of the century. In Switzerland you cannot lay your hands on it for less than 400 francs: in first-class restaurants you would have to pay at least double that. Château Mouton Rothschild is a drink for sheikhs who ask Muhammad to avert his eyes for a moment when they transgress his ban on alcohol. It is no drink for ordinary mortals.

Rico said, 'Friends, this is our last evening before the Kiribatis. We don't know what awaits us there. I'll stand you a bottle.'

The waitress was flabbergasted when she saw Rico's finger pointing to the great wine. She could not move. As Rico's finger was almost boring a hole in the menu and he gave the terrified girl a look that was almost as penetrating, she trotted off behind the buffet and whispered to her pretty colleagues who began to giggle and stare at us.

The wine waiter sneered as he took the cork out. We were already beginning to suspect its contents when he handed us the costly vessel—bottle is an unworthy description in this case—a genuine 1970 Château Mouton Rothschild, numbered and with a drawing by Marc Chagall on the label. The Rothschilds always decorate their 'Mouton' with a drawing by a famous painter.

Whenever we raised our glasses the watching girls whispered and giggled. I stood the second bottle. This wine was the purest nectar, a drink fit for gods. Behind the merry wives of Nauru an Asiatic cook bobbed up, his hearty laughter making his white chef's hat wobble. The maidens squealed as if we were unwittingly drinking castor oil that would give us a busy time that night. We checked our clothing to see if there was something wrong or ridiculous about it. We were wearing correct tropical gear.

The Air Nauru pilot who had flown us over came into the room. As he spoke the local language, we asked him to find out why we had been laughed at for two hours. He nodded and strode—every inch an aviator—to the circle of clucking hens and soon returned to our table with the result of his mission.

'They're laughing, gentlemen, because they have found three crazy foreigners stupid enough to drink such an old wine and pay 35 dollars for it into the bargain. Bye-bye.'

We were not ashamed of our stupidity. Willi ordered the third bottle and I wrote the numbers of the labels in my notebook, knowing that this would be my first and last encounter with that unforgettable 1970 Château Mouton Rothschild: 242/443, 242/444 and 242/445.

We had to tear Rico away. Although we could not speak the language, he had made unmistakable visual contact with a beautiful waitress, an Esperanto understood by men and women everywhere.

The Air Nauru Boeing 727 was supposed to fly to Tarawa, the main island of the Kiribati group, at 6.30 a.m. on 15 July, but it took off an hour late. We were going to learn on more than one occasion that time over there has a different value from that of our own hectic world.

At seven o'clock we were in the little airport at Tarawa surrounded by coffee-brown and black men and women who were starting the day in a cheerful and leisurely way. They took no notice of us. No one grabbed our cases from us, as they do in South American and Arabic countries, no one dragged us towards a taxi shouting volubly. In the equatorial morning sunlight our presence seemed pretty superfluous.

In search of the right address for my mission, I turned to a young man who was idly contemplating the motley throng. Like the rest of the islanders, all he wore was the *tepe*, a brightly coloured rectangular piece of cloth, round his loins.

When I spoke to him he smiled and said in a guttural voice, *'Ko na mauri!'*

I did not realise then, nor even guess, that during that very morning, *ko na mauri*, thou shalt be blest, would become part of our vocabulary.

The islander asked, 'You speak English?'

The language, a relic of the English colonial days, helped me out of my difficulty, but in answer to my question about taxis he replied sympathetically, 'No taxi here.'

I asked if there was a hotel. Reverend Kamoriki had not answered that question. With an embarrassed grin, the boy said there was no hotel, only a government guest-house. 'Wait here,' he said and set off at a trot barefoot, the ingrowing toenails on his big toes obviously causing him no pain.

The Air Nauru aircraft had flown on. The crowd who had come to meet relatives had dispersed. A few locals who apparently intended to spend the day here turned their curious gaze on us and offered to help. We waited for our boy, who finally trundled up in a small clapped-out lorry. He drove us to the Otintai guest-house.

A remarkably nervous man, his high forehead pouring with sweat which he wiped clear of his eyes with a large blue rag, was daydreaming behind the reception desk. In easily intelligible English he explained that the government would not decide whether the hotel would strike until that afternoon and that in the meantime he could not accept any guests owing to the shortage of staff. I cautiously asked what the strike was about.

'People want to work longer,' he said wearily and wiped a stream of sweat from his eyebrows.

'People want to work longer?' I asked, my ears still ringing with demands for 30- and 35-hour weeks, for 7 and 8 weeks'

On the islanders' doorstep nature provides everything they need for living, free of charge. The closely packed coconut palms supply material for building houses and guarantee their basic foodstuffs.

holiday and retirement on pension at the maximum age of 60. 'Work longer?' I repeated.

The nervous gentleman explained that wage earners in the Kiribatis were pensioned off at the age of 50 with a reduced income. Those now on strike wanted the pensionable age to be set at a minimum of 55, for on none of the islands did the depressed economic situation offer the possibility of supplementary work. There was no industry, while copra, island handicrafts and phosphate from the island of Banaba were the narrow basis of the export trade. The only thing there was plenty of was manpower. After the first impressions on my arrival, I wondered automatically why the islanders wanted to work longer. Everything necessary for a peaceful life was supplied virtually free by nature: fish from the sea, palm trees for building huts in the permanently hot climate and nourishing fruit. Since these idyllic islands had been blessed with officials and administrations, since they had had to export and adopt the profit motive, the bacillus of that occidental sickness, the strike, had crept in. No, civilisation does not create happiness.

It was at least obliging of the sweaty black gentleman to let us dump our luggage in a corner behind his desk. It would have been embarrassing to descend on the pastor with bag and baggage.

The island of Tarawa is a typical atoll, a horseshoe-shaped coral island which from great depths protrudes only a few metres above sea level. Between the north and south parts of Tarawa lies a lagoon connected with the sea by natural channels. As the terrain is so frequently penetrated by water, the north of the island can only be reached by boat and is almost uninhabited, whereas the south is fairly thickly populated. That was where our little van jolted over the narrow strips of coral terrain.

From our seat high up in the back of the lorry we could see only a few stone buildings—government offices, churches, the hospital and a few private houses belonging to the better-off islanders. Palm trees provided the material for the indigenous method of building: bungalow-type huts of palm trunks and fronds. Often they have only one room. The wealthier permit themselves two or three rooms. The 'communications centre' is always the living-room where people gossip, eat, sing and sleep and even beget children.

In spite of the early hour and the pleasant breeze created by our speed, the humid equatorial heat made us pour with sweat. Our shirts and trousers clung to our bodies. Plumes of smoke from open fires spiced the close salty air. Our vehicle wound its way along a narrow road between palms, breadfruit trees and huts. The islanders waved to us; children ran alongside our wheezing lorry. The island of Tarawa seemed to be a haven of peace, but there was a strike on.

On our right we could see the calm waters of the lagoon, on our left lay small villages, while right behind them the huge Pacific rollers thundered against the reef as they had done since time immemorial. There were no seasons here. Every day the sun rose and set at the same time.

Our boy stopped the lorry outside the small unplastered houses. Pink curtains waved in the open windows, something we never saw anywhere else.

'That is Reverend Kamoriki's house,' said our driver.

One old lady and two younger women were watching us from a window. They disappeared like ghosts when we looked at them. The house had no doors, only open entrances, and as the pink curtains were drawn we could see into the interior: on the right, in the largest of the three rooms, stood a large mosquito-net-draped bed that had seen better times; the other two rooms appeared to be unfurnished. Our driver had gone into the house and was talking to one of the young women. A sad expression came over his normally cheerful face. He came up to us slowly and he obviously did not relish telling us what he had just heard.

'Reverend Kamoriki is dead!'

That was a shock. The Reverend was dead. I remembered the shaky handwriting, which was that of a very old man. The Reverend Scarborough also mentioned in his letter the name of his colleague, Eritaia. I asked about him. Yes, said our guide, Reverend Eritaia lived in the other house, but was a very, very old man, who certainly could not receive any visitors. Then he asked if the children of the two clergymen could not help us and led us into the courtyard of the adjoining house.

A coffee-brown man of about 35 with the thick black hair characteristic of the islanders crouched on the ground on a coconut mat. When he realised that we were there, he stood up and said with the ghost of a smile, '*Ko na mauri.*'

'Good morning, sir,' I replied.

Bwere, Eritaia's son, understood and spoke English very well, so that I was able to tell him about my correspondence with the Reverend Scarborough, the letter from Reverend Kamoriki and my mission, in particular that I was interested in the mythology of the island and had made the long journey to examine the places with their hidden secrets.

Bwere gave his visitors a long deliberate scrutiny: Willi and Rico who stood behind me sweating, and me, politely explaining my mission. After his inspection he asked, 'How long do you mean to stay on the island?'

We drove past villages behind which the giant Pacific rollers have been thundering on to the beach since time immemorial.

Beautiful girls sit outside their huts under the palms and prepare dried fish for the next meal.

Without thinking I answered, 'About a week,' and thought to myself that we could prolong our stay if necessary.

Bwere lowered himself to the coconut mat. With a superior smile he re-examined us closely and then burst out laughing.

'A week! You're crazy. You must come from a strange country to take such a cavalier attitude to time! You want to investigate a serious subject and you've only got a week! You need months to visit our islands, which are scattered widely.' He looked at us crossly. 'Go and loaf in the sun for a couple of days and come back when you've got more time . . . In any case, you can't do anything during the strike; there's no hotel room at the Otintai and no means of transport.'

I was cross with myself, with our frantic life, the tyranny of deadlines, the professional, family and financial pressures in which we hang like spiders in a web. Bwere was right, but we *were* there and it had been no short joyride. Nothing was going to stop us seeing and examining the goal of our journey, seeing it in person and checking it, in spite of the strike and although we could not spend months there. Reverend Scarborough had warned me to be very diplomatic when dealing with the islanders. I made a quick mental review of everything I had said so far. Had Bwere Eritaia been upset by my abrupt answers? Perhaps the islands' secrets were under a taboo and they were protected from the eyes of strangers. I tried diplomacy.

'The little we have so far seen on this marvellous island has made a deep impression on us. Your countrymen are friendly and helpful. We're sorry we can't stay here long. And we don't want to give any trouble. It would mean a lot to us even if we knew whether there was a school with a library which would tell us about the local mythology. We should be most grateful.'

Bwere, who had been so prickly, positively smirked. He himself was the government cultural official; the library and archives were under his care. He would open them for us and would also help us in our search for local lore.

The first and presumably the easiest stage on the way to our goal had been reached. I thought of some islets in the Micronesian Caroline Islands, north of the Equator. They had natural landing grounds on which a small propeller-driven aircraft could land. I asked if there were such landing strips on the Kiribati Islands.

With visible pride Bwere told me that they existed on the larger islands and that Air Tungaru, a small airline, flew a regular service between the islands. But, he went on, at the moment the machines were grounded because of the strike. I could ask the head pilot if he felt brave enough to break the strike, but he did not hold out much hope.

A beautiful woman came from the house and put three coconuts down in front of Bwere. He opened them with a skilful blow of his machete and gave us the half nuts full of refreshing juice. It is amazing how many things can be made from the empty shells—the white flesh is rich in vitamins. Drinking vessels, plant pots, lamps in which glimmering wicks float in oil and even brassières for adolescent girls.

Bwere gestured to us to sit down on the coconut mat. He gave us a lesson in local history. He and his fellow countrymen were Micronesians, but their language was related to Melanesian.

Bwere said that there were various theories about the origin of the Kiribatis. Some scholars claimed that their forefathers came from Indonesia and had interbred with a dark-skinned original race below the Equator, others said that they originally came from the South American continent, while still others traced their origins directly to divine beings who had visited the island in former times. I pricked up my ears.

Magic formed part of the Kiribatis' life, said Bwere. Although he was the son of a parson and a practising Christian, his eyes assumed a cryptic, almost fanatical look, but he did not elaborate on this vague statement. I did not pursue the matter so as not to destroy his confidence. Besides I had read all the relevant literature before my journey and there had been a lot about magic in the islands.

At the beginning of this century Arthur Grimble lived in the colony as envoy of the British Crown. He learnt the Kiribati language, shared their customs and usages and was so accepted by them that he was admitted to the exclusive sun clan Karongoa, a kind of secret lodge, which was a great honour. I read Grimble's book[1] and also his daughter Rosemary's[2] who published a scholarly edition of her

Teeta, the son of Reverend Kamoriki, was our guardian angel on the roads and in the steaming jungle.

father's posthumous papers. Of the islanders' magic rituals, which our friend Bwere did not mention, she wrote:

> There is one incantation for the protection of coconuts, another for help to steal one's neighbours coconuts and yet another to prevent theft; there is a formula to conjure poison into one's enemy's food and another to prevent it. Then there is *wawi*, fatal magic, and *bonobon* to make it ineffective.

Today six churches are trying to make the islanders renounce their magical practices. Catholics, Protestants, Adventists, Mormons, the Church of God and Baha'i are competing for the right way to save the Kiribatis' souls, for their manpower and the little money they possess.[3] They take over everyday life, root out customs and usages preserved for centuries, encourage unrestrained conception to increase the numbers of their flock, compete to build the biggest churches.

By dark hints, Bwere himself did not seem to find this development altogether favourable for his countrymen.

Suddenly a barefooted giant in tattered white shorts appeared in our midst. A massive muscular chest was beating under his T-shirt with the inscription Teeta. He smiled at us like a child and shook hands with everyone at the first break in the conversation.

'*Ko na mauri.* I am Teeta, the son of Reverend Kamoriki.'

The English of his sonorous rather guttural baritone was hard to understand. You had to get used to it first, but Bwere explained that his family invited us to supper and that the Kamorikis would be glad to put us up.

We thanked him politely, but asked if we could first check with the government hotel Otintai to see if we could get rooms. I mentioned our luggage and said that we did not want to overburden his hospitality. This circumspect refusal took ten times as many sentences as Teeta's invitation.

Bwere drove us to the Otintai in a Toyota delivery truck. When he spoke after a long silence, we heard that he wanted to help us.

'You must be free to move around; you need a car. I have a friend who will rent you his.'

He did not wait for us to answer and stopped outside a hut, next to which a small Datsun was parked under a palm-leaf carport—the Japanese also have a hold on Kiribati. For a couple of Australian dollars, we drove to the hotel in 'our own' car.

The sweating manager showed us to rooms 102 and 103 for one night. The next day it would be decided whether we had to leave the hotel because of the strike. When he handed over the keys, we took our luggage up to the first floor and opened the doors to two rooms which looked completely uninhabitable. In true Swiss fashion we got down to some spring-cleaning. We emptied stinking wastepaper baskets, gathered up the contents of overturned ashtrays, used rolled-up newspapers to sweep the floor clear of nutshells, cigarette butts and ragged underwear and fastidiously removed filthy sheets and blackish-grey towels from the shower and put them in the corridor—to be removed after the strike. Above us the air-conditioning hummed its monotonous song and wafted cold air at us, making the rooms an oasis in the humid heat in spite of everything. After a good wash we left the hotel and spent the evening with the Kamorikis. We were curious. Were we going to get just a little nearer our goal?

Teeta and Bwere were in evening dress—the former wore a pillarbox-red cloth round his loins, the latter a sky-blue one. Before entering the living-room we took off our shoes and stockings, for everyone went barefoot, including an old lady who shook hands with us and curtsied. She spoke to us in a melodious voice. She nodded, we nodded, we smiled when she smiled and we tried to say a few words of English, but made a mess of it. Bwere whispered that she was Reverend Kamoriki's widow, Teeta's mother.

Her polite son, who softened his harsh baritone in her presence, invited us to sit on three chairs placed against the left-hand wall, the most comfortable part of the room because it was next to a fan. Bwere and Teeta squatted next to us, tailor fashion.

An incredibly funny pantomime began. We sat speechless as if we were hatching ostrich eggs. The merry widow's chubby face radiated cheerfulness and affection. Could she be under the effects of some kind of drug? Her eyes twinkled, she nodded confidentially, a friendly gesture we returned. Sometimes, but I don't know if it was intentional, an eyelid closed briefly as if she was winking. In case this was a local custom, I winked gaily back. Marcel Marceau, that marvellous French mime artist, should have seen us. What a number he would have to add to his programme!

This comic performance was interrupted by three enchanting girls. They danced in barefooted to unroll a gaily coloured 'tablecloth' on top of the coconut mat. They, too, kept nodding at us, then disappeared silently to return with dishes and bowls which they laid out on the floor, along with plates and beakers.

Because we were hungry, we gaped rather rudely at the lavish meal which made our mouths water: green, yellow and red vegetables, raw and cooked coconut meat, honey-coloured sweet potatoes, steamed and baked fish, cubes of meat in spicy sauces, grilled breadfuit, rice. Only the official protocol stopped us from tucking in.

Three sweet little girls aged six or seven came up to us

quite unaffectedly and crowned our unworthy heads with brilliant wreaths of flowers that smelt of jasmine and orchids. Before we could thank them, the little fairies had vanished. Then widow Kamoriki, wearing a red dress with white flowers on it, stood up near the opposite wall and made a speech which Bwere translated. I took it down on tape and brought it home with me.

Widow Kamoriki said 'My late husband, who rests out there in the garden, offered you our hospitality—as is the custom. He told me to make you welcome—as is the custom. The wreaths in your hair mean friendship and peace—as is the custom. My daughters are happy to be able to cook and wash clothes for you—as is the custom. My sons are honored to be able to help you—as is the custom. I am only a foolish weak old woman who is fulfulling her husband's wishes—as is the custom. Our house is your house, our family is at your service—as is the custom.'

Mrs Kamoriki sat down and smiled at us. We were moved by the hospitality of the good-natured old lady. Although I was as hungry as a hunter, I stood up to express our gratitude and assure her that we visitors from a small country on the other side of the globe would be happy, during our stay on the Kiribatis, to learn what we had been unable to learn so far, and I offered our condolences on the death of the husband and father. I said that we would do nothing that would displease the late Reverend.

The old lady nodded amiably and gestured to us to start eating. We left our chairs and squatted on the floor like Bwere and Teeta, next to the buffet. Groaning dishes and bowls circulated; we used our hands to heap our plates with all the delicious food. At first, in the European way, I offered dishes to the women, who were huddled against the wall at a distance, but they solemnly refused. They did not laugh and smile again until they saw that we liked the meal. We were only too happy to stuff ourselves. It was an outstanding meal, not least in comparison with those hideous spaghetti sandwiches! When we could not eat another morsel, in spite of constant pressing, the women crouched by the remains of the food on the gaily coloured cloth and began to eat. If we had known of this custom we would have tamed our appetites and left more.

During the women's snack, we discussed our plans for the next few days with Bwere and Teeta over a cigarette. Bwere thought that the stone circle was at a holy place on the island of Abaiang, as Reverend Scarborough had also intimated in his letter. Bwere said that Teeta would try to procure a boat and enough petrol for us to visit the island, which was 50 km away.

Teeta asked if I had black Papuan tobacco on me. I hadn't and asked why. I was told that the place was taboo and that I would have to offer the tobacco as a sacrifice to make the magic of the place well disposed to us. Teeta firmly refused to obtain the tobacco for me. We had to buy it ourselves if it was to have any effect on the magic.

During our conversation, more than a dozen young men and women wearing only the brightly coloured *tepes* round their waists crowded into the room, whispering and stealing curious looks at the flower-crowned foreigners. I have never seen better-looking people. We forgot the legendary circles, compass stones and myths; we were under the spell of vital animated nature. The group formed a row which gave us time to admire the graceful movements and sensuous charm of the young islanders, creatures from some paradise thought long lost. I began to understand the biblical giants and sons of the gods who had sinned with the daughters of man. Were they aware of their beauty, their fascination?

They sang. Beginning softly, then swelling to become a polyphonic choir. Two boys strummed guitars and a third drummed the rhythm on a hollow treetrunk. There were many vowels in the melodious song. After the third song boy and girl singers sat on the floor. A young girl knelt down before us and shouted in English, 'Now it's your turn!'

We had to sing! After a quick consultation, we found out that our trio would have to be reduced to a duet. Rico said even at school he had been asked to keep his mouth shut because of the horrible noises he made.

Our hosts and the choir gazed at us expectantly. Willi and I bravely rendered 'Blue Suede Shoes', not as well as Elvis Presley sang it, but well enough to be asked for an encore. Willi and I sang 'My Love Is Like a Red Red Rose'. It was a smash hit. There was a standing ovation, with applause, laughter and jumping about—a horde of happy children in paradise.

The locals live in palm huts which are open all round. At any time of day you can see women, children and their neighbours exchanging gossip.

The young islanders continued the lively programme until they broke off abruptly after a song, squatted again and the young girl repeated her challenge.

'It's your turn!'

Because this could go on for ever, but also because our repertoire was running dangerously low, I tried desperately to think of a crowning melody. I had an inspiration. I went over to the singers and asked Bwere to explain to them that we would all sing a well-known European folksong 'Frère Jacques', a lovely, but simple, melody. I hummed the tune, then sang it aloud with the words and it took only a quarter of an hour before the musical Kiribatis were singing 'Frère Jacques' at concert pitch.

Owing to this communal singsong, our soirée with Mrs Kamoriki, the close of our first day on Tarawa, gave us the freedom of the island. People waved at us when we walked down the street. When we came to the big *maneaba*, the community house, the centre of every village, people shook hands with us and pulled us—a gesture of special friendship—into the room that was open on all sides beneath the roof of brown palm fronds. It is the meeting place at which the old men do the talking and the young men are only allowed to join in if they are asked to. Women have no place here. They did not seem any the worse for it when they greeted us cheerfully. When we looked inside the open huts which were scattered around, we could see them in animated conversation with their daughters and neighbours. Often they sang and sometimes we even heard 'Frère Jacques' during our stay.

Over breakfast at his house the next morning Teeta said that the sea was too rough for a small boat and that he could not get enough petrol for a large boat because of the strike.

We ate bread from the breadfruit tree. Each year every tree bears up to a hundred fruit the size of a Rugby football. These trees grow plentifully on the Kiribatis and the whole fruit as well as its green shell can be used. When ground, it makes a pleasantly spicy-tasting porridge. Cut in slices like pineapples and grilled on hot stones, it forms a coarse-grained cake which tastes infinitely better than our industrially made bread.

It tasted good but I could not enjoy it. The idea that the crazy strike might cripple our venture ruined my appetite. I took a drink of cold coconut milk and said, 'Yesterday Bwere mentioned a small airline. Couldn't we fly to Abaiang?'

Teeta looked at me in surprise and answered in his agreeable baritone, 'Okay, let's try it.'

Teeta, who was our guardian angel during our stay, went to the airport with us so that we could meet Gil Butler, the Australian head pilot of Air Tungaru. We met a bad-tempered aviator, who was swearing like a trooper about the strike and asked sarcastically if we Swiss had a magic wand to cure the chaos caused by the misguided islanders. Fly to Abaiang? No, he could not fly today because of the strike, but tomorrow a colleague was flying a government deputy to Abaiang and if there were empty seats we could go with him and be back by evening. Being a best seller turned out to be a blessing. Gil Butler had read my book *Return to the Stars* and invited us to dine at his house the following evening. I accepted gladly as I saw a further chance of getting to one or another of the islands with him, regardless or in spite of the strike.

We sensed that Teeta was embarrassed by the strike and was doing his best to keep us in good spirits. He led us into a hut and pointed to a bundle of sticky black plugs of tobacco which smelt revoltingly of liquorice, damp cigarette butts and—I have to say it—sweaty feet. This tobacco was imported from Papua, New Guinea. I bought a bundle, convinced that the stench would drive out even the most evil of spirits once we stood on the threshold of the holy places.

After this shopping session Teeta drove us to the little village of Bairiki and left us in the library, which had an astonishing assortment of books. It contained literature from all over the Pacific. Thank heavens there was no strike here. Polite attendants brought us all the books we wanted. I was particularly interested in one book,[4] the joint work of twenty-five local authors, which contained the saga of the origin of the world and the Kiribatis. Under the humming fan which slowly stirred the heavy air in the room, I read a remarkable addition to my collection of prehistoric myths.

In the beginning, a long, long time ago, there was the god Nareau, the creator. No one knew where he came from, no one knew who his parents were, for Nareau *flew alone and asleep through the universe*. In his sleep he heard his name called three times, but the one who called him was a 'nobody'. Nareau awoke and looked around him. There was nothing but emptiness, but when he looked *down* he perceived a large object. It was Te Bomatemaki, which means 'earth and heaven together'. Nareau's curiosity drove him to go down there and he paid a cautious visit to Te Bomatemaki. There were no living beings there, no men, only he, the creator. He circled the world he had discovered four times, from north to south and from east to west, and he was alone. Finally Nareau dug a hole in Te Bomatemaki and filled it with sand and water. He mixed them together to form rock and ordered the rock, together with the void, to bear Nareau Tekikiteia. That is how Nareau Tekikiteia, which means 'Nareau the Wise', came into being at the command of Nareau.

Nareau, the creator, now ruled over Te Bomatemaki, whereas Nareau the Wise was on earth. They were able to speak to each other and decided to separate the heavens from the earth. After great efforts their plan succeeded. Then Nareau the Wise created the first thinking beings, to whom he gave names such as these:

Uka, which means the concentrated power to stir the air.
Nabawe, which means the concentrated power of age.
Karitoro, which means the concentrated power of energy.
Kanaweawe, which means the concentrated power of dimension (distance).
Ngkoangkoa, which means the concentrated power of time.
Auriaria, which means the concentrated power of light.
Nei Tewenei, which means comet.

That, then, is the commonest version of the myth about Nareau, though there are some variations. Arthur Grimble[1] supplies an important amplification: 'And when the work was done, Nareau the creator said: "Enough. It is finished. I go, never to return." And he went, never to return, and no man knows where he lives from that day to this.'

There are sparkling stones in this tradition that fit perfectly into the great mosaic of the gods-astronauts theory.

The creation god Nareau flew alone and asleep in space, when someone, who was a nobody, called him by name and woke him. Looking at this from a modern standpoint, we can imagine an ideal spaceship whose pilot has been put into a deep sleep by a special process to check the activity of his body cells until he comes to a place which makes his organism start up again at a desired point in time. For some time space travel doctors have been discussing various types of physio-chemical deep sleep to keep astronauts alive over long distances and periods of time until *x* hour. When the ship's computer confirms by radar that the spacecraft is approaching a solar system, the deep sleep is terminated. 'His name rang out and Nareau awoke.'

The newly awakened pilot looks around him, but all he can see is the blackness of space, but *below him* he sees a planet from which the gravitational attraction of a solar system is effective. 'Then Nareau looked down and perceived a large object.'

In possession of his faculties once again, the pilot decides to land on the third ideal planet of this solar system. 'Nareau stretched his limbs. He wanted to know what kind of an object it was . . . He went down and set foot on it cautiously.'

The astronaut reconnoitres the whole planet from the air and recognises the prerequisites for life, but sees no kind of life. He decides to plant the seeds of life. 'At that time there were no spirits and no men, only the mighty Nareau.' Perhaps the methods used were too complicated to find their way into popular myths and be understood. For example, Nareau could have blown blue algae out of his spaceship. He could have diffused bacteria or, but less probably, scattered the seeds of hardy primitive types of plant. 'Nareau dug a hole in the earth and filled it with sand and water, he mixed them together to form rock . . . and ordered [it], together with the void, to bear the earth [Nareau Tekikiteia]. That is how Nareau the Wise came into being.'

It may be that the nickname 'the Wise' originally stood for 'spirit' or 'endowed with a soul'. Life now begins where once the sterile void reigned. From this prehistoric beginning two creative elements were active. Nareau, the creator of all being, and Nareau the Wise, who started terrestrial development. 'Nareau the creator was now over Te Bomatemaki, whereas Nareau the Wise was on the earth.'

But it is amazing to find a creation myth with concepts such as 'concentrated power of energy', 'concentrated power of dimension', 'concentrated power of time', and 'concentrated power of light'.

My imagination is not powerful enough to guess what the first Kiribatis understood by all this. Unwittingly they handed down clues to the powers of an inconceivable god. Nowadays it is easy to realise that the concentrated power of light comes from the concentrated power of energy. We know about the researches of Professor Eugen Sänger (1905–64) into photon drive for spacecraft, which, once outside the field of gravity of a solar system, could accelerate them to incredible speeds. Today we know that all acceleration is connection with the 'concentrated power of dimension'. This acceleration implies the ability to cover vast distances, a process which is coupled by a natural law to time ('concentrated power of time') and age ('concentrated power of age'). Time dilatation is an empirically proved natural law.*

The amplification by Arthur Grimble[1] of what I noted down in the stuffy library at Bairiki is important.

'And when the work was done, he said: "Enough. It is finished. I go, never to return." And he went, never to return and no man knows where he lives from that day to this.'

On interstellar journeys at very high speeds disappearance for ever is plausible. I seemed to hear that fantastic song by the pop group Jenghiz Khan:†

> They were called gods for there was no other word for the aliens. Yet in the books of the ancients it says that when the aliens come again we shall no longer exist. Only their traces remained on the earth. Water and sand had covered everything, and no one knew what message they brought, the aliens. They were called gods for there was no other word for the aliens.

I do not know who inspired the authors to write those words. When friends ask me if I was the author, I can swear under oath that I wasn't!

The same questions crop up in all creation myths. How did our forefathers know that life on earth is of extraterrestrial origin, that it was introduced by chance or according to plan? There were no witnesses to the creation of the Kiribatis—Nareau flew to our solar system while asleep and initiated life—or of any other peoples. To whom could Nareau tell the story of his mission? Is it all the luxuriant imagination of the storytellers, with no real background?

The Bible tells us that God created heaven and earth when the earth was still 'without form and void, and darkness was upon the face of the deep'. So there was no reporter present at the biblical act of creation, either.

As none of the traditional mythological acts of creation had eye-witnesses or chroniclers, yet creation myths are concentrated on *one* major event and handed down all over the world, the logical answer to all questions was obvious. Millions of years after the creation, the god responsible

* *According to the Evidence*, pp. 201, 204.
† Jupiter Records, No. 101777.

returned to the scene and told the men he had created about the events that lay so far back in the past—told them about their own creation.

I can see ethnologists pulling sour faces as if they had been forced to suck a lemon, when they hear my simple explanation of the origin of such puzzling myths. They say that we must take all the circumstances into consideration, put many possibilities together and accept the simplest explanations first. After a headlong gallop the interpretation of pure science ends in clouds of psychological incense which bring tears to our eyes.

Myths survive in different versions. For they are retold over endless stages from tribe to tribe, from family to family, sometimes with additions, sometimes with omissions. Every criminologist knows how widely the statements of witnesses of one and the same set of facts can differ. It takes comparisons and the rejection of subjective embellishments to disclose the core of what really happened.

In the Kiribatis I also came across the story of Baby Terikiato, who was stolen and taken to the lady of heaven Nei Tetange niba. The lady flew away with the babe and brought him up as a demigod. In the west of the island, which is called 'the bird of Biiri', Terikiato, by now a young man, said to the lady of heaven, 'Look these birds are wonderful, for they look like men.' By a magic spell the young man's foster-mother made his arms strong and his body powerful. Terikiato climbed on to the back of a bird and held it fast. The bird turned in circles, then flew up to heaven and 'they came into land of the heavenly ones'. There Terikiato stood before the house of the celestial lady Ne Mango Arei, who asked him, 'Where do you come from and what kind of creature are you? No man may visit me, for I am different from mankind.' In spite of the obvious difference they produced four children. They called the first one Niraki ni Karawa, which roughly means heaven circler. The legend expressly says that after the offspring were born Terikiato returned to earth and at first settled in Samoa.[2]

This story is reminiscent of the heavenly flight of the Babylonian Etana,* who rose from the earth on the back of

* *Gold of the Gods*, pp. 120–21.

A small aircraft jolted us high over the rough sea to Abaiang. When we landed this primitive character brought us coconuts. He was the only long-haired islander we saw.

an eagle and described the globe from a great height, but also of the Japanese legend of the Island Child,* who was carried off to the heavenly fields by a fairy and later returned to earth. This theme recurs like a *leitmotiv* in many, many popular legends.

On the evening of my 'theoretical' day in the Bairika library I wondered if the tantalising myths had left tracks that were still warm, those tracks which Reverend Scarborough had put me on to. I could not wait for the morning.

At 6 a.m. Teeta, our dark angel, took us to the airport, a thoroughly misleading description in comparison with airports in our own latitudes. A twin-engined propeller-driven plane ferried us over the choppy sea to the island of Abaiang, which even in the early morning was steaming in the oppressive heat. Inside a bamboo hut, the airport building, Teeta, waving his hands about and continually pointing to

* *According to the Evidence*, pp. 124–5.

us, was talking to some men, two of whom set off at a trot and soon stopped near us with a Toyota lorry. They piled our luggage into it and rattled off with us over the deep potholes in the natural road, without sparing the vehicle.

Abaiang is a narrow atoll 32 km long, flat as a board and smothered in lofty coconut palms and breadfruit trees, from which heavy fruit dangled. It took us two hours to cover two-thirds of the island's length.

'Teeta, do you know where the circle under taboo is?' I asked, when we stopped in the village of Tuarabu. He shook his head and confessed that he did not know the place himself, although he had lived on Abaiang as a boy when his father was minister there. However his mother, our cheerful hostess, had told him who to look for to lead us to our goal. Thank heavens! Teeta left us, as lightfooted as a gazelle.

We took a look at the settlement of 451 souls. As on all the islands, the huts were made from materials obtained from the coconut palm. Many of them stood on blocks of coral which aided ventilation and kept out the vermin and crabs which abound as well as preventing the rapid rotting of the palm trunks in the muddy earth, which was even more important. Some boys clambered up palms, which at a height of 30 metres provide fronds for roofing, and threw down nuts which the men skilfully cut open to offer us the milk in a gesture of welcome. In this heat coconut milk quenches the thirst better than a whole carton of Coca Cola. It consists of 45 per cent water, the rest being valuable albumen, fat, carbohydrates and minerals, offered free and in profusion by nature.

Teeta reappeared in strange company. A skinny old woman shuffled along by his side. She was an uncanny figure in a kind of black robe, with a veil on her head. Her companion was a wrinkled old man, who carried a whimpering baby under his left arm and dragged along a boy under school age with his right hand. None of them said a word. The baby seemed to be hungry, but I did not think the old lady's bosom was still a source of nourishment, if indeed she still had one under her robe.

As we rattled off, packed like sardines in the back of the Toyota, Teeta lost his gaiety. 'Give the woman ten plugs of tobacco and a box of matches,' he whispered in his dry baritone. The nun in the black robe nodded; the old man bared his teeth which were brownish yellow stumps. Some consolation, I thought, that even on the Kiribatis old age exacts its tribute and that not all islanders are good looking.

At the southern tip of the island the Toyota braked sharply. The village was called Tebanga and here our companions underwent a sudden change, as did the young people who had run up to see us. Laughter died away. Fear showed in everyone's eyes. Even Teeta, usually so cheerful, froze up.

'What's wrong?' I asked.

Teeta silently shook his head towards the tropical green vegetation in front of us, but said nothing. The nun in the habit walked into the bush on a path the width of a handkerchief. We formed a silent procession behind her. Grandpa and the little boy began to whimper now, in addition to the baby. They were afraid.

The old lady stopped and signalled to us to do the same. She emerged from the thicket into a clearing. A curtain of luxuriant tropical bushes hid her from sight. She advanced to perform the solemn ceremony, holding the stinking tobacco. What happened next took place against a background of noises—the songs and chatter of exotically coloured birds, the thunder of the nearby surf and the smack of our hands when we killed the mosquitoes which were tormenting us. In our opinion mosquitoes prefer the sweetness of the sinful foreigner's blood.

Without wasting a glance on us, the old lady returned and walked past us. Teeta, his fear of evil spirits removed by the tobacco sacrifice, gave me a gentle push and said, 'Go on!'

The clearing was a small space free of tropical undergrowth. It was obvious to me at first glance that nothing could grow there—even without magic. The area was thickly carpeted with coral pebbles. Larger round stones marked out a rectangle in which stood a coral monolith the height of a man, like a gravestone, a suspicion which a walk round it confirmed. I saw the name and date of death of some islander carved on the stone. The plugs of tobacco were smouldering under a mussel shell the size of a tortoise. The three of us were alone. The islanders watched us curiously and fearfully from a safe distance.

What we had found here had no connection with the mysterious holy places mentioned by the Reverend Scarborough. Remembering that we must always be polite to the islanders, we swallowed our bitter disappointment, took a couple of photos and joined the phalanx of waiting natives. The old lady with the magical abilities felt that the effect of the tobacco sacrifice was confirmed and looked at us proudly. Grandpa and the baby whimpered; in fact they never stopped. Even the comparatively enlightened Teeta submitted us to a critical scrutiny. Had his friends changed? Were they leaving the burial ground satisfied? But deep down we could not help feeling angry.

Not until the Toyota was some distance from the place which was so uncanny and evil to the islanders did the spirits of our companions brighten. Teeta handed round a plastic flask containing a milky lukewarm brew. As no gift must be refused, I overcame my revulsion and took a hefty slug, closely observed by everyone. I must have twisted my face into horrible grimaces, which Teeta took for those of a connoisseur, for he laughed delightedly, helped himself generously, then held the flask to the mouths of my friends. Besides the lady magician, Grandpa and the baby let the nectar run down their gullets and became tireder and tipsier every minute.

'What's this we're drinking, Teeta?'

'Sour toddy!' he replied as prosaically as if it had been a whisky sour.

'What is sour toddy?'

He stopped the Toyota and pointed with the bluish tip of his index finger to the top of a coconut palm. Large and small bottles hung down from the branches under the leaves. The sugar-rich sap was being tapped. It had to stand for three days, then it started to ferment and knocked you over like new wine—a dangerously intoxicating drink which put the almost teetotal islanders out of action for hours. So the coconut palms even provide alcohol!

The sour toddy worked like a sedative, otherwise I should have gone berserk! Back at Tuarabu, our starting point, the old men were standing round gossiping, just as they had been early that morning. Striving to be a civil European, I asked Teeta to find out about the place where we had been taken in error. Our dark angel discovered from his fellow countrymen

The circle under taboo lies in a rectangle free of undergrowth and covered with coral pebbles. The islanders are convinced that anyone who enters the rectangle will die soon afterwards.

that we had visited the tomb of a mighty warrior, whose great spirit still protected his family today. All honour to the warrior, I said, but our goal was a stone circle without a tomb, a sterile area, where even palms could not grow.

If we could have heard the noise of the ideas revolving in the old men's heads, it would have sounded like millstones at work. One could see from their expressions how they were racking their brains. A light gleamed in the eyes of one old fellow. Yes, he said, there was such a circle in northern Tarawa. There, from time immemorial, dwelt a 'mighty spirit', who would not tolerate being disturbed, so that even birds which flew over 'his kingdom' fell to the ground dead. That was music to my ears—but was it really our goal?

Before the sun rose from the sea on the fourth morning of our island life, we went to dinner at the house of head pilot Gil Butler, as invited. Gil told us that he had not the faintest idea where we should make for. He said that the island of

Tamana mentioned by the Reverend Scarborough was 544 km away as the crow flies, whereas northern Tarawa could easily be reached by boat. He added that the next day he could fly us to Tamana for 225 Australian dollars per hour's flying time. I decided to accept this offer.

The natural landing ground at Tamana did not look too good from above and this proved to be true on landing. The runways made by Air Tungaru are no more than narrow strips hacked out of the palm forest and roughly freed of stones and undergrowth. The islanders are supposed to maintain them and chase off stray dogs and grunting pigs. They say, 'Eng, eng,' yes, yes, and a week later, the grass has grown again, the tropical rain has washed up more stones and animals are grazing and grunting again. Each landing and take-off demands tremendous skill on the pilot's part. Our aircraft did a slalom between animals and stones. Teeta made for a palm hut in which three of the ground staff were lounging. Our dark angel now knew exactly what we were looking for and explained to his countrymen, stimulating their imagination and memory with gestures and a torrent of words. Finally he approached with the three men.

'Over there are graves with very large beings!'

'Are you sure?' I asked. Teeta cross-examined them once more. They nodded and pointed straight across the landing strip to the hedge of palm trees. Draped with heavy gear, we marched off. High noon. The sun was perpendicularly overhead. It grilled our bodies pitilessly. Sweat poured off us; it even ran into our shoes. Palefaces that we were, we dared not take our shirts off or we would have been one big blister in no time. Swarms of greedy mosquitoes bit us through our clothing. Our camera straps cut into our shoulders as if into raw meat.

Graves covered with brown coral stones came into sight.

'Is that it?' I asked. My tongue was sticking to my gums with thirst and disappointment.

'*Tiaki, tiaki.* No, no, it's further on,' said the ground staff, cutting their way through the dense undergrowth, dodging round palm trees, climbing over mounds of stones and graves until they beamingly announced, 'That's it!'

We looked blank and disappointed. Teeta sensed that this was still not the right place. He turned away in embarrassment and scratched his enviably thick hair.

How were we going to make any progress? The locals were willing and doing their best. It was up to us.

'Teeta,' I began carefully, 'tell the men I am grateful for bringing us here and that we are surprised to see so many ancient graves, but that the graves we are looking for are very large, much larger than these. They were built for giants who were twice and three times as big as you and I. And these graves must be located somewhere on their own, not in the middle of a burial field like this one, for the giant men would not tolerate either life or death anywhere near them.'

Our indefatigable interpreter entered the circle of men, who looked quite cheerful in spite of the burning sun and oppressive air. I could see that Teeta was doing his utmost to explain what the white men wanted to see. One of them started to talk to our friend and assured him that there were larger graves at the end of the island, larger than the biggest one here.

'Are there other graves in the vicinity?' I asked.

'Eng, eng,' yes, yes, they agreed enthusiastically. I realised that we would only be on the wrong track again. I took paper and pencil from Willi, sat on a grave and questioned Teeta about the circle.

'Is the grave you're talking about bigger than any grave here?'

'Eng, eng.'

I called to a man and asked him to draw the burial mound. He did so with rudimentary lines.

'Now draw the other graves surrounding the big one.'

He drew the layout of a whole cemetery. It was not the place we were looking for. Obviously politeness prevented the Kiribatis from saying 'no' to a foreigner when they could not satisfy his wishes. I dreamed up a story.

'Listen. A long time ago there were two big men, much bigger than Teeta. They came from a distant land, perhaps even from heaven. They were so strong that they could throw the canoes of your fathers into the air like coconuts. Your people made them drunk and conquered them with a magic charm. Then they killed them and threw their bones into a deep grave so that they could never cause trouble again. Do you know where those graves are?'

They listened attentively to Teeta's translation. After a

lengthy silence and much deliberation, a man stepped out of the group.

'One tomb of the giants lies at the southern tip of the neighbouring island of Arorae.'

'Are there also large stones which point to islands lying far out to sea?'

Yes, the man assured me, he had seen such stones when he lived on Arorae with his father. The island was not visible from our present location. At a distance of 80 km, it was the furthest south of the sixteen Kiribati islands. Ought we to risk flying there on such vague information? Owing to the strike Gil Butler had only a limited amount of petrol, but by now he was so infected with the prospecting fever, that he overruled us. Within half an hour his aircraft was hopping down the runway. It was two o'clock and the equatorial sun was beating down as strongly as at noon.

Arorae, too, boasted three natives dozing in the shade of a shelter made of palm fronds; here, too, animals were grazing on the runway. But the ground staff had bicycles! Teeta asked the usual questions and we were directed to an old man who was reputed to be well versed in the local topography. We swung into the saddles of two rusty old bikes.

The lively old man, flattered at being asked to give information, explained with a wealth of gesture were the giants' graves and the navigation stones were to be found. With renewed hope, I reflected that the island was only 4.5 km long and a few hundred metres wide, so that anyone who'd grown old there must know it like the back of his hand.

When I asked Teeta to chase up more bicycles, the news spread like wildfire. Fourteen strong, we cycled back to the so-called airport. I pressed coins into the hands of the riders whose cycles we had asked to rent and our expedition set off on the 4 km stretch, which is no distance under civilised conditions. In Arorae it was a cross-country rally of the most testing kind—through quagmires and fine sand, across ill-kept fields through luxuriant tropical undergrowth, constantly tormented and attacked by swarms of mosquitoes.

The old man had lived up to his promise.

On the northern tip of Arorae, directly behind the *maneaba*, the community house, there was a rectangle marked out with neatly arranged flat stones. The stone wall rose one

The second giant's grave was destroyed to make room for this *maneaba*, the community house of Arorae.

metre above ground. There were no graves or gravestones. Five paces from the putative giant's grave was a square shallow hole. The sunlight was reflected from the water it contained. The Reverend Scarborough had mentioned two giant graves. Where was the second?

Teeta found out that years ago, when the *maneaba* was built, the islanders needed extra space and had removed the second grave. They were not afraid to do so, because there was nothing left of the spirits' magic or the giants' bodies. Whether terrestrial or extraterrestrial giants had been buried here, I was not surprised that the spirits had evaporated, their bones dissolved in the brackish water.

So now we stood in front of a burial mound measuring 5.3 by 2.9 m. There was no question of rummaging about under the pile of stones—what was to be found? Besides Gil Butler had to be back before nightfall. At all events we should depart with the definite impression that this was an ancient myth-

Leaving Arorae Airport.

ological grave. We paid a silent tribute to the memory of the Reverend Scarborough and asked ourselves where the navigation stones were. We were told that they were at the opposite end of the island, far beyond the landing strip.

If it had not been for the ubiquitous strike, we should have taken it easy and flown back another day, but we had to make the most of what was presumably our only chance. The rally was repeated, but there was no question of cycling, once we had left the primitive country track. Dehydrated as we were, our march through the sand dunes was torture. Sometimes I found myself having hallucinations of the kind described by desert travellers saved from death by thirst.

My heartbeats hammered in my temples and echoed in my head. Only ten minutes away from our goal, I fought down a faint-hearted inner voice which said give up. I tottered along behind Teeta and could not look at Willi and Rico whom I had enticed to share this adventure. I heard them panting

Sighting stones ravaged by wind and weather are planted in the ground, forming a diagonal in a rectangle marked out by stones.

behind me and could imagine their reproachful looks. Suddenly I was wide awake, or was I seeing a mirage?

No. The monoliths that were my goal were there, close to the surf. One lay on the ground, another stood upright. All my efforts were forgotten.

Large stones, ravaged by wind and weather, protruded from the ground, once carved into rectangles, now gnawed by the teeth of time. They were all enclosed by a rectangle of small stones. An unimportant burial field of the kind I had seen umpteen times in other parts of the world?

My senses were alert again and I noted that the upright monoliths (easily the height of a man) pointed in different

The bones of a mythical giant are reputed to lie beneath this pile of stones. In the background, participants in our cross-country rally.

A mirage? A field with monoliths close to the surf.

directions. I also discovered dead straight grooves cut into the top of the stones—signposts to distant goals.

We consulted our compass and maps.

One line pointed undeviatingly southward to the island of Niutao, which belongs to the Ellice Islands, a group of nine atolls, and is 1800 km away as the crow flies. Another groove pointed south-east to West Samoa, 1900 km away as the crow flies to the east of the Fiji Islands. A third line was aimed at the Tuamotu Islands in the South Pacific, 4700 km away as the crow flies, and after that approximately at the Hawaiian Islands. Once again a thank-you winged through the air to the Reverend Scarborough at Cape Town!

Two of the navigation stones were made of granite, which does not exist on Arorae, three had the characteristics of volcanic stone and the others consisted of material from the coral reef.

I toyed with many of the ideas which always crop up when I am confronted with prehistoric navigational problems, as I was here on Arorae. It is unanimously accepted that the islanders have always been able to solve simple navigational problems with the help of the stars and their knowledge of currents. But this does not solve the biggest puzzle of all, how the first, the very first, seafarers reached goals of whose existence they had no inkling. When they set sail from the coasts of their home island, they did not know where they would land, nor had they any idea how long the voyage would last. If the goal was just anywhere, experience gained on the outward voyage would not help their return, because the stars change their positions, and currents and winds do not stay in one direction. If we accept, as is done today, stars, currents and winds as navigational aids, we presuppose that the earliest seafarers knew about difficult aspects of astronomy, marine currents and wind movements, a state of knowledge which had not been generally reached by our early forefathers.

I remembered a recent conversation with the ethnologist Dr Robin Watt in the museum at Wellington, New Zealand. Questioned about such navigational problems, Watt claimed

Stones as tall as a man, compass stones, point to distant islands. Many of them have collapsed, eaten by wind and weather.

that he could not see any difficulty. The Maoris, for example, the Polynesian people of New Zealand, knew that there were archipelagos to the north-east, such as the present-day Fijian, Tonga and Samoan Islands. So all they had to do was steer in a general north-easterly direction in order to reach land somewhere among the network of islands. Once they had landed, the local inhabitants would help them to sail further.

At first this sounds quite reasonable, but then doubts about this 'solution' of the problem arise. Setting off in a 'general north-easterly direction' presupposes a precise idea of what that means and especially the knowledge that there are islands in the sea somewhere in that direction. Catamarans, rowing-boats, canoes and even sailing boats could easily sail right through the wide-meshed net of islands without making a landfall. A journey to 'somewhere', with no return! Obviously there are navigational aids for the experienced seaman even when there is no land in sight: refuse carried by the waves, tree-trunks, the bodies of animals. But they are minor aids which are of little use at night or in stormy seas.

When I hear all the explanations and check them, I feel that the prehistoric seafarers must have known their goal very precisely before they set forth and that they took plenty of supplies with them. Did they operate on the basis of knowledge acquired over the centuries or were they instructed by their mythological 'gods'?

Who brought the stones here? Who put them in position? Who knew about the specific directions in which 'invisible' islands lay? The only concrete witnesses in a desert of questions are the navigation stones which stand before us in the glaring sun and the mythologies of the Pacific which without exception speak of flying beings, their 'gods'.

A central myth is the legend of the bird Rupe, which is attributed to the Maoris, but nevertheless appears among other peoples in countless variations.

According to one version, Hina, one of Rupe's sisters, married Tinirau, who took his wedded wife to a distant island, made her pregnant and shut her up in a house which he surrounded with a 'protective screen'. This not only prevented Hina from leaving the house, but also stopped strangers from forcing their way in. When the time to give birth approached, there was no one to assist Hina. In her need she cried out, 'Rupe! Rupe! Come and help me.' Soon there was a whirring noise above the house and the bird Rupe shouted to his sister, 'I'm here, Hina!'

The bird Rupe could not reach his sister until he had bored a hole in the protective screen. After a difficult birth, Hina asked to be flown back home. But first Rupe was to evacuate Tinirau and his countrymen and then she would follow. Rupe explained that he would have to ascend into the sky three times. The islanders clung to Rupe's back. He flew them far away and tipped them into the sea. After three flights, he collected Hina and her baby. High in the air, Hina saw bodies and articles of clothing floating in the sea. She asked why he had killed them. Rupe replied, 'They did you wrong when you lived in their country. They imprisoned you and no one helped you during childbirth. So I was angry and threw them all into the sea'.[5]

Our Rupe was a strange charter plane!

The Kiribati legend of Te Bongi Ro, the 'Black Darkness', relates that those who dwelt in heaven landed before men existed. Before their return they left a founding father behind on every large island. The names of these legendary fathers are interesting—Bai Matoa, Matinaba and Matiriki and the rest—for they all correspond to descriptions of stars and constellations. Are these tracks that are still hot enough to lead us to the begetters of the navigation stones?

The ancient temple of Te Mahara on the island of Raivavae in French Polynesia is still considered to be the point where the mythological god Maui landed after his space flight.[6] There is a similar legend originating from the first inhabitants of Atu Ona, one of the Marquesas Islands. On it is the small mountain of Kei Ani, which is looked on as a temple, although there are no signs of a man-made building. The first Polynesians called the mountain Mouna tuatini-etua, 'Mountain of Many Gods', or Mouna tautini-etua, literally, 'Mountain, on Which the Gods Landed'.[7]

I get no special pleasure from proving my hypotheses with so many myths and legends from the Pacific. It is no effort on my part, there is such an abundance of them. So I shall play some aces from my hand.

Legend says of Ta'aroa, the god of creation of the Society Islands: 'Ta'aroa sat in his mussel, in the darkness of eternity.

The mussel was an egg which drove through endless space. There was no heaven, no land, no sea, no moon, no sun, there were no stars. All was darkness, dense all-pervading darkness.'[8]

During the last century venerable priests told ethnologists about the god Jo: 'Jo moved through the infinity of space. The universe was in darkness, there was no water anywhere. There was no trace of sunrise, no brightness, no light.'[8]

The oldest legends have this to say about the god Tagaloa on the Samoan Islands: 'The god Tagaloa floated in the void, he created everything, he was alone. Before him there was no heaven, no land, he was all alone and slept in the vastness of space. Nor was there any sea, nor did the earth exist then. His name was Tagaloa fa'atutupu nu'u which means something like "cause of growth".'[9]

Hawaii, presumably influenced by Christian missionaries, has the triune god Ku kau akahi, a contraction of the names of the gods Ku, Kane and Lono. Kane is the creator, who created men 'in his own image'.[9] Needless to say, Kane came from the darkness of space. The prayers offered to him praise his home at the firmament:

The wandering stars,
the immovable stars,
the moving stars of Kane,
countless are these stars.
The big stars, the small stars,
the red stars of Kane.
O infinite universe!
The great world of Kane,
the great sun of Kane,
they move in the vast expanses
of the universe.

Today if you ask the Kiribatis, Maoris or any other islanders about their traditions, you will meet with incomprehension. They no longer know anything about their ancient gods. Missionary activity in the Pacific buried ancient cultures, set up new ones and banned the oral transmission of 'heathen' memories. For what is left we can thank the ethnologists who, at the turn of the century, recorded what was told them. The ethnologist Robert Aitken has described what a Sisyphean task it was.[5]

'It was disappointing to find that most people admitted they knew nothing about pre-Christian sagas. Almost everyone could repeat psalms or long passages from the Bible, but very few could or would tell me what must have been common knowledge before the introduction of the Bible.'

Thus old, important, undoubtedly explosive knowledge disappears into the maws of time. It is absurd when towns and unique buildings are bombed to dust and ashes in today's crazy wars. But when important evidence of our common past is wiped out with the palm of peace in the hands of clergymen, it is downright madness. I cannot prove it, but I am sure that there must have been references to the compass stones of Arorae in the old traditions if they had not been zealously rooted out. So five stones stand there upright and point to distant goals with their grooves, while eight monoliths lie half a metre above ground. We shall never learn what technique enabled the primitive islanders to aim at unknown points in the open sea.

The government of the Kiribatis, which has not been in power long, does nothing to preserve the stones. They are known only to a few old men and they have not got the secret of eternal life.

We arrived in Tarawa as night was falling. We were met at the airport by Father Hegglin, a Swiss compatriot, and Dr Rosina Hässig, who was working for the World Health Organisation at Tarawa Hospital. The tea, relic of English colonial days, that we drank with Dr Hässig moistened our parched throats and restored our spirits. Naturally I could not wait to ask her about the legendary magical circle that was reputed to exist in north Tarawa. 'Never heard of it,' she said, but added after a moment's thought, 'If anyone knows about it, it's our medical superintendent. He is from here, grew up in north Tarawa, studied in America and then came back home.'

Without further ado she took me to see the superintendent to whom I put my question straight out so as not to bother him unduly.

He gave us a benevolent appraising look, as do all consultants, and diagnosed the case.

'Why do you want to find the circle?'

'May I conclude from your question that this magic circle exists?'

'Yes, it does. For untold generations it has been taboo and my countrymen are convinced that it is fatal to anyone who enters it. Do not get any wrong ideas, it is no enormous giant circle. It's comparatively small and its centre is laid out with a rectangle of small stones. If you will take my advice, do not visit the circle!'

That wasn't diagnosis, but therapy by a skilful doctor who knew how to wield the scalpel. 'Are you superstitious?' I asked with a grin.

He laughed. No, he said, he did not believe in ghosts and spirits. Ultimately there was a scientifically possible explanation for everything, but until one was found we should not casually dismiss the experience of his compatriots during long years of observing what went on in the magic circle. For example, they had noticed that animals which ran through the circle contracted mysterious diseases. 'Was there any question of radioactivity?' I intervened. No, that could be excluded because artificial radioactivity had only existed since the work of Marie Curie in 1903, whereas the odd happenings had been observed from the earliest times. The head doctor had no explanation for me, but he confirmed the existence of the magic circle mentioned by the Reverend Scarborough.

Although there was no service at all, we were still staying at the government hotel Otintai, in spite of the strike. We were allowed to stay and that was a good thing, because all our destinations were easier to reach than if we had accepted Teeta's repeated invitation to his parents' house.

Our dark angel came for us at 7 a.m. In spite of the strike he had laid on a boat and three cans of petrol so that we could chug off to northern Tarawa. After an hour and a half's journey through the lagoon we reached an islet barely as big as a football ground. Teeta asked for five plugs of tobacco and matches. I still had them on me and was glad to get rid of the smell. At first I had thought the stink would keep the mosquitoes at bay, but they love the scent of heathen smoke sacrifices. Teeta took tobacco and matches from me and used his right hand to throw them into the water over his left shoulder. 'Why are you doing that?' I asked. He said that this was the place where one had to offer a sacrifice to the sea god, to ensure a safe return. Although he was a parson's son, Teeta's Christian faith did not seem to have a very deep and convincing foundation. Like everybody else when the pastor was not watching, he still propitiated the spirits for safety's sake. We were half-way there when he paid tribute to the sea spirit.

Thousands of crabs were scuttling along the beach of north Tarawa. Prepared in advance, we took Teeta's polite announcement that he had to ask the natives about the location of our circle as a necessary civility. We waited. We waited three whole hours in the burning sun. Had it not been for the Reverend Scarborough's impressive warning, 'Never bathe in the sea,' we should have been only too glad to plunge into the clear water. Friendly, smiling islanders paid their respects to us and gave us coconut milk to drink.

Once again Teeta returned with a small Toyota lorry. Again he was accompanied by an old man who showed the way to the magic circle. He guided us to a clearing in the tropical undergrowth with a square marked out by stones inside it. At the top, outside the enclosure, was a large inverted mussel. Thank heavens it wasn't a tombstone! That was my first thought and then I was silent.

Our trio exchanged hesitant looks. The talk of dangerous magic had infected us. We suddenly felt rather faint-hearted but sensed that we had to put on a brave front for the anxious natives. Teeta's gaze rested on us, silently saying, 'Friends, give up! Don't tempt the spirits!'

We took our bearings. Before us lay a circle 14 m in diameter and in its centre a square with sides of 5.1 m marked out by small oblong stones. This square was the only remarkable feature. Not a plant, not a blade of grass grew in it, although there was luxuriant vegetation all round. Admittedly the square was dotted with pebbles, but there was still enough space between them for something green to thrive. In the tropical hothouse heat, ground that is cleared today is overgrown tomorrow. Moreover, no palm trees grew towards the zone that was taboo, but that could have been coincidence.

In spite of the head doctor's warning not to expect anything colossal, we were disappointed. To look as if we were doing something, we aimed our Geiger counters along both diagonals of the square. The pointer did not budge. When Willi made to enter the square, Teeta held him back in an iron grip. This was very odd, because we had not had to appease any evil spirits with vile-smelling tobacco. Like spectators watching a big match on the centre court at Wimbledon, the natives could not take their eyes off us.

We paced off the ground close to the magic circle, but found absolutely nothing worthy of note, just jungle full of rampant vegetation. It still seemed odd that it came to an abrupt halt outside the circle. Was there a family clan which kept it clear—because of tradition or to make fools of outsiders? Why should a family lumber itself with this work just for the sake of a practical joke? Conditioned by the climate, the islanders make only the minimum effort needed for existence.

I approached the old man and asked him if there was a priest or village sage who could tell us about the island's past. 'Eng, eng,' he nodded and led us to a hut outside which a corpulent man sat like a Buddha. Forewarned, I fished for tobacco and matches. The Buddha lit the smoke sacrifice and we crouched in a half-circle round him, like the others.

In guttural English that grated on our ears, the Buddha told us that the circle we had seen was reigned over by the oldest and mightiest of the spirits. He would not tolerate any kind of life in its vicinity and even killed birds which flew over it. There were a few more similar areas on the island, but the one we had seen belonged to a powerful spirit. Anyone who disregarded warnings of his power would soon pay for it with his life.

'How does he die?' I wanted to know.

The Buddha intoned, 'We do not know, no one knows, the spirit kills with his power.'

For years I have visited the holy places of all kinds of religions at which miracles have happened. These miracles happen at Lourdes, Fatima, the Convent of San Giovanni Rotonda, Guadeloupe and Iborra; they happen all over the world. The prevailing view is that faith, the ardent will to be healed, works the miracle. There must be a reason for miraculous cures attested by doctors. It is a positive miracle-working faith which only unbelievers dismiss contemptuously as superstition. I asked myself whether negative results could not be affected by similar psychological impulses. Frivolous visitors, permeated with the deadly power of the magic circle, still close to belief in gods and spirits, suffer death or disease as soon as they enter the zone which is taboo. Perhaps that is the explanation of the events which the islanders have been recounting since the distant past and in which they still believe.

I share the medical superintendent's view that mysterious magical phenomena will be given a logical scientific explanation at some time or other, but I doubt if they will be found by academic thinking. Research which seeks to measure, count and weigh everything categorically excludes what cannot be weighed or measured. But there are powers which cannot be captured even with the most delicate technical instruments. The Kiribatis' early forefathers related (and their living descendants confirm it) that the magic circle brings death. I could not find anything extraordinary, but I am not arrogant enough to claim that the islanders are the naive victims of their belief in spirits. So long as unusual phenomena cannot be measured, weighed and counted, they will be dismissed as miracles or superstitions. Until the day when a convincing explanation is given, the stone circles of Arorae can be registered as a miracle, with the proviso of Michael Faraday (1791–1867) that nothing is too wonderful to be true.

Teeta did something I would not have dared to do as a foreigner. He stopped the garrulous Buddha in full flow and urged us to leave. He wanted to finish the trip through the lagoon before the onset of darkness so that his watchful pilot's eye could steer us round the knife-sharp coral reefs which had sliced through many a boat before. In addition, sharks and octopuses wanted their supper in the evening.

We were happy to follow our dark angel, because we had no desire to watch a fight between a native and an octopus. One man acts as living bait and swims into its clutches. Then at the precise moment when the octopus wraps its tentacles, tactile organs for seizing its food, round its prey, a companion leaps into the water and kills the creature by biting it between the eyes.[1] We did not witness one of these gruesome combats, although they are still supposed to take place as a sport in the southern Kiribati Islands. Thank heavens, too, we did not have to see sharks being caught. Once they have been lured by bait of meat, divers cut up their bodies with sharp knives. Sharks' genitals are highly prized by the islanders as aids to virility—sex aids from the sea. The method of killing smaller fish as long and as thick as an arm is unchanged. The fisherman sticks the hooked fish in his mouth like a flash and bites its head off.[10] It is said that many natives only lisp because the fish bit quicker than they did.

The ebb tide dragged our boat more than a kilometre out to sea. Ten islanders waded out to us. The sun sank on the horizon in a purplish-red ball of fire. With the help of the islanders we pushed and dragged the boat in. Crabs crawling over our feet and calves felt most unpleasant. The lights of Baraiki twinkled in the darkness and were reflected in the entrance to the harbour of south Tarawa. Beach fires flickered. Oil lamps made of coconut shells smoked in the huts. The palm groves were full of lovers. Songs floated over this island paradise. Night had fallen on the Kiribatis.

My curiosity was not satisfied; there was still a trail to be pursued. I gave Teeta the Reverend Scarborough's letter to read.

> I mentioned the footprints of the giants said to be the footmarks of the gods as they walked throughout the islands. They are very large, perfectly shaped footsteps in the rocks and are found on nearly all the islands. Some are to be found just outside the village of Antebuka, almost on the sea side of the island, but there are much better examples on other islands. If you walk about 300 yards from Antebuka towards the nearest habitation you will find them in the rocks about 50 yards from the sea-line. If you have some idea that perhaps the islanders themselves have carefully carved these prints in the rocks . . . then you must ask yourself why? For what purpose should the islanders on 16 islands undertake to manufacture marks in the hard rock? Bearing in mind that they have little or no tools, that would be nonsense. The local verbal customs say that they are the footprints of gods who came from heaven.

The fact that we had not yet seen the Reverend Scarborough's footprints did not mean much, because we had not asked about them, but it seemed astonishing that even Teeta looked at us uncomprehendingly. But the hunting fever had us in its grip; equipped with such precise data, we set out hunting for the fourth time.

The area so accurately defined in the letter was an absolute abomination. If my readers might suspect from previous descriptions that Tarawa was a paradise of ideal beauty and sweet odours, I must let them see the other side of the coin. The stretch of 50 yards from the waterline was one big cloaca.

The islanders have no WCs in or near their huts. Since the days of their ancestors they relieve themselves on parts of the beach. So that the backsides of their lovely bodies are not pinched by octopuses or tickled by other water fauna, huts on piles have been built in the water. In urgent need they can reach across two palm trunks which sway like tightropes. At flood tide natives drunk on sour toddy can relieve themselves into the sea, at ebb tide on the rocks far below. These WC huts are insular communications centres. Kiribatis crouch next to each other on the thunder seat for hours, exchanging news—a community united in the same business.

This centuries' old custom of leaving human waste on the beach for the sea to remove had a logical extension when the blessings of civilisation came to Kiribati. Unlike human refuse, tin cans and Cola bottles, plastic wrappings and broken tools, do not decay, nor are they all carried far out by the tide to destruction. Back from the sea, they disintegrate on the beach—slowly or not at all.

This was the aspect of the 'catchment area' pinpointed so accurately by the Reverend Scarborough. After our previous experiences, we had to take this indication seriously, too. Whether our search was too cursory in the absence of gas-masks or because we were upset by the news that flying would stop owing to the strike, I don't know, at any rate we left the beach near the village of Antebuka without stumbling on the giants' tracks.

After lunch, Teeta came up, all smiles. He had spent the break doing some research. He said we ought to go to the village of Banreaba where there were footsteps of the kind

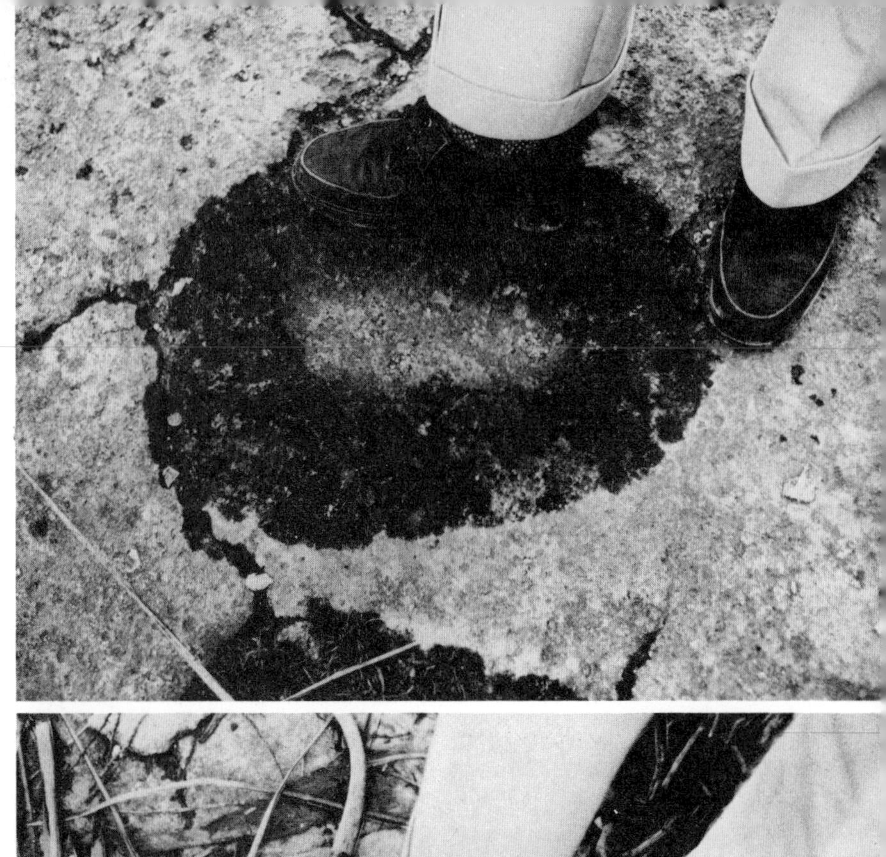

we were looking for on land belonging to a relation of his. The plot was called Te Aba-n-Anti—'Place of the Spirits'—or Te Kananrabo—'Holy Place'.

This information actually did lead us to footprints of various sizes. A giant must have walked on incredibly large feet to leave prints 1.37 m long by 1.14 m wide stamped in the rock like greetings from prehistory. One left footprint had 12 toes and a palm tree was growing out of it. Odd. The giant with the enormous feet was obviously accompanied by others with smaller feet, some of them presumably children. Most footprints had six toes on both feet and were impressed a good centimetre into the ground.

In the library I found a copy of *The Footprints of Tarawa*[11] edited by the Polynesian Society. It had informative footnotes about the giants' prints. According to legend, they were made by the giant Tabuariki, who was so tall that he could pick coconuts from the tops of palm trees without stretching. He has his place in the legend 'Te Bongi Ro', the black darkness. According to this tradition he was one of the second crew of celestial beings who are supposed to have landed on the island of Banaba. And where does the palm tree come from? In the fortieth year of this century it was planted by a clergyman so that it would overgrow the legend about Tabuariki, the gentle art of botanic missionary work.

The Footprints of Tarawa, which was scrupulously documented, mentioned several places with giant's footprints. I would have loved to visit them, but the comparatively close targets could not be reached without a boat or an aircraft. Owing to the strike they were as remote as the moon. So I had to leave the sites near Banreaba for others to investigate.

According to the most recent research, the Kiribatis have been inhabited for at least 3000 years. Three thousand years without a written tradition is a very, very long time. The 'gods' were quite right to leave the rock with permanent traces which would testify to their presence into the distant future.

We must ask ourselves how such footprints originated. An obvious idea is that they were chiselled out of the rock. The

On the edge of the village of Banreaba we found prehistoric footprints, both gigantic and normal. Most of them have six toes on each foot.

samples that we saw and photographed did not give this impression. They had natural curves round heel and toes. The alternative theory that they were made by people of enormous weight collapses. Many tons would have had to be pressing on the soles of the feet. More conceivable than that is the absurd idea that the landing legs of a scout-craft from a spaceship were perpetuating themselves. More plausible is the possibility that the prints originated when the rock was still hot and pliable—or had not yet acquired its present-day form. The prints of naked feet pressed into a layer of fine volcanic ash can become tufa by weathering and so preserve the traces. Even the outlines of feet pressed into clay can dry out over the centuries and petrify. I do not know when the giant footprints to be found in many parts of the world will find a convincing scientific explanation so long as visits by extraterrestrials are excluded.

We learnt from Gil Butler that an Air Nauru plane would fly to Nauru next morning, possibly the last for some time as the strike was disrupting flights more and more. We would willingly have tacked a few days on to our original week and—inspired by the islanders' timeless sense of time—we almost did so, if we had not faced up to our Western end-of-term feeling on the eve of the flight. We ate our supper sadly as if it had been a last meal before an execution. We tried to work out if the long journey to the Kiribatis had been worth while.

We had seen one of the giant's graves mentioned by Reverend Scarborough, we had seen the magic circle. Now we knew that this evidence of a distant past existed, that they were still taboo to the present-day islanders, even though they all profess to belong to an imported religion. We could not fathom the reasons for their fear of the magic circle. And then there were the navigation stones whose goals we had verified with maps and compass. For how much longer would they bear silent witness to the navigational abilities of primaeval islanders? Exposed to wind and weather the stone mysteries will crumble to dust. The giant footsteps also existed. The Reverend Scarborough who had spent three and a half years on the island had given us hard facts.

The best kind of proof of the former existence of extraterrestrials is in the traditions. Nareau, who flew through the cosmos while asleep and was awoken by a cry, the bird Rupe, who appeared noisily and evacuated the inhabitants of an island, the names of worshipped beings from space, whose names stand as synonymous for the first gods.

Bwere was there to say goodbye, bringing greetings from Teeta's friendly mother. He smiled indulgently.

'In a short time on our islands you have seen mysterious places which I haven't seen in my 35 years. You have achieved much, but I don't envy you—I don't want to be a European. When do you rest, when do you have inner peace? Where do you get the energy for your frenzied existence? You reach your goal, but you squander your life.'

On the edge of the runway, with the engines turning, I could not explain to Bwere what drove me on or where I got the energy from. It is the pressure present even when I am asleep, it is the desire to get on the trail of the 'gods' regardless of where in the world they manifest themselves.

Teeta, our dark angel, stood to one side. He looked at me trustingly. He asked, 'Will the old gods return?'

'They will, Teeta, they certainly will.'

Below us Tarawa floated in the ocean like paradise lost.

2 For Some Reason or Other

'What a sad age
When it is easier to smash
an atom than a prejudice.'

Albert Einstein (1879–1955)

The hanging stones of Stonehenge, near Salisbury, have inspired many different opinions about their origin and significance. I thought that nearly everything had been said on the subject, but scientific research into Stonehenge and other similar strange stone groups in recent years makes the dead monoliths as evergreen and topical as ever. It is as if they themselves were continually asking permission to take the floor. With so much new and exciting material, I feel as if the stones are addressing me; I cannot relegate them to the archives yet.

Every tourist in England is advised to look into the mystery of these silent witnesses from prehistoric times. He will not have to look far. There are more than 900 noteworthy stone circles dotted over England, Scotland and Ireland. This journey into the past along good roads is pure pleasure—once you have got used to driving on the left. For long distances you drive through what might be considered parkland.

But your holiday enjoyment becomes an adventure when you visit the alien world of the great stone blocks, the megaliths, and try to imagine yourself in the age when the mysterious complexes originated. You soon lose your way in a maze of question marks. What message have these stone monsters? Have they an intelligible meaning to us? Can they be important to us in any way?

Below I give a catalogue, a small selection of worthwhile sites to visit.

Scotland

— The stone circles of Brodgar and Stenness are on Mainland, the largest of the Orkney Islands, about 16 km west of the town of Kirkwall.

— The stone circles of Garynahine, Cnoc Fillibhir and

Callanish are on the west coast of the Island of Lewis in the Outer Hebrides, about 22 km west of Stornoway.
— The stone circles of Cullerlie and Sunhoney are 21 km west of Aberdeen on the B9119, a road branching off the A944, which runs from Aberdeen to Alford.
— The stone circle of Old Keig is located only 5 km from Alford.
— The stone circles of Balquhain and Loanhead of Daviot lie 26 km north-west of Aberdeen, 5 km from the village of Inverurie, to the right and left of the A96.
— The stone circle of Temple Wood is 1.6 km south of Kilmartin on a small country road which branches off from the A816.

Ireland

— The stone circle of New Grange is located 42 km north of Dublin, 5 km east of Slane, on the road to Drogheda.
— The stone circle of Lios is 19 km south of Limerick, 5 km north of the village of Bruff.

England

— The stone circle of Swinside is 8 km north of Millom on the north-west coast.
— The stone circle of Carles Castlerigg is 1.6 km south-west of Penzance.
— The stone circle of Stanton Drew is 11 km south of Bristol.
— The big stone circle of Avebury is 10 km west of Marlborough, in the middle of Avebury village.
— The stone circle of Rollright is north of Oxford, some 3 km north-west of Chipping Norton.
— The much discussed and much written about stone circle of Stonehenge lies north of Salisbury, 4 km west of Amesbury. Just after the A303 and the A344 fork you stay on the well-signposted A344.

Those are the fifteen best-known megalithic monuments

The stone circles of Avebury.

I have visited. To my way of thinking Rollright and Stonehenge can serve as representative of the other 900, for they were the scene of the exciting discoveries, the results of which are undoubtedly applicable to the other megalithic centres as well.

The mists and shadows of 5000 years of past enshroud Stonehenge. The experts are at least unanimous on this dating. They date the first stage of its construction to 2800 BC, in the Neolithic, the Late Stone Age, the third epoch in the history of mankind that began in the sixth millennium BC. The great pyramid of Cheops in Egypt had not yet been built, nor was the Sphinx crouching in the desert at Gizeh.

If we accept the most widely held hypothesis, some architect must have set to work around this time. It is hardly credible that he undertook the planning on his own account without a patron or employer. The complex was on too gigantic a scale for that. Who were the builders? Stone Age priests or mighty rulers? We cannot find out, for writing had not yet been invented, a state of affairs which must certainly have been a major obstacle to the extensive planning.

The brilliant architect who made a start at some point in time could refer to centuries of observations of sun, moon and stars, or so it seems if we look at the rock-hard facts. Many generations must have marked out the light and shadow of sunrise and sunset on the ground, and studied the phases of the moon and movements in the firmament. We shall never know how these astronomical data were handed down, for, as I have said, there was no writing then. All we know is that when zero hour came in Stonehenge the architect must have had a mass of proven information at his disposal and that the wealth of accurate data was collected through observations over long periods without any kind of technical aid.

Ostensibly on the basis of this traditional knowledge and with a commission unlimited in scope in the bag the architect took a look at his workmen's tools, which were made of flint, bone and wood, and realised that his task of erecting a temple for celestial observations would take a thousand years. So he relied on future generations carrying on the good work after his impressive beginning, especially as the precision he sought for did not permit botched workmanship. This Stone

The trilithons of Stonehenge.

Age farsightedness, this belief in the future, is astounding.

The first stage consisted of a circular enclosure with an entrance of two large blocks of stone and the so-called Heel Stone outside the circle. Later a second stone circle was set up inside the wall-like enclosure for accurate predictions of celestial phenomena, e.g. sunset at the winter solstice or moonrise at the summer solstice. It was marked out by 56 holes which probably held poles in order to aim at specific sight lines.

So that they could move accurately within the mathematically fixed points, the constructors adopted from the 'international bureau of weights and measures' the Megalithic Yard of 82.9 cm, which remained the unit of measure for thousands of years.

The first architect was not only a brilliant mathematician and astronomer, he was also a formidable clairvoyant. He included 4.5 tons of heavy stone colossi in his plan. Seven hundred years after building was begun, these bluestones—

so called because of their colour which shows up best when they are wet—were transported over a distance of 400 km. It is noteworthy that they were envisaged in the original plan.

When I first began a thorough study of this extraordinary structure I asked myself how did the collected knowledge get into the hands and heads of the first Stonehenge master builders when there was no writing. For all archaeologists agree that there was none. And I wonder how they could anticipate the future and make use of the theorem of Pythagoras, who lived c. 570 BC, i.e. more than 2000 years after building began, in the ground plan of Stonehenge. I do not understand it. Which came first, the chicken or the egg?

King James I (1603–25) wanted to know more about the confused mass of stones at Stonehenge. And as kings can act without parliamentary authorisation, he wasted no time in commissioning his court architect and stage designer Inigo Jones (1573–1652) to get to the heart of the matter.

Jones was impressed by the primaeval complex. He noted some 30 stones, each weighing about 25 tons and 4.3 m high, arranged in a recognisable circle, even though some of them had fallen. He observed that the standing stones had projecting pegs and that the lintels had holes to receive them.

Jones sketched a monolithic circle of five great trilithons made of sarsen, a greyish-yellow sandstone, and the massive undressed Heel Stone outside the inner ring.

What did Inigo Jones tell the king? He said that Stonehenge was the ruins of a Roman temple inscribed to Coelus.

Some years after this investigation a trilithon—two upright stones with a lintel—fell on to the so-called Altar Stone. On 3 January 1779 the next of the stone gateways collapsed.[1] The teeth of time were gnawing at Stonehenge.

It looks as if kings took more interest in our mysterious past than the potentates of our own day do. They can barely cope with the present, let alone the future. King Charles II commissioned John Aubrey, an antiquary, who had studied the stone circle at Avebury 30 years previously, to visit Stonehenge. In 1678 Aubrey registered 56 holes, which have since been known as Aubrey Holes.

What did Aubrey tell the king? He said that the idea of its being a Roman temple was nonsense; it was much more probably an ancient Druidical sanctuary.

The Druids (Irish: great sages)?

These priests of the Celts, said Aubrey, were versed in a secret doctrine and were far advanced in astronomy. They could be reasonably accepted as the master builders of the enormous complex. Members of the present-day Order of Druids still assemble at Stonehenge at the summer solstice and sing as they await the sun, which rises exactly above the Heel Stone, looking eastwards from the middle of the Altar Stone.

Over 200 years later, in 1901, Sir Joseph Norman Lockyer (1836–1920) looked into the phenomenon of Stonehenge and he was the first astronomer to make a fundamental study of the stone witnesses from ancient times. Lockyer was an outstanding expert in his field. He was Director of the Solar Physics Observatory in South Kensington, a pioneer of astrophysics and the discoverer of helium, which was unknown on earth until then.

Lockyer's astronomical studies led him to date the monument to 1860 BC, plus or minus two centuries. It makes no difference. This date was long before the Celtic period. Celts are first heard of in the sixth century BC. That put paid to the theory of a Druidical sanctuary.

Investigation of Stonehenge became more active in our own century. Scholars found flint axes and sandstone hammers, and they were puzzled about the origin of the material. There were sandstone quarries within a 30 km radius, but no place where bluestone could be found. Nevertheless, bluestones were there in profusion. In 1923 Dr Thom, working for the Ordnance Survey, took over the quest and found that the bluestones came from a small deposit in the Prescelly Mountains in Pembrokeshire. The discovery had one blemish. Prescelly is 385 km from Stonehenge.

If we accept Prescelly, we must try to solve the problem of how transport to Stonehenge was effected thousands of years ago. By common consent the archaeologists put forward the solution they always favour when they are at a loss. The gigantic blocks of stone were dragged from the Prescelly Mountains on sledges to a river where they were loaded on to ships from rafts. Professor Atkinson of the Archaeological Department of Cardiff University says that the bluestones were transferred to boats which consisted of several dugout tree-trunk canoes laid next to each other and which could carry the stones on a communal deck.[2]

An experiment was carried out in 1954. Three canoes built of elm boarding were fixed together by four transverse bearers and floated on the River Avon. A replica of a bluestone in reinforced concrete was lowered on to the vessel. Four public schoolboys punted the cargo upstream. In a second experiment, another team of 14 schoolboys dragged the block up a slope on a sledge riding on roughly fashioned rollers.

Puzzle solved. Puzzle solved?

Yes, if we attribute to the Stone Age men resources they did not have. Even the second phase of construction around 2100 BC still took place towards the end of the Stone Age. So scholars have frivolously or falsely assumed the availability of appliances and workshops that did not exist. For example, shipyards to build models for the specific task, ropewalks to make the ropes for the heavy loads, cranes, even of the simplest type, for loading, and last but not least a transport organisation with a staff of experts such as cargo foremen and skilled dockers. Altogether a couple of assumptions too many.

If anyone objects that the islanders had already left the Stone Age around 2100 BC, I must explain one thing. It has been proved that the bluestones were present *before* the second building phase, i.e. before the erection of the sandstone precinct! Then the only conclusion left is that the men of the Late Stone Age had a lot more technical know-how than scholars allow them.

This contradiction has not escaped Professor Atkinson's notice, for he admits, 'We shall never know exactly how the stones were transported'.[2] That is an honourable academic admission. Thank you.

On 26 October 1963 the scientific periodical *Nature* published an article by the astronomer Gerald Hawkins of the Smithsonian Astrophysical Laboratory, Massachusetts. Hawkins wrote that Stonehenge must definitely have been an astronomical observation station—24 horizon markers and sighting possibilities indicated astronomical connections. Hawkins proved these claims in his book *Stonehenge Decoded*[3].

Hawkins wanted to know whether the 56 Aubrey Holes in

a straight line were connected with each other and the Heel Stone, but also with the bluestones and the trilithons. He did what is the practice nowadays when many different possibilities exist. He fed 7140 possible connecting lines into a computer and programmed it to work out whether specific sighting lines were more frequently in connection with stars than the chance expectancy.

The facts are staggering! The whole of Stonehenge proved to be one great observatory, a complex which was capable of predicting a chain of astronomical data. Thus the Stone Age astronomers knew that the moon oscillated between a northernmost and a southernmost point in exactly 18.61 years. From the centre of the circle they could observe sunrise over the Heel Stone at the summer solstice. Not only could they predict eclipses of the sun and the moon, but also sunrise on the day of the winter solstice and moonrise at the summer and winter solstices.

Such a revolutionary claim has, of course, been disputed.

Professor Atkinson, the 'Pope' of Stonehenge archaeologists, made fun of 'Moonshine about Stonehenge' in the periodical *Antiquity*.[4] His world picture had collapsed!

So how could Stone Age men have built such accurate complicated know-how into 'their' Stonehenge? Hawkins and Atkinson climbed into the ring, but there was no outright winner; they sparred cautiously and came to a compromise. And when Sir Fred Hoyle had intervened with the elegant pen he wields as an SF author, to write 'Speculations on Stonehenge',[5] it was agreed, after the correction of some minor computer data, that Stonehenge was a Stone Age observatory which provided extraordinary astronomical data.

Professor Alexander Thom also used a computer in his investigation of hundreds of stone complexes in France and England. He fed masses of circles and lines marked by megaliths into the objective electronic brain and asked it for reference points in the starry sky.

The results left no room for doubt. More than 600 of the monuments examined had definite astronomical coordinates! The stones spoke and their message was that their master builders not only aligned their sights on sun and moon, but also observed the paths of many fixed stars, such as Capella, Castor, Pollux, Vega, Antares, Altair and Deneb.[6]

It was Professor Thom, too, who discovered the unit of measure which was universally used by the builders of such complexes. Thom called it the Megalithic Yard. It measures 82.9 cm. Felix R. Paturi drew this conclusion:[7]

> The almost incredible identicality of the measure of length in Scotland, Wales, West Prussia and Brittany, with occasional deviations of a few milimetres, lead to a very interesting conclusion. Four thousand years ago there must be something like a central 'Bureau of Weights and Measures' somewhere in Europe that supplied standard wooden measuring rods to different parts of the continent. For if every community had received the rods from a neighbouring village, instead of the central office, errors in length would certainly have been much greater.

The geologist and mineralogist Vladimir Ivanovich Avinski, USSR, had a fantastic tale to tell. In an interview with the news agency Tass[8] he explained that he and his team had identified a pentagram in the geometry of the five Stonehenge trilithons, the 30 stones in the circle and the 56 Aubrey Holes from which the magnitude of the five planets nearest the earth could be read off. Avinski asserted that the order of magnitude of Mercury, Venus, Mars, Jupiter and Saturn did not differ from that known today by more than 1 per cent. What about that! Naturally we ask ourselves how Stone Age men made such calculations without the aid of modern telescopes.

Astronomy is one of the oldest branches of science; archaeo-astronomy is one of the youngest. It has only existed for a few years. It is an interdisciplinary science, combining the techniques and experiences of modern archaeology with the numerical certainty of practical astronomy. A few dozen experts are already engaged on it,[9] starting from scratch, but they already include celebrated names such as Gerald Hawkins, Alexander Thom, Anthony Aveni, the physicist John A. Eddy and the initiator Edwin C. Krupp, Director of the Griffith Observatory, Los Angeles.

I like this recent branch of science. It seems to me to prove that authors like myself who cleared the ground for imaginative realism were not so far off the mark. Can it be that we were responsible for bringing archaeologists and astronomers round a single table?

My affection for archaeo-astronomy is unchanged even when its representatives are obviously unfriendly to us. Given any outlook on everything human, I even understand that they must keep Immanuel Velikovski, Däniken and others at a distance, so as not to lower their reputation in the circle of academic demigods and infallible scholars, for in their eyes we are only visionaries and cranks. Nevertheless the archaeo-astronomers themselves must stake out their claims with speculations and theories, like us, and seek proof of their assumptions, like us.

If you venture to offer the public something new, you must not be squeamish. You must accept attacks, even if they hurt. But attacks should be fair and based on facts. Dr Edwin C. Krupp has said I have cheated with my information. Dr Krupp says I claim that the tracks on the plains of Nazea were laid out by extraterrestrials. Although Dr Krupp uses quotes, my readers know that I never offered the explanation imputed to me. I merely *recommended it as an intelligent assumption.* It does not make a good impression for a new science to cheat. It is certainly not in the old academic tradition.

It would be interesting to discover from archaeological finds, in so far as they allow us to suspect a connection with astronomy, how our early forefathers acquired their astounding knowledge of the firmament. To reach that goal a young science should be more courageous. It can and should include outsiders' ideas in research. It can march forward without blinkers through the cramping legacy of professorial ballast. It does not. So I am astonished by the programme of archaeo-astronomy which leaves no room for the possibility of an extraterrestrial visit. It would only be commonsense to bear these ideas in mind so that the facts do not come as a shock one day. Perhaps Edwin C. Krupp would not then write such incomprehensible sentences as: 'Astonishingly enough, advanced astronomical knowledge is hidden in the first plan'.[9] He is puzzling about Stonehenge, but he cannot get over his astonishment.

Stonehenge is like a second home to Professor Alexander Thom and his son Alexander, and they keep an open mind when discussing it.

> It is hard to imagine how the master builders of the megalithic designed and constructed their monuments without these [astronomical] aids and yet that was exactly what happened ... The megalithic builders experimented with geometry and tabulated rules of measurement. We do not know what relation these conceptions had to their other institutions but *for some reason or other* the mathematical principles they investigated were important enough for them to be applied to the stone.

OK. To me Stonehenge is an absolutely classic example of the need to take a visit by extraterrestrials into consideration.

Who are they, where are they, the beings who thought out the buildings at Stonehenge and Rollright in advance? They are all traced back to the sacrosanct theory of evolution. In other words the builders of the megalithic complexes had predecessors who, generation by generation, collected, increased and handed on small portions of knowledge. So where are these climbing monkeys on the ladder of wisdom? They do not exist. The megalithic architects had all the necessary mathematical and astronomical basic knowledge at their fingertips, and even had a unit of length. From the start and without further-education classes they knew all about types of material, since they brought special stone for special purposes from a distant site. Because it had special properties?

The pseudo-scientific fairytale hour can now begin!

I read[10] that around 2800 BC the northern half of Europe was drier and warmer than today and that large tracts of England were covered with dense forests in which herds of cattle grazed, and that the scanty population was the reason for the considerable wealth of the stockbreeders.

This restricted state of trade and husbandry continued. It is assumed that the population density in 2500 BC was two persons per square kilometre. There were no villages or small towns. So where was the demand for meat when there were no buyers at the market?

Take it easy. The fairytale hour about political economy has a point. The stockbreeders' wealth gave them a lot of leisure and they used it to produce creative ideas about the struggle for existence. 'We can ascribe the idea of Stonehenge to these stock farmers simply because their life was monotonous and primitive.'

Idleness is the beginning of all wisdom! If we actually follow the culture of the stockbreeders, it is not revealed in its materials, but in its great feats of memory. Rabbits out of a top-hat—memory must appear. Obviously, for the Stone Age men could not read or write. Stonehenge—magicians of the world unite!—the product of a brand-new culture, the so-called memory culture. Good heavens! Stone Age geniuses!

Stockbreeders and farmers tilled their fields with sharpened stones or antlers. Naturally a king ruled over them and their families and alone or with the help of his wise priests controlled everything. Then one fine day he ordered a start on the incredibly productive work of covering the British Isles with stone circles à la Stonehenge.

Why? For some reason or other. One of the most stupid reasons is that the priests asked for the complexes so that they could at last predict the seasons, calculate neap-tides and spring-tides and foretell eclipses of the sun and moon. In other words, the priests were demanding a calendar! The result being that gigantic stones had to be set up, in the absence of writing, so as to reveal what everybody could observe without any trouble: the daily rise and fall of the tide, spring-tides occurring at two-weekly intervals, the rising of the sun on the days of the summer and winter solstices. Stone Age men, being closer to nature than we are today, could follow all that from their huts or caves. They needed these gigantic complexes which took centuries to build to determine such recurrent events? Sheer nonsense.

In 1979 the highly regarded American periodical *Science*[11] carried an article about a simple calendar, thousands of years old, which the Indians invented in Chaco Canyon, New Mexico.

The Indians noticed that the sun's rays described a recurring curve through a crack in the rock during the course of the year. They marked this by scratching a spiral at the point where the light rays reached the highest point. If the light rays traversed the 40 cm high spiral in exactly 18 minutes, it was the summer solstice. From a nearby crack in the rock another ray of light cut a smaller 13 cm spiral. That meant the onset of autumn or spring. If both strips of light formed a tangent to left and right of the big spiral, it was the winter solstice. It was as simple as that.

This article proved that monumental buildings for calendar purposes were unnecessary even for simple societies. Yet the Stonehenge architects were by no means primitive, as their legacy shows. Stones were not shoved about for centuries just to make the priests a present of a massive unwieldy calendar. Even Stone Age men were endowed with *reason*.

In all ages one really important reason has inspired men to impressive extraordinary achievement—religion. So we should ask in which gods' honour monstrous buildings were erected in the Neolithic period, and we should check whether certain localities seem to be predestined for the purpose and why heavy stones and not light wood were used. Why were certain types of stone preferred—at Stonehenge dolerite and rhyolite.

A scientific by-product points the way to a trail that is still warm.

Ancient traditions tell the story of the magician and prophet Merlin. In the year AD 573 he is supposed to have been wounded in battle, to have fled to the forests of northern Scotland and lived there among the wild beasts for half a century. It is said that he acquired the gift of prophecy during this compulsory seclusion in the bosom of nature.[12]

Merlin the magician emerges as counsellor to the fabulous King Arthur, who is recorded in legends from the sixth century. There is no definite information about him but the Arthurian legend persisted and acquired literary fame, from the king's birth when Merlin protected him to the Round Table at which Merlin sat as adviser. The court of King Arthur has been celebrated as the model of knighthood, from Wolfram von Eschenbach's *Parzival* to the musical *Camelot*, in which Richard Burton starred on Broadway.

King Arthur is supposed to have held court with beautiful ladies and noble knights at Castle Camelot in the county of Monmouth. Twelve ambitious knights with no distinction in rank could sit at the *round* table, at which wise Merlin gave advice. So the round table was invented for knightly heroes. It has salvaged protocol in many a tricky diplomatic situation. Every power is at the head of a round table!

If Merlin only appeared at the Round Table meetings, he would be uninteresting in connection with Stonehenge. But this multi-purpose magician also appears in a work by Geoffrey of Monmouth, Bishop of St Asaph: *Historia de Gestis Regnum Britanniae*. It is not a historical work, but a historicising narrative in the style of Homer's and Virgil's epics.[13]

Geoffrey introduces Merlin as the magician and steward of the British usurper King Vortigern. This fine monarch had 460 nobles treacherously murdered at a council. When he himself was beheaded, his rightful heir King Aurelius Ambrosius wanted to erect a monument to the 460 murdered nobles. Magician Merlin gave this advice:

> If you want to grace the burial place of these men with a work that shall endure for ever, send for the Giants' Dance that is in Killaraus, a mountain in Ireland. For a structure of stones is there that none of this age could erect unless he combined great skill and artistry. For the stones are big, nor is there stone anywhere of more virtue; and, so they be set up round this plot in a circle, even as they now be, they shall stand for ever . . . For in these stones there is a mystery, and a healing virtue against many ailments. Giants of old did carry them from the farthest ends of Africa and did set them up in Ireland, when they lived there.[14]

The King took Merlin's advice and sent a whole army to Ireland, but they had to give up trying to move the gigantic stones. According to Geoffrey of Monmouth, it was Merlin the magician who managed to transport the stones to Stonehenge by means of a spell.

Whatever may be discovered about the legend, Merlin cannot have given his advice in the sixth century AD. Building at Stonehenge was demonstrably begun 2000 years earlier. The 'hard core' of the saga must be dated much further back.

That is often the case. Since I have been delving into sagas, myths, legends and old popular tales, I am constantly finding that the substance of such traditions, i.e. the hard core, is often submerged by the embellishments and imaginative additions of later narrators. The hard core is history that has been experienced and endured. Later generations no longer understand it, they were not present at the event, they added to it or made omissions, but, because the central point of the traditional story was so astonishing, it survived beneath its many accretions.

The hard core of the Merlin legend says that an inexplicable force is at work in certain stones set up in certain places. The 'circle' of the royal Round Table, too, acquires more significance than that of courtly etiquette. People communicate well in a 'circle'.

What special quality do the megalithic stones possess?

Are they merely dead matter?

Can they be 'addressed', once they stand in a specific circle?

Can the stones 'hear', and perhaps even 'answer'?

If only one of these questions could be answered affirmatively, how did the Late Stone Age man see the phenomenon of the stone circles?

The British chemist, Dr G. V. Robins, who specialised in investigating stones, also asked himself some strange questions. He published the first results of his researches into Rollright in the periodical *Alpha*.[15]

The Rollright stones can be reached from London on a pleasant half-day excusion. You take the M40 to Oxford, bypass the old university town and swing off north on the A34 to Chipping Norton. From there you continue on the M44. Four kilometres to the north in the direction of Adlestrop the stone monuments lie to the left and right of the road, on private ground. The owner of the land willingly opens the complex to visitors from all over the world.

The Rollright complex has three parts. It consists of a perfect stone circle with a diameter of 31.6 m known as the King's Men. About 70 m distant from the circle there is a weathered upright menhir, a typical product of the Late Stone Age, called the King Stone. In spite of the teeth of time which have gnawed at it for millennia, it still stands upright, 2.60 m high and 1.44 m wide. To the east of the stone circle there is a group of standing menhirs, though some of them have fallen over. They are called the Whispering Knights.

What can the saga tell us about the goal of our visit?

The ancient Rollright stones are only a half-day excursion from London.

One saga rumours it that the Rollright stones are a king and his soldiers who were turned to stone by a miracle and that there are graves in which the king and his men sleep until one day they awake to life again.

The saga also says that on New Year's Eve the Whispering Knights march downhill to a spring to drink. Another tale relates that an attempt was once made to remove one of the large stones at night to fit it into the pier of a bridge that was being built. Many men and their horses managed to do this, but every morning it lay on the grass again. On repeated occasions it could not be kept in place, so that the bridge builders finally gave up and took the recalcitrant stone back to its original site. Oddly enough only two horses and four men were needed for the return transport.[16]

Equally nebulous stories circulate in our own day. For example, people who have touched the stones claim that they felt giddy. Road-menders talk about hallucinations, illusions of the senses in the waking state, which came over them at certain times of the day, when they were inside the stone circle. Sensitive people are even supposed to have suffered shocks.

Altogether enough puzzling phenomena to make a scholar like Dr G. V. Robins investigate Rollright.

Dr Robins and his team took as their starting point the fact that most of the stones are silicates, from the Latin *silex* (hard stone). They form about 95 per cent of the structure of the earth's crust. Their own structure exhibits a three-dimensional net of silicon-oxygen chains, atoms that are permeated with ions, such as natrium, kalium and aluminium. The analyst speaks of stones with faulty physical structures, because the geometrical relation between the various atoms in the stone is never the same. Under the electron microscope a fragment of stone gives the impression of a disparate crystal and atom lattice with many holes. The holes in the lattice act like a coarse filter. Where such holes are found, the filter catches other atoms, ions, simple molecules . . . and *electrons*! Like men, animals, trees and all organic matter, stone has a small amount of radioactivity, which comes from the atmosphere, a constant quantity of the radioactive carbon isotope. This radioactivity in the stone is constantly disintegrating and causes continuous change in the atomic lattice. Holes originate, to be immediately filled with ions and electrons. The lattice releases the captured electrons as soon as energy is applied to the stone, say by radiation or great heat. This basic pattern by which 'captured' electrons remain in stone and materials like stone led to a new method of dating things, analysis by thermoluminescence. The material under investigation is heated, electrons are released, reduce their activity to a lower level and give off the difference in energy in visible light. The amount of light can be measured with the technically highly complicated photomultiplier[17] and from that we can find out when a potsherd, for example, was fired hundreds of years ago.

The method can be used on any kind of stone. Stone *x* or *y* or *z* is heated, the electrons leave it and give off light. The amount of light set free is in direct relation to the emission of radioactive rays and so to the stone's age, for the disintegration times of radioactive rays are known.

In other words, the thermoluminescence method reduces

The 'Whispering Knights' can no longer leave their site. They have been railed in.

released electrons to a new level of energy. But, if the electrons are to be measured at their original level, we make use of what is known as electron spin resonance. The transition between two states of energy is effected by microwaves. The stone is exposed to a magnetic field and once again we have a measurable electromagnetic radiation which varies according to the amount of electrons and enables us to decide on the age of the stone.

The earth has had a natural magnetic field since its existence. Magnetic fields originate through veins of metal in the ground. Stones have been exposed to these weak forces for millennia. At all times, we are told, they have minute amounts of electrons captured in the lattice and released again by long-term radiation.

Making use of this knowledge Dr Robins took a decisive step forward.

The transformation of electromagnetic energy into sound is a known physical effect. So Robins looked for ultrasonic

waves near the Rollright stones. In 1978–9 he carried out measurements on the site at various times of the day and night with a perfectly normal ultrasound detector. The detector's protected head prevented interference by chance waves in the micro-range. The scale was graduated from one to ten.

First of all Robins ascertained the basic level of ultrasonic frequencies in the district near Rollright. The values oscillated between nought and one on the scale.

Robins knew that stones radiate rather more strongly at sunrise than dring the day. At daybreak there is a predominance of long-wave rays activating the electrons in the stone.

Then came the first surprise!

The Rollright stones did not begin to emit rays slowly and continuously at sunrise. Unexpected pulsation began in the King Stone and the group of Whispering Knights half an hour *before* sunrise, but not in the precinct of the stone circle. The pulsating effect of the stone and the group reached an incredible seven on the scale, whereas the ultrasonic emission around the stone circle fell *below* the normal level for the district. Two or three hours after sunrise the pulsation suddenly stopped. But, while the reading on the scale at the King Stone diminished, it increased in the stone circle. In the spring of 1979 the ultrasonic activity in the stone circle increased steadily and built up an electric field between the King Stone and the Whispering Knights that pulsated in synchronisation with the ultrasound.

Now for the second surprise!

When a member of the team entered the stone circle during the measuring, the pulsation stopped abruptly. Dr Robins states:

> During all visits at dawn strong pulsation around the menhir as well as on the road and the field between menhir and circle could be observed, yet it stopped as soon as anyone entered the stone circle. This change from intensive pulsations to very weak oscillations below the basic values was repeated during the whole period of observation and was confirmed by a number of observers.[15]

Today the King Stone still towers 2.60 m above the ground. A single menhir, it stands about 70 m away from the circle.

Rollright—stone witnesses from antiquity.

In his final report Robins confirms the hypothesis according to which the stone circles are energy-activating centres and states that Stone Age men who built the Rollright complex consciously made use of the energy produced.

That is a fantastic statement! It opens up dimensions which *measurably* oppose the theory of evolution. That doctrine will have it that all development, regardless of in which sphere, results from tiny steps, that every advance arrives via a sequence of stages and over thousands of generations. According to it nothing can simply and suddenly be 'there'.

If Late Stone Age men—to think in terms of the dusty old dogma—produced complexes like those at Rollright, Stonehenge and elsewhere and are assumed to have been at a comparatively low stage of evolution, their predecessors must have been even more simple-minded. That's what the religious dogma of evolution says. Therefore there was no one on earth from whom the builders could take over manuals of instruction, measuring apparatus and tables that would have

enabled them systematically to create the pulsations from stones proved by the latest physical and chemical techniques and deliberately release them. No one told our Stone Age men which stones emit the energy effect at a particular site in a particular order. Yet they must have known about the effect before they made use of it. The fact that their stones also communicate with the stars does not solve the puzzle, it only makes it more uncanny—especially in view of the world-wide distribution of such sites!

As I am assured that the collaboration of extraterrestrials is out of the question, something must have snapped in the sick brain of a Stone Age dictator, making him force his countrymen to install giant stones in playgrounds, and, since all dictators are imitated, other madmen emulated him and whipped their populations on to similar feats. That is roughly how stone circles originated over many many centuries in England, Scotland, Ireland and less numerously on the continent, or so people would have me believe. If this absurd origin and development is accepted, the stone circle phenomenon would have remained confined to a comparatively small geographical area, a purely European stone plague. But that is not the case. Stone circles must have been an international fashion. They are found in India, Africa, Australia, Japan and the Pacific. Here are the addresses of the most important megalithic stone circles:[18]

The stone circle of Brahmagiri lies to the south of the Narmada and Godavari Rivers in south India.

The stone circle of Sillustani is located near Lake Titicaca in Peru.

The stone circle of Msoura is in north Morocco.

The stone circle of Nioro du Rip in the province of Casamance lies in Senegal, south of the River Senegal.

The biblical stone circle of Gilgal lies on the eastern city limits of Jericho. It was mentioned in the Bible. The prophet Joshua is supposed to have set up 12 stones in a circle in memory of the crossing of the Jordan. The stones are supposed to symbolise the twelve tribes of Israel.

The stone circle of Ain es Zerka is in east Jordan.

The stone circle of Ajun uns Rass is in the steppe plateau of the Nejd in Saudi Arabia.

The geographical location of the Australian stone circle south-west of the Emu desert: latitude 28° 58′ south, longitude 132° 00′ east.

There are several stone circles and stone wheels on the Japanese mainland and near Nonakado on the island of Hokkaido.

Professor Marcel Homet discovered the stone circle of Quebrada of Queneto[19] at sea level on the border between Peru and Ecuador.

There is a stone circle on Naue, one of the Tongareva Islands. In the literature it is specifically pointed out that the stone circle was neither a grave nor a tribal sanctuary comparable to a *marae*.[20]

The stone circles of Portela de Mogos and Boa Fe lie 16 km to the west of Evora in Portugal.[18]

For some reason or other the Late Stone Age men made building stone circles into a world-wide cult. *For some reason or other*—that is too nebulous, too vague, too inaccurate for me. I should dearly like to know *the* reason that led the pre-

Inca tribes in Peru to do the same as the aborigines in Australia, as the blacks in Senegal, the Indians, the Japanese and the isolated islanders in the Pacific. The stone circles all over the world do not all stem from the same period, but the builders were all simple journeymen who had not the faintest idea about radiation technique.

It is said that stones have always been sacred to mankind. Correct. *Certain* stones were worshipped and still are today. Gravestones and memorial stones, for example. Jacob, one of the three patriarchs of Israel, even—so Moses tells us—erected a memorial tablet to a dream experience:

> Jacob left Beer-sheba and went toward Haran. And he came to a certain (holy) place, and stayed there that night, because the sun had set. Taking one of the stones of the place, he put it under his head and lay down in the place to sleep.
>
> (Genesis 28.10 *et seq.*)

We do not have to read anything into this passage. It says in black and white that Jacob came to a holy place and put one of the stones, which presumably had collapsed, under his head. In other words, it was a special stone from a consecrated site on which Jacob slumbered and had this dream:

> And he dreamed that there was a ladder set up on the earth, and the top of it reached to heaven; and behold, the angels of God were ascending and descending on it! And behold, the Lord stood above it and said . . . 'and your descendants shall be like the dust of the earth and you shall spread abroad to the west and to the east and to the north and to the south; and by you and your descendants shall all the families of the world bless themselves'.
>
> (Genesis 28.12 *et seq.*)

The next verse says: 'For I will not leave you until I have done that of which I have spoken to you.'

What had the Lord promised? Simply that Jacob's descendants would spread all over the earth and the Lord would not leave Jacob. Whatever generative power we attribute to him, Jacob could scarcely have distributed sons, daughters and grandchildren over every continent in one lifetime, so the Lord must have supported him actively, for the Lord did not make his promise for an indefinite future. He would not leave Jacob until his mission was accomplished. Jacob found the affair mysterious. He does not sense that he can speak to the Lord at 'this place':

> Then Jacob awoke from his sleep and said, 'Surely the Lord is in this place and I did not know it.' And he was afraid, and said:
>
> 'How awesome is this place! This is none other than the house of God, and this is the gate of heaven.' So Jacob rose early in the morning, and he took the stone which he had put under his head and set it up for a pillar and poured oil on the top of it.'
>
> (Genesis 28.16 *et seq.*)

The facts:

On his march Jacob came to a place with holy stones.

Jacob takes a stone and sleeps on it, without having any idea of the magic power of his 'pillow'.

Jacob has a vivid dream. Angels are climbing up and down the ladder leading to heaven.

The Lord makes Jacob a tremendous promise.

Was all that a dream or a real event actually experienced?

If it were only a dream, the Lord's promise would have been meaningless. Dreams are disconnected, stuff without substance.

So what if it was not a dream? If the stone on which Jacob rested developed a picture of the heavenly ladder in his brain? Had the heat of his body released pulsations in the stone?

Undoubtedly every stone in these holy places was a special stone with a special history. Did the stone have the property of strengthening currents in the brain? Was Jacob a particularly suitable medium? Could a privileged being communicate with human brains through the stone? Do certain stones work like 'transmitters' and receptive men as 'aerials', when they are coupled to other human brains?

Those seem to be purely speculative questions. It remains to be proved that they are not, that they are more than wild ideas winging in the blue.

Men did not get the idea of erecting stones and monuments spontaneously. They were often inspired by God (or gods). In the Book of Joshua, the Lord orders the erection of memorial stones at a certain place:

> And the men of Israel did as Joshua commanded, and took up twelve stones out of the midst of the Jordan, according to the number of the tribes of the people of Israel . . . and they carried them over with them to the place where they lodged, and laid them down there. And Joshua set up twelve stones in the midst of the Jordan, in the place where the priests bearing the ark of the covenant had stood; and they are there to this day.

These stones were not to be considered simply as memorials. They were obviously intended to tell a story down the ages:

> And Joshua wrote these words in the book of the law of God; and he took a great stone, and set it up there under the oak in the sanctuary of the Lord. And Joshua said to all the people, 'Behold, this stone shall be a witness against us; for it has heard all the words of the Lord which he spoke to us; therefore it shall be a witness against you, lest you deal falsely with your God.'
>
> (Joshua 24, 26 *et seq.*)

The stone had 'heard words'? Joshua makes it virtually an 'aural' witness. But what use is a dead stone as a dumb witness? Did Joshua know about this special ability to repeat the words it had heard at some time in the future? It is still to be shown whether we are on the track of something working like a tape.

In Asia Minor the goddess Cybele, the great earth mother, supplied her Greek countrymen with prophecies which she made with the help of a 'holy stone'. On the Syrian coast her collague Laodicaea compiled her news with the same assistance.[21] At Delphi Pythia worked through the omphalos in the middle of the temple, the semi-ovoid stone called the navel of the world, and made daily statements about past and future which she had learnt about through the stone.

Mohammed Ibn al-Chatib from Kufa tells us in his *Book of Idols* about ancient Arabic holy stones, miraculous stones, the most famous of which is set into the wall in the south-east corner of the Kaaba in Mecca at a height of one and a half metres. This is the mystical religious centre of the Islamic world, worshipped in an empty windowless room. Muhammad himself made the Kaaba the central point of his religion and the 'Black Stone' (Arabic: *Hajar al-aswad*) the goal of all Muslims' thoughts. All over the world 650 million Muslims daily prostrate themselves in prayer in the direction of this stone. Their prayers carry wishes and hopes over seas and mountains to the 'Black Stone', from which they expect some kind of return. At least once in a lifetime every Muslim must make a pilgrimage to Mecca and touch the stone, otherwise he will never share the bliss of paradise. For the faithful are 'recorded' by the stone when they touch it. No wonder then that millions of Muslims still touch and kiss the 'Black Stone' in its silver setting, as they have done for more than 1200 years.

What is there about the 'Black Stone'? What can it do, what effects can it produce? What is the unique property which the prophet recognised in it?

As legend claims that the 'Black Stone' fell from heaven, it was at once assumed that it was a meteorite, an aerolite or nickel body of extraterrestrial origin, which did not burn up completely on its passage through the atmosphere.

That is a totally unproved assumption, for there has been no chemical analysis of the 'Black Stone'. The Muhammadans do not allow non-believers into the Kaaba, so they certainly would not permit an investigation of their sanctuary. Perhaps it really is an ordinary meteorite, for its uninterrupted power of attraction since Muhammad (570–632) is inexplicable. Meteorites of all sizes fall daily on to the earth, including Arabic countries, yet no one has ever heard of them being sanctified. Perhaps it is a quite special stone which did not *fall*, but *came* from heaven. There is a very big difference between the two.

In his excellent picture book about the prehistoric stone circles of England and Ireland,[22] Aubrey Burl turns his attention to me: 'The von Däniken approach of making mysteries out of non-mysteries.' Arthur C. Clarke, first-rate SF author, makes this generalisation in a magazine:[23] 'The world is full of real mysteries. I am irritated by the idiots who try to make mysteries out of things for which there is a perfectly simple explanation.'

There it is, this miserable trick of dismissing 'heretics' cursorily and frivolously. If we realistic dreamers are so mediocre, why does anyone at all accept us? Because we hurt with our persistent questions, because we are not prepared to swallow the illogicality of many current explanations, because we do not look on highly dubious dogmas as taboo, because we doubt them.

I read with pleasure a newspaper column 'Science 100 years ago' and sometimes catch myself thinking presumptuously, 'Good grief! Was that the ultimate conclusion of scientific knowledge?' I at once curb myself and think, that was the latest state of knowledge *at that time*. Time corrects errors and replaces old results by new more correct conclusions, which in turn will be polished up and superseded in a couple of years. That is a normal and honourable process.

I have to marvel at the sublime self-satisfaction of my critics. They possess the ultimate definitive knowledge about everything that really holds the world together. Their elitist arrogance, their naive state of mind is enviable. I share the aims of the curious who think ahead, who are not afraid of being able to prove *tomorrow* what is unthinkable *today*. 'We cannot renounce the combustion engine because the prophet Muhammad rode on a camel,' said Datuk Husein Onn, the Prime Minister of Malaysia.

The construction of transport problems of the megalithic complexes are dismissed as solved in many erudite tomes. Such problems can be solved in many ways. What worries me about the explanations put forward is this: people always proceed from the possibilities conceivable *today*, as if they could go back in their imagination, scientific imagination, of course, to former times. But no one was actually there. What is put on the table as a solution is still only one of many other possibilities. Those who have thought themselves back into the past always offer the same set of aids: sledges, ropes, rollers and inclined planes of tightly packed sand or clay. As all our conceptions of possible types of transport are firmly fixed on such aids, doubting them is looked on as sacrilege, as blasphemy. I have a high opinion of our scientists, but I cannot believe in them. They are human and hence subject to error, as you are, as I am, as we all are. Even when they happen to sit on the throne of eminence, that does not make them gods.

This question is meant to shock. What if men, thousands of years ago, could liquefy stone to a pulp and harden it again on the building site, just as we do with concrete today, delivering it from the factory in big tankers? Excuse me, omniscient ones, it is only a question. I wrote it down without thinking, for I can already see it, torn out of its context, being quoted by my smart opponents! So I do *not* claim the megalith builders worked in this way.

No, I think that stones weighing tons were dragged centimetre by centimetre over hundreds of kilometres by ropes attached to the necks of Late Stone Age men. If belief makes us blessed, the great beyond is teeming with incorporated archaeologists. We shall not meet there, for I doubt their often utopian assumptions. From early times holy stones seem to have been associated with the 'gods'; at least they are associated with the firmament for they, like the stone circles, were aligned on the stars. Were the heavens under perpetual observation because the 'gods' had promised to return? In terms of a religious cult that would be a sensible motive for the tremendous expenditure of work on erecting the stones. However, it does not explain the astronomical knowledge, the choice of sites or the special materials. Or does it?

Nor does a religious cult explain the story of Genesis—although the 'Lord' had a hand in it—according to which Jacob set up his stone pillow after use and poured oil over it. Why did he anoint the stone? He performed a sacred ritual which pertained to the priests. What had Jacob in mind, since he knew that the oil would evaporate and burn up in the heat of the sun? Was it his thanks to the stone that 'spoke' to him? Undoubtedly Jacob was in a trancelike state when he raised his head from the stone. Was that also true of Pythia when she brooded over the omphalos? Did she owe her prophecies to this stone 'Navel of the World'? Ancient texts say that Pythia fell into her visionary trances by inhaling vapours which emerged from a fissure in the rock. In spite of industrious searches in and around the Delphic temple no cracks giving off vapours have been discovered. Did Pythia communicate with the stone omphalos? Did she act as a medium to whom it gave ambiguous answers when questioned?

I am looking for indications that extraterrestrials influenced Stone Age men. According to the way of looking at things so far, megalithic complexes show no proof of anything at all. Anyone who blissfully believes this has only to read a single clever book about Stonehenge to know that extraterrestrials are not needed to solve the mystery. Everything is known. On the other hand, if we think just a little further than the 'assured doctrine' then the extraterrestrials, inopportune yet helpful in tricky situations, hold an outstanding position.

There are countless traditions which tell of promises by the 'gods' to return in the distant future after their stay on earth.* Hope of this return has survived among mankind. No one has so far tried to find out if a mathematical key to the date of the return is hidden in megalithic structures. More than 600 of the complexes examined by Professor Thom are laid out according to astronomical rules. So far only the 'gods' know why.

There should be no doubt that hard stone was ideally suited as a deposit for news of the extraterrestrials. It is plentiful, it survives the millennia, it made possible monumental structures which constantly attract attention. So my hypothesis is:

Thousands of years ago 'gods' explained to the inhabitants of earth *how* to lay out stone circles, what material to use, in what arrangement and where the stones had to be erected, so that the inserted messages could be deciphered in days to come.

The 'gods', who created us in their own image, placed traces of their intelligence in the descendants of the new species genetically manipulated by them. They made a mistake. We have understood nothing.

If Dr Vladimir Avinski is right in thinking that the magnitude of the five planets nearest the earth can be read from the Stonehenge complex, the extraterrestrials must have given

* *Signs of the Gods.*

a helping hand. There is no getting round it. If Late Stone Age men, as Louis Charpentier[24] and Robert Wernick[25] mention, erected important structures at the crosspoints of electric currents in the earth's interior, extraterrestrials must have given a helping hand, for they only become measurable with modern physical apparatuses. If it is true that trained priests or gifted mediums could communicate with pulsating stones, extraterrestrials gave a helping hand.

For some reason or other.

What reason?

3 Mind: The Fundamental Basis of All Matter

'We are wrong to ask why. What we really ought to ask is "Why not?"'

George Bernard Shaw

At question time in the Illinois Institute of Technology in Chicago, a student asked me, 'Do you really believe in your theory?'

'As I am convinced of it, I am precluded from believing in it. "Belief" is the prerogative of religions; it is emotional trust in an authority, in a doctrine. In this sense belief simply means that the secret of nature must be accepted as it is. I have to convince by facts, step by step, for I am not the leader of a sect and still less the founder of a religion.'

I am an indefatigable moonraker, yet time, evolution and research support me. What were bold hypotheses, tightrope acts without a net, when I began to write 14 years ago, have gradually been confirmed by scientific recognition. It is not always a bed of roses. Sometimes I have to invite my readers to a strenuous climbing party. Once we reach the summit the view becomes clearer and paths that are easier to negotiate lead through the plains of theory. No one should 'believe' that titanic courage goes unrewarded. Let us set out on a new road. Unfortunately I cannot help it if it is rather hard going.

On our climbing trip we shall take with us the statements of six leading scientists as tasty food for thought.

1. The molecular geneticist and Nobel Prize winner Professor Werner Arber says:[1]

> The results of molecular genetics . . . show us that spatially and temporally creation is infinite . . . Moreover creation is at work here and now, ubiquitously and continuously, in the independent choice of details during the accomplishment of specific vital processes.

2. Professor Joachim Illies of the Max Planck Institute of Limnology says:[2]

We are all infatuated with objectivity. We behave as if 'objective proof' were the ultimate in possible evidence, the highest of all attainable values, and we imagine we live in an objectively proven world which we then proudly call modern science. Some basic demythologisation must take place here so that we do not block access to our own selves and the truth behind all science.

3. Professor Max Thürkauf, a physicist from the University of Bale, says:[3]

Recently the natural sciences have been trying to reduce everything to physical and chemical processes. Nevertheless, paranormal phenomena are connected with what we call life or the spiritual world and that is superior to physical and chemical processes.

4. Professor Erwin Chargaff, the biochemist, says:[4]

A viscous avalanche of information pours into every gap in our consciousness. The mindless babble of idling machinery drowns every thought . . . Naturally there is always something more to do. As we know, small fleas have even smaller fleas, but how small can we chop up atoms and atomic nuclei? I have an uneasy feeling that if the Nobel Prize for Physics were abolished, no more elementary particles would be discovered.

5. The theoretical physicist Jean E. Charon says in his book *The Mind of Matter*:[5]

Scientists are seldom prepared to deal with 'metaphysical' questions, for the simple reason that the high priests of 'official' science forbid it. Now, as in the past, to occupy oneself with metaphysical questions is considered unscientific. Personally I find this attitude scandalous.

6. Professor A. E. Wilder-Smith, guest professor at various celebrated universities in different countries, says:[6]

Natural science exclusively studies objects that can be researched within our material dimensions. If anyone suggests that God, who is a logos or ideas of a personal kind, stands behind the coding of life, the scientist generally rejects the suggestion immediately and decisively because it is outside his research possibilities . . . But what would we think of an astronomer who was unwilling to explain the orbits of the heavenly bodies with the help of gravitation, because he would not accept the idea of such a force on *philosophical* grounds? By its very nature we could not produce such a force or study it in a laboratory. Admittedly, we could put the effects of this force under the microscope, but not the *nature* of the force itself. Consequently the whole subject of gravitation is scientifically intolerable.

Let us now make an experiment in the darkened room of an ophthalmologist and direct an electron microscope at our eyes.

It penetrates the cornea, the iris and the retina. We slip through the lens, which is attached to a fine mesh of fibres, and perceive the optic nerve which looks like a tree with many branches when magnified several thousand times. A fascinating world is revealed. Small crystals, which look like the stone debris of a bizarre landscape, are attached to the nerve fibres. Our microscope brings out molecular chains, hundreds of atoms linked to one another. While looking at an atom, it suddenly gleams brightly; we see a world in perpetual motion, we see the atomic nucleus, around which even smaller particles rush at great speeds. They are protons, neutrons and electrons. Between atomic nucleus and particles a universe is revealed like that between the sun and the orbits of its planets.

Let us catch an electron. If we couple it to a measuring appliance, which slows down its velocity as if in a slow-motion film, we see that in one second our electron enlarges by 10^{23} and then contracts. In other words it pulsates. The figure 10^{23} is a 10 with 23 noughts! This world of constant movement and diffuse radiation is the mysterious dimension of all matter.

Our ovular experiment can also be carried out with a piece of human skin, a bit of wood or a stone. The journey begins differently, but in the end we shall always find atoms and their subatomic particles. For in the last event, everything is energy, radiation and movement, as Albert Einstein postulated 75 years ago.

This unalterable eternal fact makes many scientists despair, but forces others to be modest.

Supposing we reduced (almost) everything to its component parts and molecules were turned into the smaller unit of the atom. If we then studied its behaviour and that of the subatomic particles in a gigantic accelerator that splits atoms and releases radiation, we should still be faced with the same result in the end. Behind the smallest unit there would be a new order, a new law, which seems to obey instructions unknown to us given by the guiding force which all philosophers call 'mind'.

The French mathematician and physicist Jean E. Charon proved that mind and matter are inextricably connected! Charon speaks the precise language of mathematics.[7] Colleagues who have not yet made use of his work to form a revolutionary new conception will have to take notice of it. There is no way round it, for Charon's way *also* points back to prehistory, which leads to the 'gods', I am glad to say. Charon's proof means a significant change.

Matter is material, mass, the substance of all life, everything that exists. Regardless of its consistency, matter can be reduced to atoms and elementary particles. All that is old hat. But where does matter come from? How does it, how did it, originate? How did everything begin? Those are the exciting questions.

In the beginning there was nothing, the infinite void—black body radiation, as physicists call it. This radiation was in a waiting state from time immemorial, before any beginning so to speak. We may ask what existed *before* this state, but we shall find no answer. It may be imparted to us in a different dimension—after death. But that is a solution dependent on belief. As we are trained to think in terms of four limiting dimensions—length, breadth, height and time—the concept of infinite time has no place. If we posit a creator before any beginning, the new, yet age-old, question crops up. Who created the creator? Presumably a physical *perpetuum mobile* will never be found, but the question behind the question is a philosophical *perpetuum mobile*.

Mathematics and physics are counterpoints to philosophy. Physical calculations and observations show that the first pair of particles-cum-matter were an electron* and a positron.† Negatively and positively charged, the particles hardly needed any energy to unite as a pair, to form the first matter.

The first electron pulsated, as it still does today, at the incredible rhythm of 10^{23} expansions and contractions per second, a movement that led to extremely high temperatures of some hundred million degrees. Once again the physicists called the electromagnetic radiations so released 'black body radiation'.

On the basis of known physical reciprocal action, the positron can link up with the neutron to form a proton—one of the two building blocks of the atomic nucleus. Then the electron combines with the proton and produces a hydrogen atom. Seventy-five per cent of the matter in the universe is hydrogen. As there would have been no hydrogen atom without the electron, it follows that the electron existed *before* hydrogen. The slogan 'In the beginning was hydrogen' is wrong. In the beginning was the electron. It was present at the origin of the first pair of particles and it asserts its unchangeable role during the penetration of all matter, including mind.

Jean E. Charon proved mathematically that the electron exhibits similar properties to a 'black hole'. We must go into that further, for we do not want to lose sight of the electron.

What is a black hole?

We must go a long way back. After the origin of the world, the so-called Big Bang, gas, carbon and cosmic dust swept through the universe. Particles met and whirled round in a kind of cloud until, owing to the constant rotation, they formed a ball which perpetually attracted more matter. The increasing density caused intense friction among the particles. Tremendous heat was engendered and as a result a glowing red star. The young star increased in density still more and finally shone like a sun. Light atomic nuclei fused to form heavier ones. In the burning melting-pot helium grew out of

* A negatively charged elementary particle.

† An elementary particle with the same mass and charge as the electron, but positive.

hydrogen, then carbon, oxygen and nitrogen. Finally increasingly heavy elements were formed, including iron.

During this smelting process energy was constantly produced and emitted, a process like that which has been taking place in the sun for milliards of years and during which, says the English astrophysicist John Taylor,[8] 'our sun pours out 4 million tons of its own mass every second, ten thousand times more than the amount of water that flows under Waterloo Bridge in the same time'.

Even a sun cannot go on expending forces so lavishly for milliards of years without damage. As soon as the lighter elements are exhausted, nuclear fusion (the construction of heavier atomic nuclei from lighter ones) comes to an end, because there is nothing left to fuse. The star inflates, explodes and becomes a big, new star, a supernova. During the explosion its brightness increases ten-million-fold. Stellar matter is sprayed into space, but in the last phase of extinction the majority of it falls back on to the star. This compresses it; it becomes smaller and owing to its small magnitude joins the group of white dwarfs. But such a white dwarf has a special characteristic. Its weight increases the speed of rotation around its own axis. In spite of the original mass preserved in the turbulence, its diameter shrinks to a few kilometres and the white dwarf becomes a pulsar, so called because it is supposed to emit brief electromagnetic signals with each rotation. Whether it actually does or not is unimportant; it does rotate and lose energy, which gradually slows down the rotation around its own axis. The top stops spinning.

The star is finished; it suffers a collapse. Its internal pressure can no longer withstand the gravitation of space. It collapses and not a ray of light is left to tell of its former existence. The astrophysicist Reinhard Breuer defines it as follows:[9]

> A black hole is what we call a star that has become so extremely heavy by contraction that no particle, not even light, can pass its surface. The contraction of a star that leads to the birth of a black hole happens in a flash—in fractions of a second—in what is called a gravitational collapse.

We owe our ability to ascertain the violent hour of birth of a black hole to the astronomer Kark Schwarzschild (1873–1916), who, as Director of the Astrophysical Observatory at Potsdam, made important discoveries about the movement of fixed stars. The limit (event horizon) to which a star must be compressed and from which space closes around it is defined by the Schwarzschild radius. Thus Schwarzschild confirmed what Einstein had calculated and what astronomers and astrophysicists have observed on countless occasions since then.

The black hole is a space inside space, rather like a bubble in water. Anything captured in the space of a black hole can never come out again. This sinister Moloch does not even allow light quanta to escape and is, therefore, invisible. Its existence is only betrayed by the curvature of our space which approaches the space of the black hole in the shape of a funnel. In this alien world, the physical laws prevailing are totally different from those in our environment.

Compared with the unfolding of time in our universe, time in a black hole runs in reverse.

In a black hole space has a *temporal* nature and time a *spatial* nature.

In our universe all processes unfold with increasing *entropy*. Entropy is the measure of heat content that is no longer available for mechanical work when energy is transformed. This is based on the second law of thermodynamics and means that the 'order' in every closed system always reaches a state of equilibrium of total disorder, what is known as maximum entropy. In simpler terms, if we pour a can of cold water into a bath full of hot water, the hot and cold water mix. We call this mixture a 'disordered state'.

In black hole space everything takes place the other way round—the processes unfold with *decreasing* entropy. The 'order' gets steadily higher.

In a black hole time unfolds cyclically, which means that all states keep on beginning anew. All information returns to its starting point. As nothing ever leaves the 'treasury', no information is lost. 'Order' is timeless. In this cycle information and order increase, like human experience which gains a little more information every day.

As early as 1963–4 the Nobel Prizewinner Richard Phillips

Feynman, Professor at the California Institute of Technology in Pasadena, showed that the space in an electron is not empty and that neutrinos and black body radiation are at work in it.

Jean E. Charon proved in addition that the electron behaves like a black hole, that it deforms the surrounding space in exactly the same way. Space curves and closes round the tiny electron like water round a bubble. The electron possesses all the properties of the black hole, plus one of its own. From its enclosed space it can connect with the enclosed spaces of other electrons.

Is that a contradiction, seeing that I have described the black hole as permanently cut off from surrounding space?

Black photons, light quanta with very short wavelengths and no mass, exchange their velocities with the black photons of other electrons. The fascinating and important thing from our point of view is that the processes in the electron continue with *decreasing* entropy, i.e. with increasing order. If electrons exchange black photons with each other—and it has been proved that they do—the state of information inside an electron increases steadily. The resultant conclusion is tremendous. The electron has been present since the creation of the universe. Whatever stages it may have gone through, it has not 'forgotten'; its information has increased all the time.

The electron has *always* been a stable particle. If we look on it as a carrier of memory, it has experienced everything since the very beginning. It permeated the universe and penetrated all kinds of matter. It is a component of all living beings, all plants, all stones and all brains. Its order increased. It amassed information and knowledge which it can exchange with particles of its own kind.

In connection with his description of black holes,[10] Rudolf Kippenhahn (1926), Professor of Astronomy and Astrophysics at Göttingen, wrote: 'Even the matter from which our bodies are built up has certainly bubbled about in the interior of a star at least once.'

We must understand and accept the full significance of that. The matter of the electron is immortal. Since it forgets nothing, took part and still takes part in past and present, knowledge and experience are also immortal. The electron preserves all the message of joy experienced and suffering undergone. It permeated (and permeates) the earth, every stone, every plant . . . and each and every one of them are bearers of information. Bodies die and disintegrate; the electron lives on and hands on knowledge and information from the past to the future, as if in a relay race without beginning or end.

Jean E. Charon asserts:[5]

> This means that all matter that took part in the building of a living or thinking structure and during the relatively short lifetime of that structure possessed the qualities of its consciousness cannot simply return to its original diffuse minimal psyche after the death of that structure. The information and the 'consciousness' once acquired can never be lost. After the death of a complex organised structure no power in the world can ever effect a retrograde development of the elementary particle's consciousness.

Although in the past we have had no idea how to tackle many paranormal, parapsychological and metaphysical problems, now a cosmic system suddenly appears behind everything.

Albert Einstein stipulated that his body should be cremated and his brain donated to research. In 1978 the shameful news appeared in the press that his legacy to science was preserved in formaldehyde in a glass jar kept in a cardboard box in an experimental biological laboratory in Wichita, Kansas. At the time, when I read the terrible news, I thought automatically that a chance for humanity would be squandered once the cells died off. Now we know that the electrons of this superbrain whir through the universe, lodge in plants and stones and penetrate brains in which they resurrect the knowledge already stored there. Then electrons whose knowledge Einstein increased flash out and stimulate ideas in a new brain that its owner would not have had from his own experience.

The sudden illumination of a lightning idea happens to many of us. Suddenly up comes an image or a situation which we say we have experienced, although our memory says, I was never in that place, I never took part in that event. This mystery, too, is explained with the discovery that the knowledge of the electron is immortal. Electrons of the long since dead nest in our brains and unreel earlier memories.

The incomprehensible is now an actual event. The confusing, the mysterious, the inexplicable become intelligible. Time in the electron runs backwards, as it does in a black hole, therefore it can also announce events that lie in the future. Clairvoyance, precognition and prophecy become explicable. Nearly all West Europeans have read the name of Gérard Croiset, the clairvoyant who died recently. Police investigators from various countries used his services when they had to find the trail of a kidnapped child or the corpse of a murder victim. Croiset's proportion of successes was improbably high. He was the medium for something he himself could not explain. He did not know what went on in his brain at such moments. The power of electrons explains the phenomenon. A kidnapped child thinks and emits electrons charged with memories into the environment. These tiny omniscient particles are everywhere; there are no fences or walls which they cannot penetrate. If the brain of a suitably receptive medium managed to 'tap' even one of these electrons and allow it to penetrate his brain, it would find the trail that others sought in vain or know whether a victim was alive or dead. Others will be able to emulate Croiset in finding a hidden corpse.

It may be that a brain that makes contact with the knowledge of the electrons needs a specific talent, but I suspect that the ability lurks in each one of us.

What was science fiction material yesterday is explained now that the electron has been revealed as an information carrier. Then the question, 'Who are *we*?' arises. To put it crudely, like all matter, we are the allotted vehicles and parking places for the electron to collect and store information and experience, so that the timeless particle can hand them on from eternity to eternity.

In the mid-fifties a similarly astounding discovery shook the world. Francis C. Crick and J. D. Watson succeeded in unravelling the secret of heredity.

Every body contains the genetic code, the building plan for the construction of the whole body. This miracle of nature has long entered our life as the DNA double helix, although microbiologists still do not know why the DNA molecule passes on information for the construction of a body, just as so far scientists do not know which law makes the female egg cell admit one specific seed among the 200 to 300 million spermatozoa which invade the vagina at ejaculation. The cause at work here is the mind behind matter, the consciousness in the electron. While female egg cells and male sperm are approaching each other, electrons exchange information through their black photons in fractions of a second. They are seeking carriers suitable for evolution.

Utopia? No longer. As Wernher von Braun said: 'In hindsight nothing looks so simple as a Utopia made into reality.'

The astronomer and physicist Arthur Eddington (1882–1944), who initiated research into the internal structure of stars, wrote that the matter of the world is the matter of the mind.

A distinction is made between dead and living matter, a distinction which should not really be made. Living or dead, it consists of atoms, protons and electrons.

Let us recall the investigations Dr Robins made into the stone circles at Rollright. The stones pulsated; an electromagnetic field was formed—the world of electrons! If anyone stood in the centre of the stone circle, the pulsation stopped. Were the electrons communicating with the person at the centre? Is it not conceivable in the light of recent research that a medium sensitised for the reception of the electron message could 'talk' to the stones? The stones oscillate, release electrons and transmit information—they comprehend mankind, the whole of nature and the vast universe. For the matter of the world is the matter of the mind.

There are primaeval stone sanctuaries on nearly all the islands in Melanesia and Polynesia. These religious sites are called *maraes*. The *maraes* have no characteristic architectural style. Sometimes, as on the island of Raiatea, the *marae* is a large rectangle of massive monoliths, then at Arahurahu on Tahiti it is a terrace-style temple and an orderly arrangement of monoliths on the island of Tubuai in the South Pacific. Before Christian proselytising, the *maraes* were 'the official places of meeting between Polynesians and the realities of another world'.[11] The rites that were celebrated in the *maraes* are not known, but the islanders told the first European visitors that they were very *tapu*, very holy places. *Tapu* means 'the strongly marked' as opposed to the normal. We have adopted our word 'taboo' from the Polynesian.

What was taboo about the *maraes*? What was strongly marked?

The South Sea islanders had a second concept that was sacred to them, *mana*, which means effective. Dictionaries say that *mana* is a word to describe a power or effect that is not physical and is in a certain sense supernatural. *Mana* is effective in men, or organic and inorganic nature, and is usually inherited. *Mana* can be concentrated in men, the divine king for example, or in objects. *Mana* also means the power that inspires terror and awe.

A *marae* was not only taboo, it also possessed considerable *mana*. Wilhelm Ziehr wrote:[12]

> *Mana* can also manifest itself at certain places, such as spooky clefts in a cliff, dark places on the beach or in the jungle. Such an impersonal *mana* is then embodied in the spirits and demons that haunt these holy places. By holding secret ceremonies, for example by using the *mana* of a cave in a coral reef in the New Hebrides (Port Olry), one can make oneself invisible and invulnerable. One overhanging cliff conceals so much *mana* that anyone who stands under it can change his sex. Strangely shaped stones are set up at special religious sites, for they, too, contain mysterious powers.

When highly regarded personalities died, such as a wise priest, an honoured chieftain or a brave hero, a mysterious *mana* possessed them even in death. Their skeletons were more taboo than those of ordinary men. Their graves were especially taboo compared to other graves, because there was more *mana* in them.

This strange spooky world which has had to be catalogued as an esoteric mystery until now has a plausible explanation. The *mana* that filled the experienced chieftain or the wise priest consisted of imperishable electrons. A priest had even more *mana* than other men and therefore radiated more wisdom and knowledge. What once seemed to be superstition turns out to be an advance presentiment of the effective forces behind matter. Much of the *mana* of the dead is not lost, for electrons continue to work in the matter composing the body. May we not ask ourselves is this the reason why our feelings in a cemetery are different from those we have in a theatre or a restaurant? Is that why we are overcome by memories of the past and ideas about the future in a mortuary? Does a heightened exchange of electrons take place?

Did the primitive peoples still have immediate access to nature? Did they still sense the vibrations of the whirling electrons? Were they still able to 'talk' to plants, animals and objects (fetishes!)?

A Polynesian legend says that the god Maui came from the Tuamotu Islands to Raivavae to install a large *marae*. When it was finished, Maui took a stone from it to Tubuai, set up another *marae* and inserted his heavy present into the structure. The god must have been bitten by a craze for *marae* building, for immediately after finishing the one at Tubuai he again took a stone and flew to Rurutu, then to Rimatara and Rarotonga (the Cook Islands) and so on and so on. Everywhere he took with him a stone from the *marae* he had just completed. An absurd legend? Today we know why the god Maui acted as he did. With every stone, he implanted *mana* into the new structure. That is why Maui sought out certain special stones.

For stones vary greatly. Basalt has a different atomic structure from andesite, granite a different one from coral. It is true that ultimately everything terminates in the atomic world, the world of diffuse radiation and the electron, but the atomic lattices—we mentioned them in connection with our visit to Stonehenge—differ from each other in the rough state. There are types of stone which, with less applied energy, exchange their electrons more rapidly than others which can only release their electrons with difficulty.

Did the primitive peoples know this? Is that why our early forefathers brought a selection of special stones to special religious sites? Is that why bluestones brought from 400 km away had to be used at Stonehenge? An article by Dr Hans Biedermann supports this assumption.[14]

> The archaeologists who specialise in the remains of Guatemala's prehistoric period have found several stone sculptures representing the heads or seated figures of ex-

tremely obese men. These statues, which they call 'fat boys', are characterised by a property that had remained unnoticed before. Certain parts of their bodies are magnetic, a discovery which we owe to the geographer Vincent H. Malmstrom (Dartmouth College, Hanover, New Hampshire, USA).

In the case of the stone heads, which are to some extent reminiscent of the later sculptures by the Olmeks on the Gulf of Mexico, the concentration zone of natural magnetism are near the temples; in the figures of obese men crouching or sitting they are in the umbilical region.

Stonemasons or sculptors must have been familiar with the phenomenon of magnetism around 2000 BC, for they sought out basalt blocks that clearly showed natural magnetism in places as raw material for their work.

That's it, I said. In magnetism electrostatic fields have a reciprocal action. Electrons are exchanged. Modern investigators used modern measuring apparatus to show that primaeval stones had a magnetic effect. What kind of apparatus the scholars of 4000 years ago used to determine magnetic radiation at a certain point in a rock is a question I should like some omniscient being to answer, please!

Research into a magnetic sense in human beings has just begun.[15]

In June 1979, at Barnard Castle, 31 boys and girls were blindfolded, put into a bus and driven to an unknown destination on a sunless day which precluded orientation. Longish objects, half of them containing bar magnets, the other half merely dummies of the same weight and appearance, were attached to their heads. When they reached their destination, the children, still blindfolded, were asked to indicate the direction in which they thought their starting point had been. The object of the experiment was to find out if the human capacity for orientation was influenced by magnetic fields.

The result was astounding and created a sensation in England—as the *New Scientist* reported in October 1980. For the test children who wore dummies on their heads could point out the direction easily, while those who wore magnets had no sense of direction.

After further experiments, Robert E. Baker, of Manchester University, was firmly convinced that human beings actually possess a magnetic sense which can be disturbed by magnets.

Although there is no doubt about the existence of a magnetic sense in various creatures, bees, doves, dolphins, birds of passage, etc., the biophysical mechanisms have so far remained a mystery to science. Last year, researchers at Princeton University in New Jersey, USA, demonstrated the permanent presence of magnetic material in the dissected heads and necks of doves.

The researchers, writing in *Science*, said it was not clear whether the magnetic structures of living beings were actually used as detectors of the earth's magnetic field and their perceptions then passed to the senses. 'At least six laboratories in different parts of the world are already engaged in investigating human magnetism,' the report concludes.

As soon as Jean E. Charon's epoch-making discovery is made use of in these researches, the circle closes. Magnetic fields are the operational territories of electrons. The original mind, the mind of God, knew that. He made his creatures and all matter receptive to the eternally active force of the electron. The mind behind the matter left nothing to chance during the milliards of years when the universe was coming into being—the creation was not a 'game'!

As Albert Einstein said, 'God does not play dice.'

Critics are particularly fond of dismissing my astronaut-gods theory with the deadly remark that the distances from other inhabited planets alone made the cooperation of extraterrestrials in the creation of life on our planet impossible. They say that spaceships could never reach the velocity close to the speed of light that alone would make the transportation of 'life' possible.

Without repeating what I have already written about this attitude in my book *Signs of the Gods*, a spaceflight by a technically superior intelligence (though still conceivable) is no longer necessary, according to the latest scientific findings, for the importation of the extraterrestrials' knowledge and experience into our planet and their effective action during the 'creation' of the earth. The atom, as the vehicle for electrons charged with all knowledge, existed *before* the creation of the earth. Through electrons the brains of our forefathers could also have learned about the origin of the universe. Perhaps electrons were messengers bringing news about distant solar systems and alien beings.

George Bernard Shaw wrote that we were wrong to ask why and that we really ought to ask 'Why not?'

The masterly answer to this was given by Max Planck (1858–1947), whose radiation formula inscribed the law of black body or full radiation in the bible of physics. In 1918 he won the Nobel Prize for Physics for his quantum theory. Towards the end of his days Max Planck made this statement:

> As a physicist, in other words as a man who throughout his life has served the most rational of sciences, namely the investigation of matter, I am surely free of the suspicion of being taken for a fanatic. So I say this to you after my research into the atom, there is no matter as such! All matter originates and exists only through a force which sets the atomic particles oscillating and holds them together to form the minute solar system of the atom. But as there is neither an intelligent nor an infinite force in the whole universe, we must assume a conscious intelligent mind behind this force. This mind is the fundamental basis of all matter.

The electron.

4 Chasing Little Green Men (and Canards)

'A man should never be ashamed of admitting an error. By doing so, he shows that he is developing, that he is cleverer today than he was yesterday.'

Jonathan Swift (1667–1745)

The American journalist Henry Gris, who speaks fluent Russian, interviewed the Soviet mathematician and astrophysicist Professor Sergei Petrovich Bozhich. At the beginning of August 1979 UPI (United Press International) sent the sensational conversation on the wire all round the world. I came across it on 20 August 1979 in the *Rand Daily Mail* when I happened to be staying in South Africa.[1] I read the article and held my breath. 'There is no doubt in my mind that a crippled alien spaceship is orbiting our earth, a tomb from outer space with a dead crew aboard.'

Had Professor Bozhich gone out of his mind? So when my clipping service sent me the *National Enquirer*[2] with the same interview, I wrote to friends on the editorial staff in Latana, Florida and asked for a transcript of the taped interview which they promptly sent me, translated into English.[3] I reproduce parts of it here word for word.

Gris: Professor Bozhich, your colleagues are very upset by the results of your researches. Will you tell us in the West something about them?
Bozhich: I have definitive astronomical data concerning various important discoveries.
Gris: And you're convinced of them?
Bozhich: Yes, I'm convinced. A crippled extraterrestrial spaceship from an alien solar system is orbiting our earth and it has been doing so since it fell into difficulties. It exploded. Two large and eight smaller parts of it are circling the earth. Our scientists have been following the two large parts by telescope for years. We assume that your people in the West have done the same. I think that a Russo-American project should be started to bring to earth

whatever remains of the alien spaceship and its inhabitants. It can be done and it must be done before the bits fall to earth and burn up in the atmosphere.

Gris heard the Russian Professor Bozhich express the astounding belief that aliens from another galaxy might still be alive in one or other of the two pieces hurtling through space. He also considered the possibility that the alien reconnaissance crew, while observing our planet, could no longer manoeuvre their craft owing to the breakdown and died as the victims of their mission. All the indications seemed to Bozhich to be urging us to seek contact with the aliens (or at least the objects) in order to advance our technology by decades.

On hearing this self-confident statement Gris made sure that the professor was really convinced of what he was saying. He received the reply that there were no terrestrial objects in space before October 1957, whereas the fragments in question had been observed for much longer. The possibility that they might have been fragments of a meteor that exploded had been eliminated, because the speed at which they move would either have made them plummet into the earth's atmosphere and burn up or hurled them into outer space. Gris's attempt to get a simpler more plausible explanation from Professor Bozhich failed. No, he said, all the other possibilities have been checked out and I stick by my statement. Originally the alien fragments were taken for meteorites, but then scientists asked themselves over and over again, what is it? What is staying in orbit and not leaving it? Not until Russian satellites were diverted from their courses by the unidentifiable objects were the relevant data fed into a computer. Then, with the objectivity possessed by computers, it emitted the astonishing conclusion (which shook him and his colleagues) that the ten parts were all united at one point on 18 December 1955. Consequently 'something' must have exploded in our orbit on 18 December 1955. Once they had acquired this information, they kept silent for years, calculating and recalculating before they made the sensational news public.

Henry Gris asked other Russian experts for their views of Professor Bozhich's remarks. Dr Vladimir Georgeivich Azhazha, commander of the first Russian submarine to sail under the North Pole, who has published several scientific books, said:

> It is quite possible that the dead crew of an alien spaceship are still on board. If Russians and Americans put their heads together, we have the technical know-how to bring parts of the spaceship back to earth. We ought to do it and the sooner the better, if we hesitate it may soon be too late. The fragments will plummet to earth and burn up in the atmosphere. In my opinion there is absolutely no doubt that we are dealing with parts of an alien spaceship. We must not confuse these parts with meteors. And meteors don't have orbits!

The geophysicist Professor Alexei Vasilievich Zolotov, well known for his investigation of the Tungusku meteorite which exploded at about 7.17 hours on 30 June 1908 over the Siberian taiga, confirmed, 'There can be no doubt that we are dealing with the remains of what was once an alien spaceship. We have studied the case for years; now there is no time to lose!'

Are we losing the first real proof of an extraterrestrial technology through negligence?

Are the Russians on the right track, have they judged correctly?

Are the parts they have been observing for so long fragments of an extraterrestrial spaceship?

Why don't the Americans make a move to clear up the phenomenon? If there is anything in the most fantastic story of the century, why is it not constantly hitting the headlines in the press?

Would not this research be worth a scientific 'summit' that might justify that pretentiously overworked concept.

I wanted to know what there was in the 'sensation'.

Here is the story:

In October 1969 the American scientific periodical devoted to astronomy, *Icarus*, published a nine-page article: 'Terrestrial Satellites: Some Direct and Indirect Evidence'.[4] The author was the astronomer John P. Bagby, who works at the research centre of the Hughes Aircraft Company in Culver City, California.

For years Bagby has been observing the space around the earth, an important task, for as from the beginning of the sixties Russians and Americans were putting more and more satellites into orbit. The flight paths of these artificial heavenly bodies allow of no deviation from the paths calculated in advance. 'Wobbly' satellites must be prevented from colliding. That applies equally to the geostationary satellites which relay television programmes and telephone conversations round the globe and which, seen from the earth, apparently always 'stand' at the same point on the horizon, although they do move as well. No matter how accurately the orbits were calculated and although there were no technical problems, individual satellites did not stick to the precalculated path. Something was diverting them, altering their courses and causing not a few of them to burn up prematurely in the earth's atmosphere. Russians and Americans covered every point in space above us with their precision radar. What was the cause of the course alterations?

Even before the first Sputnik was sent up on 4 October 1957, it was known that natural 'micromondes' orbit the earth. Ten such *natural* satellites were registered: eight small and two larger fragments. John P. Bagby examined these micromondes, published tables, compiled over a lengthy period, with orbital data and fed them into a computer to ascertain whether the *natural* satellites were responsible for the course deviations of the *artificial satellites*. Bagby and his computer produced an amazing result. If the path of a heavenly body is known, as well as other physical influences such as solar winds, the earth's attraction and centrifugal force, the deviations from its path that the satellite will make in the future can be calculated in advance. (Using similar calculations it was possible to predict in 1979 where and when the remains of Skylab would fall to earth.)

Bagby explored every possibility. To avoid the artificial satellites having orbital collisions, he not only made the computer calculate ahead, but also ran it backwards. Where did the natural micromondes come from? That was his query. And how much longer would they orbit the earth?

Calculating the orbital data retrospectively showed that all ten parts were united at one point on 18 December 1955. There was no doubt. There was an explosion in a terrestrial orbit on 18 December 1955. But in his *Icarus* article Bagby put forward the view that natural *fragments* were involved; there was no mention at all of an extraterrestrial spaceship. The Russians were the first to come up with that idea. Why?

The Russians keep tabs on all interesting scientific publications in the West, which often publishes its findings in a rather casual way. To be sure Professor Bozhich said that he had followed the two larger pieces by telescope, but it was a fact that John P. Bagby was the first man to write about the phenomenon. East and West both agree that there are fragments, but they disagree about what they are.

The great powers like to pull the wool over each other's eyes, but there are facts which cannot be concealed, not even explosions deep underground. If a technical heavenly body had been sent into orbit, there would have been even less chance of concealing it. That is what launched the speculation that the ten obscure fragments might be artificial.

The first launching of a terrestrial satellite took place on 4 October 1957, two years *after* the explosion of the mysterious object. After the publication of Bagby's article, the Russians also began to calculate and they came up with the same date for the explosion: 18 December 1955.

What gave them at first sight the extraordinary idea that this disturbance of the peace in space was caused by parts of an alien spaceship?

The wily Russians thought a little further than the Americans. They wanted to find out what path the original object had followed before the 18 December 1955. In order to do this, they first had to know the size of the separate parts, which would enable conclusions about the size of the object when it was whole. Radar and laser measurements gave the two larger fragments a diameter of some 27 m, whereas the eight smaller parts could only be estimated roughly. Our reliable friend the computer knew in a flash that before the 18 December 1955 the object must have been between 70 and 80 m in diameter.

The Russians went still further. If the object consisted of meteoric iron it would have logically had a different weight from a hollow sphere. According to their findings, the exploded body must have been hollow.

Who is right, the Russians or the Americans? Was the object artificial or natural?

I wrote to Western scientists, questioning them at length on the subject.

Professor Dr Harry O. Ruppe, Wernher von Braun's right-hand man for many years, now holder of the Chair for Space Travel Technology at Munich Technical University, answered as follows:[5]

Lehrstuhl für Raumfahrttechnik
Technische Universität München
Professor Dr Ing. Harry O.
Ruppe

Richard-Wagnerstr 18 III
8000 München 2
Telefon (0089) 2105 2578
Telex 5 22854 tumue

I know the *Icarus* article you mentioned. Retrospective orbital calculations are always a bit dubious. To that extent, the 'unity of the object' is to be taken with a grain of salt. Measurements of the 'original' are easily arrived at.

Naturally such an object could be extraterrestrial in theory; nevertheless we always try to hit upon a less 'exotic' explanation if humanly possible.

Jesco von Puttkamer, a NASA engineer, answered similarly, but in more detail.

NASA
National Aeronautics and Space Administration

Washington, DC
20546

Up to the present there is absolutely no proof that the earth has any natural satellites except the moon. The statements made by Bagby in the article in *Icarus* you mentioned have since had considerable doubt cast on them and Dr John O'Keefe of NASA's Goddard Space Flight Centre, one of the leading experts in this field, says categorically that Bagby's data are wrong. He held many meetings with Bagby and convinced him that the orbital deviations he cited and which his hypothetical satellites are presumed to cause in artificial satellites do not correspond to reality. Since those days many intensive searches for other satellites have been undertaken. Without exception, they have been fruitless. Naturally we keep a very accurate log of all artificial satellites—more than 4500 at present—many of which are of 'unknown', though not of extraterrestrial, origin (fragments, USSR, etc.).

You ask why such objects must have a natural origin. Because logically that is the most obvious answer. We know that the solar system is full of them, so it is not unlikely that the earth has some, too. To date extraterrestrial spaceships only exist in our imagination and it would be completely baseless and meaningless to scientists to call these figments of the imagination real so long as there are simpler, more firmly based, more normal and more logical explanations.

So the bubble of the 'extraterrestrial' spaceship bursts and honestly leaves nothing behind. But this will not stop many people, including the credulous and professional liars, from dragging out new evidence which does not exist at all in reality.

Professor Frank Drake is the leading astronomer in the world. In Ithaca, New York, he is Director of the National Astronomy and Ionosphere Centre of Cornell University, which has the biggest radiotelescope in the world at Arecibo in Puerto Rico. Professor Drake wrote to me:[7]

National Astronomy and
Ionosphere Centre
Office of the Director,
Cornell University,
Space Sciences Building,
Ithaca, NY 14583
Telephone 607–256–3734
Telex 932454

Arecibo Observatory
Post Office Box 995
Arecibo, PR 00612
Telephone 809–878–2612
Telex 385–638

If these objects did indeed come from a single object, there is, of course, at present no clear-cut evidence concerning the origins of the original object. This must await a direct examination. However a natural origin is obviously much the most reasonable and in fact is entirely consistent with the existing knowledge of the objects. Of particular importance is that the roughly estimated semi-major axis of the orbit places the objects just inside the Roche limit of the earth. This makes a consistent picture in which a natural object broke up due to the tidal forces when it passed within the Roche limit.* This is also consistent with the fact that the objects seem to have very similar orbits, suggesting that if a parent object broke apart, the mechanism of the break-up was very gentle, and not highly explosive. This fits a tidal break-up picture.

I have no information about measurements of the objects, sizes, present whereabouts or any attempts to study them in detail. I hope the above is helpful to you.

These three convincing self-assured answers seem to make the matter clear. But do they really?

It is a time-honoured principle of science to use the first available item of 'instant' knowledge to answer open upsetting questions before 'exotic' explanations (Ruppe) are aired. The letters quoted above are based on this principle. Without this basic principle of scientific logic there would be a danger of the forces and means available for research being dissipated. Problems might be tackled that only waste time and money in the end.

And yet an undiscovered bacillus seems to lurk in this attitude. The 'logically most obvious' (Puttkamer) only agrees with 'the existing knowledge' (Drake). 'Up to the present there is absolutely no proof' (Puttkamer)—that means an outright renunciation of constructive imagination (by which even NASA was originally spurred on to make its bold plans) and attractive speculations. When I had the privilege of a conversation with Wernher von Braun, he was ready to listen to such ideas. The most 'obvious' answer always comes *from the present-day viewpoint*. In order to call in question the extraordinarily conservative principle, may I quote the

* At the Roche limit the gravitation of the earth and the gravitation of the moon work against each other.

American scientist and diplomat James Brian Conant, who wrote in his book *Modern Science and Modern Man* (1952): 'The history of science proves beyond all doubt that really revolutionary and significant advances come from new theories, not the empyrean.'

Examples will clarify the errors that can creep in when only the 'most obvious' possibilities are considered.

A prospector, i.e. a man who looks for the locations of iron, copper and other metals in the ground, fell sick 40 years ago. He complained of attacks of vertigo, his eyes hurt, his hair dried out and a leaden tiredness overcame him more and more often. Using the most obvious answers in their bags, doctors first diagnosed a cold, then anaemia and finally an indefinable virus. The prospector was treated according to these diagnoses until he died a rather painful death.

What had been overlooked by accepting the 'most obvious' answer?

Without knowing it the prospector had been working for a long time in an area with an underground vein of uranium. Naturally uranium emits radiation. Nature, which has the radioactive element inherently, does not protect it with concrete walls and water chambers. Because the 'most obvious' precluded the suggestion of the decisive possibility—given such an occupation—the man was treated with powders for influenza and haemoglobin preparations against anaemia, instead of drugs to counter the damage caused by radiation. The 'most obvious' had been done.

Or:

For more than 25 years thousands of people have claimed that they have seen UFOs. These things to not fit into the most rational framework of present-day science, therefore they do not exist. The 'most obvious' phrase of dismissal is taken from psychology. The people are cranks, they suffer from hallucinations, wishful thinking or delusions. Heaven knows I am no UFO fan, but I do think that by using the 'most obvious' method the problem is not solved, but merely shunted into a siding.

Or:

There are traditions which give both broad and detailed accounts of 'gods' who came down to our planet from heaven. The ancient chroniclers name them by name and describe their functions, relate their achievements, as well as giving accurate reports of their arrival and departure. But because 'no proof' of their 'actual existence' can be given in 'our present-day state of knowledge', the 'most obvious answer' is relegated to the credulous sphere of religions or given a pseudopsychological interpretation.

If constant reminders bear no fruit, it should be borne in mind that pioneering revolutionary discoveries are so often made by outsiders who—unencumbered by 'present-day knowledge'—break into exotic neglected fields and are successful there. These outsiders are not satisfied with the 'most obvious' answer. Uninhibitedly they ask questions beyond the 'most obvious' answer—utopian questions beyond the state of 'present-day knowledge'.

I discussed this problem for hours with scientists I knew. They said, what are we supposed to do? Should we chase every hairbrained story? Wouldn't our financiers—universities and the state—stop our funds pretty quickly? Given this weighing up of material benefits, science seems to me to be on the horns of a dilemma between the 'most obvious answer' and chance correct answers on an empirical basis. A fatal situation.

Although I'm imaginative, I'm not a crank. I understand the dilemma, I am not pleading that every farfetched idea should be examined, but there is a broad field between the 'most obvious' answer and the speculative *possible* answer. Before the trace of a possible answer is pursued, the probability of its being fruitful should thoroughly be checked, that does not cost money, only a little brain grease. Scholars should investigate most carefully to check if the *possible* answer has a chance in comparison with the 'most obvious' answer.

To put it in concrete terms, two divergent statements are in opposition to each other. In the West the most obvious answer is that the ten unidentified fragments are *natural* 'satellites'. The Russians say, 'We have carried out all kinds of research, we have calculated and recalculated . . . they are parts of an alien spaceship.'

It is not up to me to assess the quality of the standpoints of either side, but my normal common sense tells me that the scientific high-ups should get round the conference table! I am against losing a chance that may have incredible results. I am all for the Russians' suggestion to put at least one of the objects under the microscope before it burns up for ever in the earth's atmosphere. Millions of dollars were spent on collecting a few samples of stones from the moon that no one talks about any more. But very close to us, among 4500 registered artificial satellites, ten unidentified fragments are orbiting, with no one in the West giving a damn about them, because they have been explained by the 'most obvious answer'.

I, too, incline to the view that the ten fragments are of natural origin, but they must have come from somewhere. And definitely not from the earth. The complete object which exploded on 18 December 1955 in the miraculously coincidental view of both East and West had made a very long voyage. Does not its mere presence bring up the question of the existence of extraterrestrial life again? Could not mini-bodies also be the bearers of alien distant forms of life.

Did 'Bombs' from Space Bring Life to Earth?
Die Welt, 11 January 1980

In November 1980 a number of well-known academicians met at the University of Maryland, USA, to discuss the question of whether life on earth originated through 'seeding' from space.[8] When I modestly put this possibility up for discussion in 1973, bucketfuls of scorn were poured on my thick head; now scientists are discussing it seriously. I'm delighted.

Definite proof of extraterrestrial life is still lacking. According to Professor Hans Elsässer, the fact that the question of the existence of cosmic forms of life has become a serious subject for research is connected not least with the view held by many scientists who think it crazy to assume that we are the only intelligent beings in the cosmos.

Speculation about extraterrestrial life is not all that new. Hermann Ludwig Ferdinand von Helmholtz (1821–94), physicist and physiologist, wrote, 'Who knows whether or not meteorites and comets rushing through the universe carry seeds to places where worlds have developed subsequently, that they give beings a future.' At the Maryland symposium in 1980, Sherwood Chang of the NASA Ames Research

1 Like their forefathers, the locals relieve themselves on the beach at Tarawa in palm huts on stilts in the sea and reached over swaying palm trunks.

2 Phosphate, the island's only wealth, is over-exploited. In the harbour of Tarawa it is loaded on to big freighters bound for Australia and New Zealand. But for how long?

3 On the beach at Tarawa—one of the 16 island paradises in the Pacific. But they go on strike, even in paradise!

4 All the material for the huts in the small settlements comes from the coconut palm. Open on all sides, they mostly consist of one room, the meeting place for the whole family.

5 Wherever we went in our little Datsun truck, the youthful islanders were our constant companions, cheerful, lively and always ready to help—so long as they could understand us.

6 Teeta, our dark angel, opens a coconut with a blow of his machete. The milk is thirst-quenching, the white meat is good to eat—healthy all-round nourishment.

7 Reverend Kamoriki's widow invited us to supper—a colourful meal of island delicacies.

8 Apart from some government and administration buildings, the Kamoriki's is one of the few stone houses on the island—small, but bursting with hospitality.

9 The *manaeba*, the community house, is the centre of every village. Here the old men do the talking. Young men speak when they are spoken to and women are excluded. They chatter away in their huts.

10 Like all the airports on the islands, the 'airport' on Abaiang is a clearing hacked out of the jungle; the landing strips are bumpy. Animals graze on them, 'tended' by sleepy herdsmen.

11 Two of several compass stones on the island of Arorae. Anchored deep in the ground, for untold ages they have been pointing to distant islands far across the sea.

12 The site under taboo on the island of North Tarawa, in which nothing grows, is marked out in a rectangle with small stones. The tops of the palms actually do turn away from the circle.

13 Stonehenge as we know it—the monumental trilithons.

14 The investigations that led to brand-new discoveries began at Rollright. The lines with the 'speaking stones' run to left and right of the road.

15 Although the millennia have taken their toll, the Rollright stones still have a remarkable message for us.

16 The *marae* of Arahurahu on Tahiti consists of several terraces made of small stones. Today the *marae* is still a holy place to the Polynesians.

17 The god Maui also took a monolith imbued with *'mana'* to the *marae* of Raiatea in French Polynesia.

18 Twice a week an Aero Peru plane lands in the dust clouds of Huanuco's primitive airport, at a height of 1800 m—twice too often for the tourists, for the only worthwhile sight is the marvellous mountain panorama.

19 Kotosh, the plundered archaeological site from pre-Inca days, on the edge of Huanuco, now green fields and a playground for Indian children, strictly but lovingly guarded by their mothers.

20 In the Indus valley camels, cows and of course sacred cows have the undisputed right of way. Unfortunately they have no idea of the highway code.

21 The Pakistanis paint their lorries and buses all colours of the rainbow to propitiate their 'St Christopher', the patron saint of the roads. As the passengers packed into the buses reach their destinations alive, the colourful vehicles seem to fulfil their purpose.

22 At a height of 2180 m you drive through the Baniha Tunnel. As soon as you emerge on the other side, you have this breathtaking view of the valley of Kashmir.

23 You drive through many small villages with a Tibetan character. Their streets are welcoming and clean, like their friendly inhabitants.

24 Streams which still serve as open sewers flow through the outskirts of Srinagar—nice to look at, nasty to smell.

25 Hundreds of houseboats are moored in the canals of Srinagar. It is called the 'Venice of the East' because of its numerous canals.

26 The church in which Jesus is supposed to be buried is called Rauzabal Khanyar. It is a place of pilgrimage for Christians, Moslems and Hindus.

27 I climbed down into the vault, which is normally forbidden ground, through a small latticed door.

28 Tradition has it that the sarcophagus containing the body of Jesus of Nazareth lies beneath this stone monument.

29 The ruined site of Parahaspur suggests massive destruction from the air.

30 Here as in South America the dimensions and weight of the stone colossi do not seem to have caused the builders any transport or dressing problems.

31 The heavens open their sluices. The road to El Baul was soon under water, turning into a raging river.

32 'El Baul Monument No. 27.'

33 This strange monolith, known as the 'writing desk' in specialist literature, is located in Puma Punku.

34 The prehistoric master builders of Puma Punku were certainly familiar with the circle as a technical draughtsman's aid.

35 The mysterious band with many thousands of holes for which there is no explanation runs from somewhere to somewhere in the Pisco valley, Peru.

Institute, California, described how it may have happened. The earth was hostile to life, like other heavenly bodies, which had been analysed by space probes—bare as the moon, ice-bound like Jupiter, with a dusty crater landscape like Mars, with no atmosphere. But comets and asteroids hit the earth like 'bombs' and supplied the basis for every form of life with material rich in carbon. Sherwood Chang is convinced that the first life developed from these biological building blocks. The objection that space radiation and great heat would inevitably have destroyed the molecules is contradicted by Don E. Brownlee of Washington University who is convinced that the carbon-rich particles could withstand the long journey. With the help of their characteristic radio radiation Brownlee was able to find at least 50 chemical combinations as the basic material for the origin of life—of the kind meteorites and comet tails bring with them.

Professor Yeheskel Wolman of the Hebrew University of Jerusalem held the same view.[9] At a congress in the summer

Jerusalem Conference on the Origin of Life
Did Adam Come from Outer Space?
Die Welt, 25 June 1980

●

of 1980, more than 100 scientists discussed the question, 'Did Adam come from space?' Although they agreed on the development from lower to higher forms of life, they disputed the question of how the step from the purely mineral abiotic world to the first low forms of life was taken.

Professor Wolman:

> We know from chemical analyses that the basic building blocks of life are chemical combinations with monster molecules. Each of these molecules consists of many hundred thousand or even millions of atoms. We call this chemical substance polymer. As soon as we know how and when the first polymers originated, we shall be closer to the origin of life . . . We suspect that the basic substance from which nature created the first polymers came from the cosmos, not from the surface of the earth.

In the discussion Professor Emanuel Gilav of the Weizmann Institute of Sciences admitted:

Like all research, our own began because we were curious. As soon as we know how the first living cells originated, it will become easier to fight cancer. For cancer is nothing more than a diseased multiplication of the cells.

All right. The existence of vital building blocks is discovered, but that does not bind us to admit that extraterrestrial life exists. Bits of space junk are revolving almost next door to the earth and we don't even take the trouble to find out whether this extraterrestrial stone—let's forget the parts of a wreck of the (Russian) alien spaceship—contains micro-organisms which might at least supply irrevocable proof of life in space!

Don't these dear scholars realise that here is a tangible chance of turning theory into fact? We have the technical know-how to investigate the ten mysterious fragments. Why don't we do it? In view of the incomparably greater problem, does it really matter whether the parts are of natural or artificial origin? Let us go in search of the origin of the first form of life. It is worth any amount of effort. In this sense the previous researches of East and West are of great importance. It is simply a question of switching to a new target. That should not be too difficult. If the UN (and its affiliated organisations) were not such an impotent rubberstamping set-up, it could summon members to a great communal effort: search for the first life in space!

We know that science is busily concerned with the question of how life reached our planet from the universe.

When the idea dawned on us that we are not the only intelligent beings in the universe, many comic and speculative ideas were put forward. What would the gentlemen from other stars look like? In the hope that the assumption of extraterrestrial life could be killed by ridicule, the 'little green men' hit the headlines. This kind of humour was of no avail, because more and more scholars were adopting the view that our civilisation was only one among millions or milliards of others.

In the meantime the men who according to my conviction only recently were literally reaching for the stars are backtracking . . . for example the Soviet astrophysicist Yosif Samuilovich Shlovski. He once told me in his Institute at

Universitetskiprospekt 13 in Moscow that he suspected planets with intelligent life within a radius of 100 light-years and he spoke of a cybernetically steered spaceship which could withstand a thousand-year journey undamaged. Today Shlovski describes the earth as a 'rare exception in the universe' and estimates the distance to the next civilisation at 10,000 light-years.

The Russian's statement[10] that our earth and its life form a 'rare exception in the universe' is not so new. It is as rancid as the postulate put forward in 1974 by Jacques Monod in his book *Chance and Necessity*. He claimed that we citizens of earth were the only intelligences in the universe—by chance! I offer some reflections which in my opinion do not emerge in the public discussion.

Scientists do not have to prove that life must have begun somehow, somewhere and at some time. We ourselves are proof of that. We are here!

It is a law of all life that it spreads and multiplies. That happens—yes, but since when and why?—around us every day and we contribute to it in a pleasurable way. That life perishes only to rise anew is an axiom that does not need proving.

Unintelligent life, the lowest forms of life, can only spread on its own planet, although owing to a physical event (earthquakes, volcanic eruptions, the destruction of a planet by the impact of a giant meteor) seeds of life, spores of the low unintelligent forms of life may be hurled into space.

Intelligent life has a tendency to spread. As soon as the technical prerequisites are available, it strives to leave its home planet to steer for new, distant destinations. Our own reconnaissances of the moon, Mars, Jupiter and Venus are examples of such beginnings.

Intelligent life does not have to spread necessarily and exclusively by manned spaceships. Intelligent extraterrestrials can also send out 'life bombs', light capsules, which they fire out of their solar system with rockets. Such capsules can contain micro-organisms, cells with the genetic code of their own species. By this process intelligent inhabitants of other planets could 'seed' an infinite number of solar systems, as was assumed at the Maryland symposium in 1980.

Many capsules reach no destination, roaming through the

cosmos for all eternity or burning up in a sun. This possibility of spreading life could already be an actual practice in our case. By the time the reader of this book holds it in his or her hand, the Jupiter probe launched in March 1972 will have already passed Saturn and left our solar system. If the probe had been equipped with a small container filled with microscopically small balls that were diffused by a radio signal, our 'life envoys', genes and micro-organisms, could be floating in all directions in the universe and—perhaps—reach a planet suitable for life, on which after millennia beings 'in our own image' would develop.

According to this scenario life following the original pattern can develop in various solar systems. The scientific view is that this development on other planets is beyond our ken.

Consequently the question, 'How great is the probability of the development of life on other planets?' is unanswerable. Once in the universe the life sent forth by us (or by other intelligent beings) continues to evolve according to the primaeval law. Life multiplies by snowballing. Ceaselessly. Irresistibly.

Taking all the criteria into consideration, we have, in my opinion, a choice between three possibilities.

First, life is infinitely complicated. Our existence was a unique piece of good luck—coincidence! (Monod.)

Secondly, life can have originated at different times in different places in different forms. This possibility is so minimal that it can happen at the most every 10,000 light-years (Shlovski).

Thirdly, life evolved *once*, somewhere, at some time, and spread by addition and multiplication. This assumption is assured by the evolutionary principle according to which all developed intelligent forms of life are similar (Däniken).

Possibilities one and two are not demonstrable at the present. Admittedly we exist, but we do not know for certain whether there are other intelligent living beings. Three is demonstrable. We exist and all intelligent life tends to spread and multiply. We—like nature—practise this.

Without the little green men!

Anything that lay in the earth for millennia must await an encounter with me till the day of judgement. It will not be forgotten, for my archives are marked with tags of different

Father Gustavo Le Paige, who is supposed to have found the skeletons of dead beings from other stars.

colours to remind me. Thus a sensational news item published in 1975 languished in the 'Unlikely' box.

Dead people from other stars in ancient graves:

> The Belgian priest Gustavo Le Paige is convinced that beings like men who came from other planets were buried on our earth many thousands of years ago. Le Paige lives in Chile as a missionary. For 20 years he has been carrying out archaeological research. The 72-year-old mission leader has excavated 5424 graves of men some of whom died more than a hundred thousand years ago, according to him. Padre Le Paige recently told a Chilean reporter: 'I

believe that extraterrestrial beings were buried in the graves. Some of the mummies I found had facial characteristics that we do not know on earth.'[11]

In a very ancient grave in the far north of Chile the priest found a wooden figure whose headgear resembled an astronaut's helmet on a cylindrical torso. In the holy man's opinion the funerary adjuncts came from an extraterrestrial. 'People wouldn't believe me if I were to say what else I found in the graves!'

To be honest I did not believe it myself, but as a matter of routine I picked up the phone and rang the magazine's office in Hamburg. They knew nothing more about the padre than what was in the article, moreover they had only had a telex from Chile that formed the basis for the story. Nor did questioning two journalists I knew in Santiago produce any result. They did not know the padre. The report went into the 'Unlikely' box.

It would still be there today if the Mexican paper *Vistazo*[12] had not published pictures of a skeleton and claimed that it was in the possession of Professor Ramón de Aguilar in Panama. A name at last!

Precisely at Christmas 1979 the reputable Brazilian magazine *Gente*[13] once again made us a present of the alien skeleton and mentioned Professor de Aguilar as the owner. The sympathetic face of a man in the prime of life, with an intelligent look, did not suggest a charlatan. And he is not, for I have met him since.

With some delay I received a report in the Spanish periodical *Mundo Desconocido*,[14] which again referred to the padre and his skeleton.

The tag on the 'Unlikely' box was flashing at me encouragingly.

I have been friendly with the editor of *Mundo Desconocido*, Andreas Faber-Kaiser, for years. I asked him for help. He knew nothing about the padre, but he could obtain Professor de Aguilar's address for me. Although further questions in Mexico and Brazil were fruitless, the professor answered by return. He would be glad to show me the skeleton and I could photograph it, too, from all sides.

But who and where was Padre Le Paige, the finder of the primaeval message?

The Swiss Embassy answered me on 4 March 1980 in a letter from the counsellor, V. Vuffray:[15]

Swiss Embassy
in Chile

Santiago, 4 March 1980
Calle J. Miguel de la Barra 536
Casilla 3875
Telephone 3 20 09

Ref: 642. O-VU/ke
Dear Mr von Däniken,

I confirm receipt of your letter of 23 February and beg to inform you that the Belgian Padre Gustavo Le Paige, who is known personally to the undersigned, is at present at Colegio San Ignacio, Calle Alonso Ovalle 1480 in Santiago. As he has been very ill in recent months and had to undergo protracted medical treatment, he will probably never be able to return to San Pedro de Atacama.

In this northern settlement at the foot of the Andes and in the vicinity of the saltpetre deserts, the above-mentioned built a museum which houses a wealth of skeletons that he found and excavated in the region as well as countless artefacts.

I very much hope that it will be possible to put you in touch with Padre Le Paige and I shall be glad to receive you during your stay in Chile.

Would that all embassies were so accommodating!

The same day I sent the Spanish version of all my books to the counsellor and asked him to transmit them to the sick padre with my best wishes for his recovery and announced my visit. Our ambassador Mr Casanova answered me on 7 May 1980:[16] 'I was going to take your Spanish books to the padre who is also known personally to me, when I was told that unfortunately he was dying and had been in a deep coma for several weeks.'

My South American travel programme, conceived to take in many destinations, planned a meeting with Padre Le Paige for the second week in August. Then on 6 June the following news[17] by express airmail hit me like a sledgehammer:

Dear Mr von Däniken,

Thank you for your letter of 27 May confirming your arrival in Santiago on 8 August.

6

ROVER
721
PINDIG GUSHTI Goods FORWARDING AGY.
R.P.
P G G

23

CHERRY STONE
NEW AUSTRALIA

2 3 4 5 6 7 8 9 10 11 12 13 14 15 16 17 18 19 20 21 22 23 24 25 26 27 28 29 30 31 32 33 34 35

I regret to inform you that Padre Le Paige died on 19 May. The Archaeological Museum which he founded in Atacama comes under the Universidad del Norte, Casilla 1280, Antofagasta.

I enclose three newspaper articles about Padre Le Paige.

Yours sincerely,
the Swiss Ambassador,
M. Casanova.

This time the account had languished too long under the heading 'Unlikely'. The obituary notices confirmed that the padre had the absolute confidence of the Indios. They emphasised that people had always been able to rely on the word of the man of God. But he had taken the secret of his funerary finds and hence the miracle of an extraterrestrial skeleton with him to the eternal hunting grounds.

I made a heartfelt wish that all the gods who looked on me with favour would preserve Professor de Aguilar's health.

At the end of August Professor de Aguilar received me in his well-stocked library with his family. I soon realised that he knew all about me from my books, while obviously I knew nothing about him. This charming bearded gentleman, whose bonhomie made me feel quite at home, laughed understandingly and took his five-page curriculum vitae from a drawer in his desk. De Aguilar graduated in medicine in Seville in 1953 and took a further degree in psychiatry in Madrid in 1960. As medical superintendent many doctorates were conferred on him *honoris causa*. I was in good hands and waited feverishly for the moment when I would set eyes on the first extraterrestrial skeleton.

The professor put me on the rack. Champagne was served; we toasted each other, his wife, his two daughters, talked about the humid heat in Panama, the stress of children at school, the wretched international political situation. I could not stand it any longer, interrupted the small talk, pulled newspapers and magazines out of my briefcase and asked rather impolitely, 'And what about the skeleton?'

Professor de Aguilar smiled, damped my ardour and explained that first I must hear the story of the find, a story that made me wonder if the learned man had lost his reason.

The year 1972. De Aguilar said that a skeleton very similar

Professor Ramón de Aguilar, Medical Superintendent in Panama.

to the one in his possession was found near Erendira in the Bay of California on the Mexican side of the border. The 1972 skeleton was taken to the world-famous Anthropological Museum in Mexico City, examined by reputable anthropologists and classified as 'not terrestrial'.

Then a strange thing happened. The skeleton vanished without a trace and the same scientists who shortly before had described the object as 'not terrestrial' changed their minds overnight. None of them stood by their former statements. The professor smirked, perhaps because such 'resoluteness' on the part of his colleagues was familiar to him.

Shortly after this incident, a farm labourer came to Ramón de Aguilar, bringing a 'skeleton' which he had found on the beach at San Carlos on the Pacific coast of Panama. The professor immediately discovered similarities with the Mexican find, which he knew well from numerous photos. Then, he recalled, a swarm of reporters arrived asking questions and frequently putting words into his mouth as he discovered from what was printed the following day. Up to this point I understood him very well, for unfortunately I have fallen into such traps only too often. So far the story seemed rather dull, but I listened to it without interrupting in order to see the skeleton, for then the excitement would begin.

One afternoon three years ago three men dressed in black from head to foot rang his front-door bell, pushed the secretary who opened it to one side without a word and forced their way into his study. His colleagues were petrified with fear and de Aguilar admitted he did not feel too good, either.

The thought flashed through my mind of the three men in black,[18] those occult figures who haunt the international scene in sensational literature. They are linked with mysterious murders, are looked on as 'time travellers' who appear suddenly, carry out their terrible mission and disappear without a trace.

Even though the three men in black fitted perfectly into the professor's story, that distinguished scientist had never heard of those obscure figures before. Nevertheless, three men in the same clothes had been in his study in the flesh. Several eye-witnesses had followed their behaviour. Barely half an hour later the drama was over. The men in black withdrew as they had come without a word, as if the ground had swallowed them up.

'What did the men want? What were they looking for?' I asked.

'I don't know,' said de Aguilar. 'They did not ask for anything; they never said a word. The whole business was uncanny.'

'Did they take the skeleton with them? Did they look for it?'

'No,' smiled the professor. 'Naturally I thought at first that that was what they had come for. I remembered the unexplained Mexican story, but no, the skeleton was not touched.'

'So you still have it?'

'I'm going to show it you now.'

A load of Cyclopean dimensions fell from my heart, after all one only has the chance of seeing an extraterrestrial skeleton once in a lifetime!

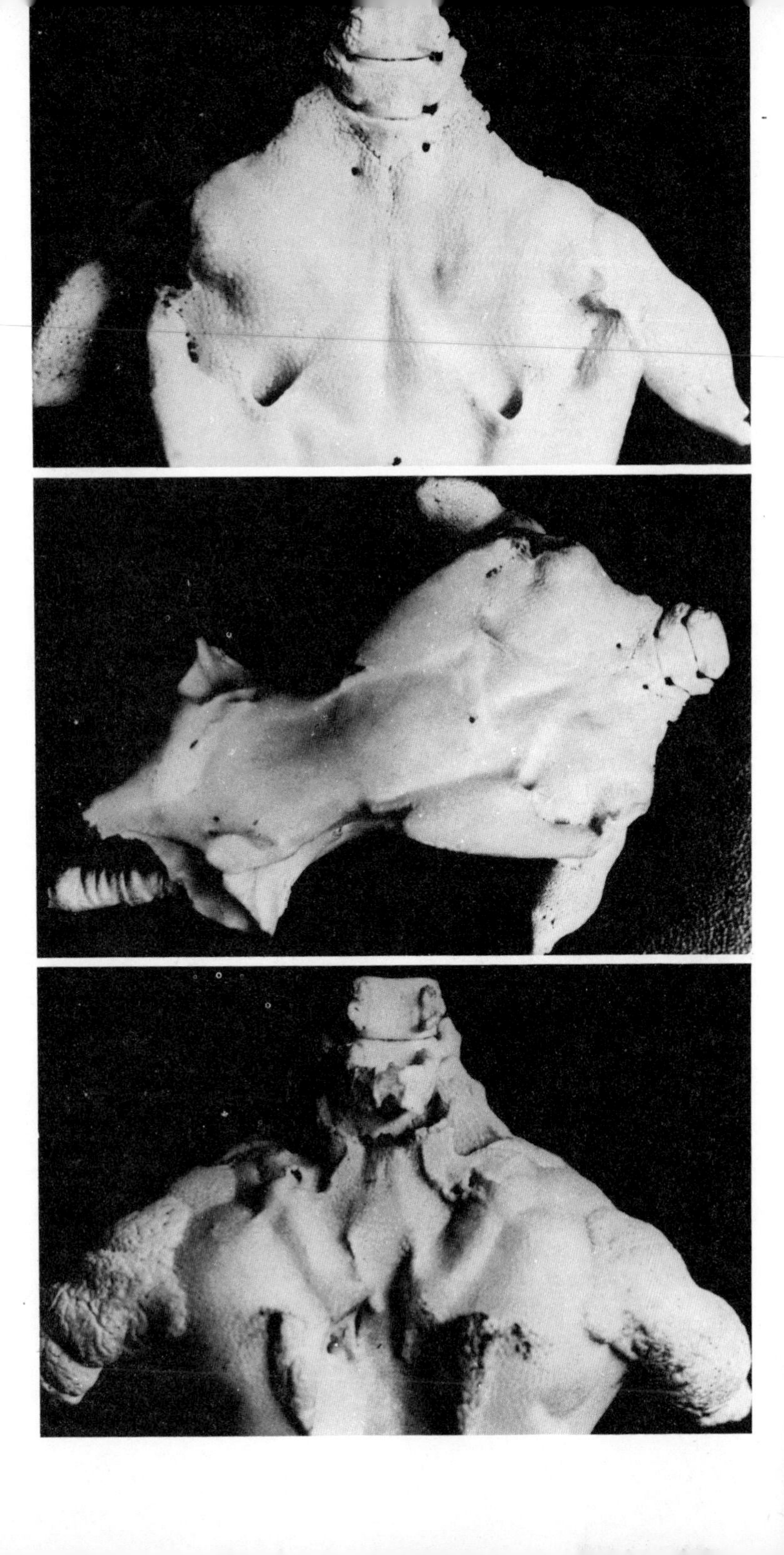

Professor de Aguilar placed a plexiglass box on the table. It was 15 cm long and 10 cm wide. He took the top off.

My eyes nearly fell out of my head. I was staring at a piece of bleached large-pored skin, a full 8 cm long! A rat's skeleton covered with skin, I thought, and picked it up with revulsion, looking at it from all sides. It weighed only a few grammes. It could have been sent by ordinary mail without paying excess postage.

In front on its 'chest', I noticed two holes on which the thing had presumably been spitted. Small stunted beginnings of arms were reminiscent of a foetus; I could see clearly that they had been sewn on to the white skin. The only remarkable feature I saw was the shape of two extremities on the back at the height of the 'shoulder blades', like Dracula's teeth or tired-looking nipples.

I kept giving the professor questioning and disappointed looks. He observed with obvious amusement how the nasty remains of what was probably a small mammal disgusted me.

'Is that the skeleton that hit the headlines?' I heard myself ask hoarsely. I knew that I was on the wrong track.

'That's it,' answered the professor.

'Then why do you think it's extraterrestrial?'

'Extraterrestrial?' Ramón de Aguilar shook his head vigorously. 'Extraterrestrial? *I* don't believe that it's extraterrestrial, nor have *I* ever claimed that it was!'

Who had sent this canard fluttering through the newspaper forest? The professor laughed, his wife and daughters laughed—liberating merriment that swept away my disappointment. The professor assured me that he had never said the 'skeleton' was of extraterrestrial origin. He had described the find as a curiosity, but had not linked that remark with any fantastic embellishment. Sensational journalists had added so much pepper to make 8 cm of white skin into a

The 'skeleton' turned out to be a piece of bleached, large-pored skin.

In front, 'on the chest', I noticed two holes on which the thing had presumably been spitted.

The only feature worthy of note was the strange extremities on the 'shoulder blades'. It was all a silly canard!

saleable newspaper canard that it was offered on editorial menus as roast of the day in distant continents.

It is best to laugh at yourself when you find you've been led up the garden path.

Postscript:

1. I unmasked the 'extraterrestrial skeleton' in Professor de Aguilar's possession as a pure newspaper canard.

2. When I photograph objects—for example, giants' footprints—which do not give an accurate impression of their size, I put a centimetre scale next to them. If it had been reported that the 'extraterrestrial skeleton' was only 8 cm long, the canard would have been unsaleable.

3. I doubt that Padre Le Paige's extraterrestrial relics will ever crop up again.

On 5 July 1980 I stumbled across a three-column article with the headline: 'Did the Incas Know the Secret of Making Diamonds?'

The Inca, nowadays the plural 's' is omitted, are old friends of mine and always good for a surprise. Why should they not have known about artificial diamonds, in addition to other inexplicable abilities? To my amazement I read:

> In the 500-year-old Inca temple of Cuca which lies in the inaccessible mountains north of Huanuco in Peru, a climbing expedition under the leadership of the South African ethnologist Dr Maath has made surprising finds on a site for sacrifices to the Sun God of this legendary South American people. After the Spaniard Lepico who reached the temple ruins of Cuca in 1925, Dr Maath from Cape Town became the second Inca scholar to penetrate to this 'holy masonry', as the correspondents of *La Cronica*, Lima, calls it. Apart from the fact that no one has yet worked out how the Inca transported giant blocks of a stone not found in this wild mountain region from the valleys to a height of nearly 5000 m to build a temple for the Sun God—they worship the sun—it is incredible that diamonds described as 'synthetic stones' by some experts should be found under the floor of a place of sacrifice.

According to the article the Inca ornamented their sacrificial chalices with valuable diamonds, stones cut from natural finds that are priceless today. What was new was that the splendid sacrificial chalices were set in diamond-ornamented bases, two examples of which Dr Maath discovered; he removed seven stones to have them examined in Lima. I was not surprised to read that the diamond specialist and chemist Collins flew from America on hearing the news and travelled to Huanuco to meet the expedition. Later Collins said that he felt like an alchemist faced with the biggest discovery of his life. 'I have never seen such diamonds,' said Collins. 'During my long years as a specialist I have never hesitated so much in giving my judgement. I take them for half-diamonds, not synthetic stones, although they could be the latter. But it would be too incredible to claim that the Inca knew the secret of manufacturing synthetic/real diamonds. In any case they are genuine carbon diamonds. But there are characteristics which contradict a natural origin.'

Mr Collins did not want to elaborate, but Lima was awaiting specialists who intended to put the previous finds under their special microscopes. Their report concluded in this optimistic and speculative vein:

> Perhaps decipherment of the hieroglyphs also found at the temple of Cuca above the tomb of the 'Prince of the Sun Stone' will solve the puzzle and throw light on the mystery. Cuzeca, the eleventh-dynasty ruler, was reputed to worship the diamond in which he saw a sacred gift from the Sun God.

A report full of names, places and facts!

The contradictory epithet of 'synthetic/real diamonds' had obviously been inserted by a reporter. Diamonds are either 'synthetic' or 'real'. What irritated me, for I think I know Peru pretty well, I looked on as a gap in my education. Before then I had never heard of an Inca temple called Cuca. The mention of Cuzeca as the eleventh-dynasty ruler must have been a slip. The eleventh dynasty lasted from 1493 to 1525 and its ruler was called Huayna Capac.

But that counted for little in comparison with the exciting news—diamonds, possibly manufactured synthetically. Good heavens!

I phoned my friend Rico Mercurio, who had proved himself on the journey to the Kiribatis, and dragged him away from his diamonds, which he was just sorting or dressing.

'What's the score on synthetic diamonds? Do they exist? How are they made, what do they cost?' I asked and was told:

Antoine Laurent Lavoisier (1743–94), a member of the Academy of Sciences, was the founder of modern organic chemistry. In 1776 he proved that diamonds consist of carbon and are materially identical with the graphite frequently found in nature.

This piece of knowledge stimulated researchers at the end of the nineteenth and during the first half of the twentieth centuries to patient and expensive attempts to manufacture diamonds synthetically. They had no success. Not until 1954 did the Belt apparatus provide the technical requisites for manufacturing synthetic diamonds under high pressure at great heat. It worked like this. A test-tube is let into a high-pressure press that is under pressure of 35,000 atu at 1600 °C. Under these extreme conditions graphite turns into diamond, with the help of a catalyst of nickel or the chemical element tantalum, a very expensive metal. Rico explained that the process was complicated and expensive and that the diamonds so produced could not compete with real ones.

That was just what I wanted to hear. The production of synthetic diamonds demanded a technical know-how which the Inca did not possess. If such stones were actually found in the temple of Cuca, we must posthumously ascribe an ultramodern technology to the Inca . . . or assume that they were gifts from representatives of a highly developed technological civilisation.

The article which so pleased me mentioned the newspaper *La Cronica*. An airmail letter to the editor was already on its way, promising payment in return for granting my request to send me the original report. In spite of the self-addressed envelope and the international reply coupons I enclosed there was no answer from Lima. I also asked the Gemmological Institute of Santa Monica near Los Angeles about the method of distinguishing natural stones from synthetic stones and imitations. Not a murmur.

During my lengthy stay in Peru in the summer of 1980 I had a few days free when I meant to take a mini-holiday.

One morning in Lima I took a battered old taxi to the building housing *La Cronica*, a popular paper with a big circulation, as I discovered. The sceptical friendship of the editor changed to extreme politeness when instead of flowers I gave him a signed copy of my book *According to the Evidence* in Spanish. I told him about the report of the Cuca diamond find in a German paper, which said that a reporter from *La Cronica* had supplied the information. The editor knew nothing about it and summoned a colleague. The conversation revealed that no one knew anything about Cuca, not to mention synthetic diamonds up there in the mountains.

'That's impossible!' I interrupted. 'We roast that sort of fat canard on April the first, not in the middle of the summer!'

Through the cloud of smoke in which his thick cigar enveloped him, the editor put a colleague at my disposal and said, 'During the last few years since I have been in charge that item has not been in the paper. Take a look in the archives for as long as you want!'

When I entered the long narrow room in the next-door building with shelves full of documents, files, annuals and boxes, my hope of finding anything in this classical South American disorder were dashed, but were pleasantly restored with the support of three kindly archivists. Much like my own archives, there was a dual classification, by date and by captions. In addition to *La Cronica* all the Lima newspapers had been taken apart and filed in orderly fashion.

I was faced with mountains which were assembled under the heading 'Archaeology'. With the assistance of the archivists and the volunteer we covered every report. There was nothing about Cuca. Did Cuca really exist? I began to wonder. It was not mentioned in the Peruvian lexicon, but given the thousands of Inca sites that did not necessarily mean anything.

From the hotel I phoned all the archaeologists and ethnologists I knew in Peru, including men who have devoted their lives to the Inca. None of them knew the Inca temple of Cuca in the mountains of Huanuco, but they all consoled and comforted me. There were so many Inca ruins in Peru that if they did not have something really out of the ordinary to offer they found no place in the literature.

A good boy scout since my childhood, I picked up some maps. According to the German newspaper article the Cuca temple was supposed to lie at a height of 5000 m, i.e. in the eternal ice and snow. All right. Huanuco is 3000 m lower down, north-west of it rises the Cordillera Blanca, the white cordillera, with Huascaran, 6768 m high. Within a radius of 100 km from Huanuco there are some five-thousand-metre mountains on which the Cuca temple might be located.

Aero Peru flies to the town of 50,000 inhabitants twice a week. The tourist guide,[20] which otherwise recommends a visit to every heap of stones, warns: 'The provincial capital on the upper Huallago, prized for its pleasant climate, has no worthwhile sights to offer the foreign tourist.' That is an understatement. Huanuco is dreary, yet I stayed at the Hotel Turistas for three days. State hotels with this name are found in all the larger towns such as Ica, Nazca and Cuzco.

In an old house near the hotel was a museum privately owned by a skinny nervous man with a goatee. The four rooms were crammed with all kinds of junk: stuffed animals, including a sheep with six feet, absurd archaeological figurines, skull-bones, etc. The bearded gentleman, who travelled around the countryside buying his trinkets, had never heard of Cuca.

The local Huanuco paper appears when needed, once a week if necessary. The editor and his wife had plenty of time to think seriously about my quest. No, they had no knowledge of Cuca, a temple or a diamond find. There were no archaeologists around, no excavations had been made for a long time.

Was I on a wild goose chase?

Toward evening I sat on a green bench in the marketplace and stared dully at the colourful crowd. Schoolgirls and schoolboys of all ages, with books and satchels under their arms, were running home. They were uniformly dressed, the girls in white blouses and dark-grey jackets, the boys in dark-grey trousers and white shirts. Three young girls stopped in front of me. They asked: 'Where do you come from?'

We were conversing. More schoolchildren came up, alert brown faces with hair as black as boot-polish. They asked, I answered. They asked me to sing the Swiss National Anthem. I promised I would if they would sing one of their folksongs first. The song they spontaneously broke into is called *El Condor Pasa*. The song or rather my rather flat version of our national anthem attracted more curious children. For a moment I thought I had become a good missionary. I suddenly popped a question into the general discussion.

'Does any of you know the Inca temple in Cuca? It must lie somewhere here in the mountains . . .'

The children looked at me blankly and whispered to each other. None of them had ever heard of Cuca.

I asked them to ask their parents that evening and their teachers the next day. I would wait for them at the same time in the same place and if any one of them could tell me where Cuca was he or she would get ten American dollars.

To make a pretence of work on the next day of my holidays, I drove to the ruins of Kotosh on the town limits of Huanuco. I knew from the relevant literature that Kotosh is considered to be a pre-Inca settlement, about whose builders absolutely nothing is known. The little site on a hill is not a place about which one can say anything much. The pre-Inca builders could not handle monoliths or dress great blocks. They had not yet been 'kissed awake' by technology. On this particular day I was the only visitor. Warned by the tourist guide, others did not even go to Huanuco, let alone to Kotosh. And they were right.

My late afternoon rendezvous with the children gave me no information. Neither parents nor teachers had ever heard of Cuca. I was advised to visit other Inca temples, but I was only looking for Cuca.

The sensational article in the serious German paper lacked any foundation. If it appeared on 1 April, I would have laughed about it, as I did at the report in *Sterne und Weltraum* for April 1980,[21] scientifically presented under the title 'Archaeology at La Silla' and supposedly coming from Hungarian sources. With three academically sterile photos, the reader was referred to a 2400 m high mountain on the edge of the Atacama desert north of Santiago de Chile. Indian settlements from the pre-Columbian period were to be found there. Stone drawings showed a ball with a ring like Saturn's. The text read:

Should it turn out that the two drawings are more than a

few centuries old, perhaps even older than the European technical civilisation, the writings of Erich von Däniken, who has done a great deal of research in South America, will have to be discussed anew.

The source quoted was: 'D. Niken et al., Ver. Arch. Ung. 11, 222 (1979).' Can you imagine?

Jokes are allowed on 1 April. On all the other days of the year readers should not be fobbed off with apparently serious, but in fact purely sensational, articles. I have unearthed three cases here. I had been on the wrong track, but I returned home a wiser man.

5 In the Promised Land?

'Belief is not the beginning but the end of all knowledge'

Johann Wolfgang von Goethe

I knew India and Pakistan from visits that were only too brief. From the literature I knew about the prehistoric city of Mohenjo Daro in Pakistan and the ruined temples and pyramids in the Indian highlands. But I had never been there long enough to get out into the country. My previous visits were confined to cities which were easily and comfortably reached by air. Perhaps I never would have gone into the countryside had not several reasons for doing so cropped up simultaneously. I heard about speculations that the tomb of Jesus was in India. A startling piece of news. Then my publisher Ajitt Dutt wrote to me from Calcutta that my long-planned visit was now due and when I came would I please bring him a portable typewriter which he could not get over there.

Often in my life chance and luck have been the deciding factors which made me take a particular course. The letter from my Indian publisher was still unanswered when the post brought a letter from Tehran. My correspondent of many years Dr Kamil Botosha wrote that he had just returned from a desert trip which had taken him 80 km into the west of Persia, to the town of Kermanshah. There he had seen hundreds of cave and rock drawings which reminded him of flying beings and astronaut-like figures such as I had presented in my books.* The caves are only known to the locals and are virgin territory, archaeologically speaking. Dr Botosha recommended me to make the journey in a cross-country vehicle, unless I was keen on a long camel ride.

I reflected. The ruins of Mohenjo Daro are in Pakistan; the caves recommended by Dr Botosha beckoned me in the west of Iran, 150 km as the crow flies from the Iraqi border. On a globe every location looks neat and close to the next one, but there are 2500 km as the crow flies between the two

* *In Search of Ancient Gods.*

destinations. Brooding over the maps I discovered a chain of archaeological points of burning interest to me that lay precisely on the stretch between Pakistan and the Iraqi border. I noted the following down:

Tepe Yahya lies in the Soghum valley in southern Iran. Six thousand years ago the city is supposed to have been a centre of the Elamite kingdom. It played its part in history from the third century BC. The oldest written tablets, older than those of the Sumerians, were found at Tepe Yahya. In 1971 a joint American–Iranian excavation team decided that the place was already a trading centre around 4000 BC. They had convincing reasons. The written tablets proved to be receipts for the import and export of goods. Several hundred seals, as well as potsherds with mysterious motifs, were taken from the hill of ruins. There was no doubt that Tepe Yahya was worth a journey.

The old Sassanid town of Ardashir Khurra is located barely 100 km south of the present-day town of Shiraz in the plain of Firuzabad. I knew of this circular town with a diameter of 2.16 km from descriptions. Ardashir Papak, the builder from the Sassanid house, had the city divided into four equal sectors by a road forming a cross and considered it an image of the cosmos. In the centre stood a 30 m high tower without doors or steps. Archaeologists puzzle about the purpose of this peculiar structure. This round edifice had always fascinated me, all the more because I know that the Parthians, forerunners of the Sassanids, knew and used electricity. I have already written about a Parthian electric battery which is in the Baghdad Museum.*

The tomb of Kashmir, the ruins of Mohenjo Daro, the ancient city of Tepe Yahya, the Sassanid Ardashir Khurra, the caves of Kermanshah formed a line which could be covered in one journey. I had to go, but how?

Far more luggage than I usually take was needed for the long journey conceived on a surprise basis. In India and Pakistan, road conditions, with a few pleasant exceptions in the big cities, are at least as bad as in South and Central American countries. Outside the big cities—full of gigantic blocks teeming with humanity—one cannot get anywhere in

* *Chariots of the Gods?*

an old bone-shaker. A cross-country vehicle is indispensable, one of the kind you are never able to rent.

If I travelled from Switzerland in my own car, the round trip would take more than four months. Taking into account local stops and possible political unrest I could count on half a year which had no place in my calendar. How could I reduce this period to a more reasonable one? After much deliberation, there was only one solution. I would have to buy a Range Rover, send it on ahead by ship or air, start driving from the landing place and return to Switzerland on four wheels following the line between my various destinations.

Buying the Range Rover was a matter of a telephone call. Two weeks later it stood outside my front door, in its imposing size and massiveness. It is faster than a jeep and has four-wheel drive, and a differential gear. In addition it is roomy and comfortable. I shut myself up in my den with the technical handbook. Soon I discovered many Achilles' heels when it came to mountain and desert journeys. What to do if the petrol pump failed? Would I find a spare pump in a country with an area of 3,046,000 sq km and more than 500 million inhabitants? Was the normal battery charge enough? Could the bearings be protected against fine desert sand? What about the spark coil, the oil filter, the V-belt, the inner tubes? A guardian angel made me do something that friends mocked me for. I took two of everything with me, not to mention a winch which could haul the expensive vehicle out of mud and slime if necessary. I do not know what we would have done without the winch. Perhaps I should have done my critics the favour of vanishing without a trace.

In the century of tourism everyone knows that a passport is needed for travel abroad. It is not so well known that an international passport, a *carnet de passage*, must accompany a car. On payment of a considerable deposit, you are issued with this document. The deposit is supposed to prevent the car being flogged *en route*. In accordance with the international agreement of 8 June 1961 the Chamber of Commerce of the home country issues a '*carnet* for the temporary import of professional equipment'. I was yet to learn that international agreements are not worth the paper they are written on.

Before our Range Rover was loaded on to an Air France plane bound for Karachi at Orly Airport near Paris, we had

We said goodbye to our Range Rover at Orly Airport near Paris. See you again in Asia!

to empty the petrol tank, let half the air out of the tyres and disconnect the batteries. I asked the freight manager to contact the Air France office in Karachi and ask them to store the Range Rover in the shade on arrival so that our first-aid medicines would not be spoiled in the steaming heat.

Stowed in a container, we saw our fully packed vehicle disappear over a ramp into the cargo hold of the aircraft.

See you again in Asia!

16 January. We landed in Karachi shortly before midnight in a Lufthansa DC 10 . . . into a hothouse of clammy humid air.

We formed a queue in front of half a hundred white-clad customs men. It took a long time to get our passports stamped. We reached our hotel about three o'clock. The next day we would fetch the Range Rover.

17 January. Air France sent Mr Lakmiehr, a lanky Pakistani, to the hotel to help us with the customs. Why? We had a *carnet de passages*. At once he asked for Form A. I didn't have it, hadn't heard of it and showed him the *carnet*.

Mr Lakmiehr said wearily that it meant nothing and that besides we ought to have 'declared' the car last night. I informed him that the car had not flown with me and my secretary, Willi Dünnenberger, but had arrived days before on a cargo flight. The Pakistani thought our omission was a bad business. He drove us to the airport customs. There he deposited a letter in my name which read roughly as follows:

> Most honoured and venerable Mr Customs Inspector!
> I, Erich von Däniken, a Swiss subject with passport XY, arrived here last night and omitted to declare my car immediately on arrival. I sincerely regret this and beg you in your immeasurable generosity to overlook my fault and issue me with Form A.

After three hours I got Form A and filled it in in 30 seconds. Mr Lakmiehr took us into an office in which Form A was stamped after a lengthy delay. My Pakistani signalled us to follow him into the next office. There the first stamp was validated by a second. The 'offices' are open sheds. Weary fans turn under the ceiling. There is never more than one chair which is always occupied by an official. Cats are busy hunting mice, and sometimes rats as well. Waving Form A like a proof of victory, Mr Lakmiehr made for a building at the other end of the airport. Why didn't we take a taxi? Our helper silently pointed to the distant house burning in the sun. I was fed up to the teeth. And I did not hide my feelings. The man behind the desk smiled! Making extravagant excuses, he had a chair brought, looked at my passport, asked for a signature and handed me the car keys. Well, well. I was happy because I thought I was nearing the goal.

Mr Lakmiehr started a new hike. 'Where to?' I asked and was told that the car was still in the customs area and now it would need a customs agent to release it. He found him at the end of the diagonal right across the airport. His brown face lit up in a smile and assured us that he would take the matter in hand, but that it was too late to do anything today. We drove 25 km back to the hotel, cursing.

18 January. We were at the airport at nine o'clock sharp.

Mr Lakmiehr flourished a bundle of forms and said he had been working on them half the night. I cut into this self-praise. 'Where is my car?' He asked us to follow him to an enormous shed. Even from a distance I could see the inevitable endless queue. Stubbornly I marched straight past it and went to the first man at the desk. 'Excuse me, I have come a very long way and must continue my journey. All the formalities have been complied with. Here is Form A, here is the *carnet*.'

The man in white grinned at me. '*Carnets* are not dispatched at the airport, only at road customs posts or in the port. Normally cars do not come by air!'

If I had not already been perspiring like a shower from all pores, I would have broken out in sweat.

An angry silent Mr Lakmiehr, Willi and I drove for one and a half hours through Karachi to the harbour and there entered the customs house, a gigantic hall with a hundred officials at a hundred desks. Below the ceiling 41 useless crippled fans—I had time to count them—were humming. No one there had ever heard of the internationally valid *carnet de passages*. With the courage born of desperation I shouted as loud as I could above the din: 'Is anyone here responsible for a *carnet de passages*?' The effect was tremendous. Suddenly there was total silence. The gentlemen stopped their work and stared at me. Right at the back a bald official wearing glasses stood up.

'Are you responsible?' I shouted.

Apparently he was very frightened. I switched from anger to amiability, chatted him up, asked him to sit down again and said mildly that I had been chasing up my car for two whole days and was not going to put up with this circus any longer. Baldhead said, 'Your car will be outside the hotel in two hours!'

You only have to pick out the right man. He handed Mr Lakmiehr three new forms, told him to have the car inspected in the hangar, and then return with the forms so that car could be released.

Mr Lakmiehr assured me that all we needed now was an official to inspect the car, then we could go back to the harbour. Once again right across the city, then we stood in the same hut. I approached the bald official cheerfully.

'Voilà. Here is Form A, here are three more forms. Put your stamp on them.'

I could see that he was terrified. No, he said, he could not stamp them, that was the inspector's prerogative. I gave Mr Lakmiehr one of my ugliest looks.

'Where is your car?' asked the customs inspector in Building 4.

'In a hangar,' I answered.

Then he was not responsible, lamented the inspector. The hangar came under its own police. But the hangar police swarmed round us. Their colleagues' information was false, the customs for freight despatch in Hall 7 was responsible for my car, there I would get a release document and I could get into my car straight away.

Hall 7. Inspectors arguing. I went up to one group.

'Gentlemen, I appreciate your hospitality, but what goes on here is giving me a nervous breakdown. Have any of you heard of a *carnet de passages*?'

Shoulders were shrugged. I showed the bundle of forms and asked for the last decisive stamp. Another official went to the hangar with me.

I saw my Range Rover again. On a platform two metres above me, still firmly held by the blue strap. The inspector shook his head. 'The car must come down. How can I inspect it?'

'Everything you want to know is in the *carnet*!' I said.

'Can you prove that the details in it are identical with those of the car?'

I clambered on to the platform, with the *carnet* in my left hand. Out of his sight I shouted down to the inspector all the details from the *carnet* with a slight hesitation each time as if I was reading from the parts of the car. He gave a quick look at the car above him and scrawled his signature on the form. It was in the bag.

I asked the hangar guard who did the work there. He sent me to a little hut in which a man was sleeping. I woke him up gently and told him I was going to drive to the harbour to fetch the 'licence'. Would he please get the car down from the platform and I would pay him well.

Once again right across Karachi. I went up to my baldhead in the customs house. 'Right. Here are all the forms. All stamped; there's nothing missing.'

He smiled and offered me a chair. Had I got three minutes . . . It didn't really matter to me any more. I waited for two hours. About 1900 hours my *carnet de passages* was stamped. Mr Lakmiehr said gently that it was pointless to go to the airport now. It was the only remark he made that day during our hunt for the stamps.

19 January. At eight Mr Kakmiehr was happy to announce that everything was settled. All we needed now was a gate pass. 'What's that?' I asked. New snags were looming up. Mr Lakmiehr said that the hangar was cut off from the street by a barrier. Soldiers guarded it and in order to drive out one needed a gate pass.

As no one was prepared to issue me the blasted gate pass until noon, I said I was going to the hangar to get in the car and crash through the barrier. Mr Lakmiehr, who by now believed I was capable of it, beseeched me not to do it. I would be shot at and he would get into trouble with Air France who had seconded him to me. I went to the hangar.

The Range Rover was still on the platform. I asked some workers to get it down and I would pay them well. After a lengthy conference three men began to undo the blue strap, taking their time. About 5 p.m. the car was on the ground again. Then I had an eye-opener. The petrol tank was empty, the batteries were not connected and the tyres were at half-pressure—our disastrous work at Orly! I asked a taxi driver to buy a can of petrol, then I opened the tool kit and connected the batteries while Willie pumped up the tyres. At 7 p.m. the taxi driver returned. Knocking off time at the airport. Leaving now was out of the question.

20 January. In the airport at 8 a.m. I asked Mr Lakmiehr, 'Have you got the gate pass?' No, he croaked, it could only be issued by the airport director and he could not be reached at the weekend. What did he mean, weekend? Was it Saturday already?

'Where does the director live?'

That really upset the Pakistani. He was an important gentleman. I would have to wait until Monday. After forking out a goodly bundle of notes, I obtained the address of the almighty one. After a taxi ride of at least 30 km we stopped outside a villa with a lovely park. A female with a veil over her face said that the director was absent. 'All right,' I said, 'I'll wait in the park till he returns.'

Soon afterwards a young man put an end to my sit-in. I

handed him three English versions of my books and asked for two minutes' conversation with the director. I was shown in, described the four-day battle for my car and asked for his signature on the gate pass so that I could at last be master of my own property, my freedom and my valuable time. The director took the form, scribbled on it with a green felt-tipped pen and handed to me without a word. Perhaps he did not speak at weekends.

Mr Lakmiehr looked at the directorial signature as if it was the sign of a miracle.

At last! Into the car and out of this bureaucratic hell. I reached the barrier. The soldier wanted to know what the contents of the car were. I told him in a tone that suggested I was worried about his future not to make any difficulties, because the car had been cleared by the very highest authority. The soldier slunk into the guard house and the barrier rose—automatically.

We were free. After four and a half days spent in 23 offices getting 23 signatures and covering 300 km in taxi rides.

We made Lahore in west Pakistan our first destination, a city of 1.3 million inhabitants, and an important industrial and cultural centre with the famous Punjab University.

To get to Hyderabad on the lower Indus, the map promised us a road 100 km long, which the Pakistanis enthused about as a super-highway. We got a taxi driver to guide us out of Karachi to the main road through bustling streets with bazaars and slum districts teeming with people. It turned out to be a badly asphalted country road. Although all the car windows were open, the thermometer inside read 41 °C!

The Indus is one kilometre wide near Hyderabad. Its waters are a frothing brown broth which flows through Pakistan from north to south. It is what makes the country viable.

Although it was long past noon, the heat got even worse. About every 40 km we passed small settlements where soft drinks—naturally Coca Cola like everywhere else in the world—were on sale at stalls. That afternoon we both drank 14 bottles, but our tongues were still stuck to our palates.

There are as many buses in Pakistan as there are Fiats in Italy. They are painted in glaring colours, bedecked with Christmas tree decorations and crammed as full as if everybody in the Indus valley was travelling. Herds of goats and camel caravans share the traffic as do carts drawn by buffaloes and oxen. At the roadside people cook, pray and sleep. Many travellers carry their beds with them. A wooden framework with ropes lashed across it. A practical idea which ensures ventilation all round, something that undoubtedly benefits these travellers.

The buses run on diesel fuel and from their exhausts float black banners which would drive Western environmentalists to protest marches, but the climate is too oppressive for such activities here. People only demonstrate where it is no effort, where they can drive to the scene in their own cars and go home comfortably after the great battle. Protest needs a certain comfort. Wasn't it Lenin who recommended that demonstrators should be served a good hot meal, because it is hard to demonstrate against hunger on an empty stomach.

There are hardly any private cars. We counted only four on the 1300 km trip to Lahore. That is why all the pumps supply diesel even when they proudly announce petrol. You have to take damned good care that the attendants do not fill the tank with a mixture your engine cannot digest.

Although day-time driving demanded my full attention, night-time driving was the worst I have ever experienced. The buses drive in the middle of the road with their headlights on. Camels, oxen, buffaloes and goats have no luminous strips on their flanks. They pound through the darkness regardless of the highway code. Large groups of men sleep right up to the road surface. If you are blinded by lights, you can only stop or jolt into the fields.

At three o'clock at night we came to Multan, a town of 350,000 inhabitants on the Chenab, one of the five rivers of that part of India that rises in the Himalayas. Strangely enough I have never come across the name in a crossword puzzle.

In the hotel we could not sleep because of the clammy humid air. Like ourselves the fan had given up the ghost.

We had to follow our nose or use the compass for the signs are mostly written in the Persian variant of Arabic script, *Nastaliq*. You cannot ask for information because the Pakistanis either speak one of their 32 dialects or at best the official language Urdu, and of course we did not understand that. One consolation was that after Lahore, the border town with India, we could get by with English.

About nine o'clock we drove through a wrought-iron gate, signposted the 'Frontier of Kashmir', and only 500 m further on we passed through a much bigger iron gate painted in the Indian national colours, 'Welcome to India'.

The 250 km long Indian road from Wagah to Jammu differs only from the Pakistani super-highway in that large numbers of cows swell the animal traffic. Cows always have the right of way here. They can do as they please. If they feel like it, they lie down in herds in the middle of the road. Gradually you begin to hate these harmless bovines.

In India you learn a great many facts about the sacred cows that change any preconceived opinions. When I said that the sacred cows should be slaughtered, I was told that these miserable skinny creatures still play an important and irreplaceable part in everyday life. I wondered how that could be, thinking of the beautiful fat cows in the Swiss meadows with their bursting udders. The wretched cows on India's streets supply only half a litre of milk daily, but that is an important source of nourishment in a country where hunger dogs people like a shadow. I had already noticed that dried cowdung was busily collected as fuel by the natives, but I was amazed to hear that it supplied more heating fuel than all the coal won from the West German coalfields. The third reason for the presence of cows on all the streets was particularly illuminating. They eat all refuse that is in any way digestible. So they are simultaneously dustmen and hygiene inspectors! But why are they holy? Because Hinduism strictly forbids the slaughter of cows and the 300 million people Hindus in the Indian union watch carefully over this religious law.

From Jammu you can see the giant mountains of the Himalayas. Jammu has more than 3½ million inhabitants and is the capital of Kashmir in winter, a role adopted by Srinagar in the summer. This move by the authorities is easily understood once you have spent January in Jammu. We were dried out by the heat at this time of year and enjoyed Srinagar in Kashmir, a region the travel guide calls the Asiatic Switzerland.

The map gives 300 km as the distance from Jammu to Srinagar. By the evening we would be able to breathe in refreshing air at a height of 1768 m.

This hope dwindled with every kilometre. I have never seen

so many soldiers on the march. Even these military columns were not allowed to frighten or crowd the cows. Perhaps they can prevent wars—and then they would indeed be 'sacred'. We wound our way up to a height of some 2000 m past mountain villages with a Tibetan character. In a flash the hothouse air of the Indus valley was blown away. Spicy clear mountain air made our spirits rise. We were in the foothills of the Himalayas.

Srinagar!

Factually and without exaggeration one could describe the town as the 'Venice of Asia'. It is traversed by many canals teeming with boats, gondolas and moored houseboats, especially on Lake Bal which borders the town to the east. Srinagar lies on latitude 34, the same as Gibraltar and Damascus. The average summer temperature is 30 °C, in winter 3–4 °C.

Srinagar lies at the outlet of Lake Wular in the Kashmir valley. There is every justification for calling this valley 'heaven on earth'. Former rulers laid out parks of exceptional beauty, great extent and unusual floral richness, especially the garden of Shalimar, praised by poets, in which wooden bridges cross still pools.

However delightful it looks, it is all on the surface. There is something wrong with this holiday paradise. Kashmir's Asiatic tradition cannot adapt to modern ways. Up here the streets are choked with the same filth (Srinagar has half a million inhabitants) as down in the valleys. The most primitive hygiene is lacking. Although the drinking water is filtered, it is still a yellowish colour. Revolting.

Here as elsewhere one senses how many expensive shipments of foreign aid are wasted pointlessly. Medicines perish because of a shortage of refrigerators. If there are any, they do not work, with few exceptions. Surrounded by dirt from birth, the natives are immune to the bacteria and viruses prevailing here. They are dangerous to foreigners. Mortally dangerous. If this delightful region is to be opened up, as the intention is, to money-spinning world tourism, there is a lot to be done first.

The population are industrious. From the age of six, chil-

'Are you sure you don't want a girl?' asked 12-year-old Mahmud.

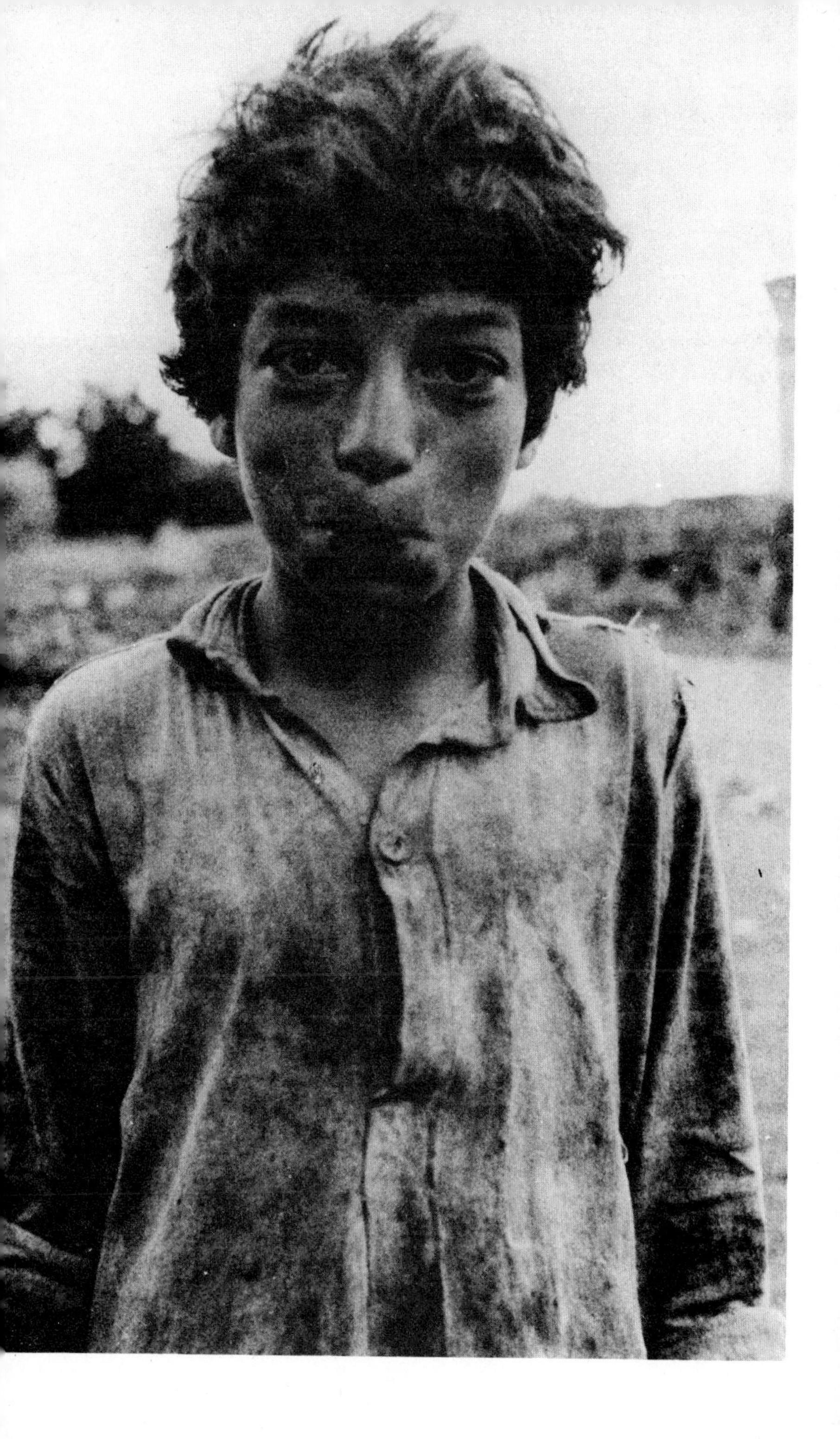

The men in Kashmir wear the *kipa*, like the Jews of the Old Testament and present-day Israel.

dren work in the fertile fields and many small workshops. Mediaeval. At a filling station I was served by a 12-year-old, Mahmud, a nice boy. He asked what services I wanted. As I needed nothing except petrol, he asked if he could procure a girl for me. I asked, 'Why aren't you at school?'

'I have no parents,' he answered, 'and we've all got to live. Are you sure you don't want a girl?'

The little pimp was disappointed when a rich foreigner—all foreigners are rich—refused his offer.

The physical similarity between the Kashmiris and the Israelis is astonishing. They are of the same stature, have the same almond eyes and similar noses. The boys are circumcised here, too. As in ancient Israel the dead are buried in an east–west direction. Like the Israelis, the Kashmiri men wear a *kipa*, a little cap, on the back of their heads.

As we drove through the valleys of Kashmir (without snow in the winter), we constantly felt that we were travelling through a biblical landscape and living among the biblical folk of the Old Testament. Kashmiri itself, the language of the country, has much in common with Old Aramaic, the oldest branch of West Semitic, in other words the language that Jesus and his disciples spoke. I give some examples below:

Hebrew	*Kashmiri*	*Meaning*
akh	akh	alone
ajal	ajal	death
awa	awa	blind
ahad	ahad	at once
hamah	humaham	noise
loal	lol	love
qatal	qatal	murder
qabar	qabar	grave

There are too many features common to Israelis and Kashmiris for them to be explained as coincidences.

A legend firmly held by the Kashmiri people says that the Kashmir valley was really the *promised land* that Moses promised the children of Israel. Moreover they claim that the present-day Kashmiris are direct descendants of an Israeli tribe. Popular tradition here astonished me. The Kashmiris say that the Exodus—contrary to the biblical account—did not start from Egypt and wind through the Sinai Desert for 40 years to end up in Palestine. According to them, the Exodus started from Egypt and traversed the (present-day) countries of Jordan, Syria, Iran, Afghanistan and Pakistan to the highlands of Kashmir.

We must take this version seriously, for if you look at the map, it makes more sense than the chaotic and aimless movement of masses in the deserts of the Near East. If we consider the Kashmiri tradition, many of the battles which the Israelites had to fight for 40 long years begin to make sense. What battles would they have been exposed to in marching round the Sinai Desert? There were no enemy alien peoples there. On the long trek to Kashmir, on the other hand, the wandering Israelites would really have had to fight their way through against opposing forces. The land frontiers they reached were under the dominion of kings hostile to nomadic peoples who poured in with bag and baggage and a train of carts and cattle.

The legend also states that Moses died in the Kashmiri

highlands. Traditions have it that the prophet was active there and that Solomon had his throne there, too. Following this legend the local mountain near Srinagar is still called Takht-i-Suleiman, the Throne of Solomon, and 30 km south-west of Srinagar lies the tomb of Moses on Mount Booth, as every Kashmiri knows! This fact is also noted in the Bible:

> And the Lord said to him (Moses), 'This is the land of which I swore to Abraham, to Isaac, and to Jacob, I will give it to your descendants. I have let you see it with your eyes, but you shall not go over there.' So Moses the servant of the Lord died there in the land of Moab, according to the word of the Lord, and he buried him in the valley in the land of Moab opposite Beth-Peor; but no man knows the place of his burial to this day.

What if . . .

Suppose that Moses had not led the Israelites to Palestine, but to the highlands of Kashmir. Tradition assures us that Moses acted on the orders of the Lord, the same Lord who destroyed the attacking Egyptians and preceded the Israelites in a pillar of cloud which glowed red at night. The Lord provided the Israelites with manna from heaven on their long wanderings, so that men, women and children would not perish in the wilderness. There are many deserts to cross on the way from Egypt to Kashmir. Could the Lord have had an interest in guiding the Israelites to Kashmir?

I remembered the mutiny described by the antediluvian prophet Enoch—the rebellion of 200 'angels' against their 'Lord'. In Chapter 6 of his apocryphal (Greek for 'hidden scriptures') book the prophet Enoch writes:

> After the sons of men had multiplied, beautiful and pleasing daughters were born to them in those days. But when the angels, the sons of heaven, saw them, they lusted after them and said to each other: 'We want to elect wives for ourselves from among the daughters of men and beget children.' But Semyasa, their chief, said to them: 'I fear that you will not carry out this deed, so that I alone will have to atone for a great sin.' Then did they all answer him and say: 'We shall all swear an oath and bind ourselves

> mutually by curses not to give up this plan, but to fulfil the work we have intended.' Then they all swore together and bound themselves mutually by curses. In all they were 200, who came down on to the summit of Mount Hermon in Yared's days. And they called the mount Hermon because they had sworn on it and bound themselves mutually by curses. These are the names of their leaders: Semyasa, their chief, Urakib, Arameel, Akibeel, Tamiel, Ramuel, Danel, Ezeqeel, Saraquyal, Asael, Armers, Batraal, Anani, Zaqebe, Samsaveel, Sartael, Turel, Yomyael, Arasyal . . . These and all the others with them took themselves wives, each of them chose one, and they began to go in to them and to defile themselves with them. They taught them charms, incantations and how to cut roots, and revealed healing plants to them.[1]

Further on Enoch describes the conspiracy and even the functions the unusual 'angels' had to exercise. I did not need my imagination stimulated to recognise these 'angels' as something quite different. None of the qualities described by Enoch tallies with the benevolent and helpful attributes ascribed to biblical angels. Biblical angels did not beget children, did not seduce the daughters of earth and did not bind each other mutually by 'curses'. Enoch's angels were mutineers against the Lord. A considerable team of 200 members rebelled against their commander, who—as Enoch knew—finally vanished into space in a spaceship and left the mutineers behind on the earth.

What did the mutineers have at their disposal, how could they maintain their existence? They still had tools, a few technical apparatuses, perhaps a caterpillar track vehicle, a craft like a helicopter, but they had nothing to conquer interstellar space. Nevertheless, they had something left: their knowledge! The mutineers would have had some valid reasons for their rebellion. Perhaps the commander was too strict with them. Perhaps they were fed up with the monotonous everyday work on board. All these are purely speculative assumptions. But now they were on a planet with men on it who were very like themselves. The mutineers decided to turn these men into servants and serfs who would enable them to lead a riotous life.

The mutineers did not stay together long. They split into groups, divided up the remaining appliances and decided to keep each other mutually informed about their activities by radio. Then they went off to different points of the compass. One group sailed over the ocean to South America, another to North America, a third to the Pacific and a fourth to Asia. Dividing up the earth caused them no problems. They behaved exactly like the mutineers on the *Bounty* thousands of years later. Its crew took over the ship in the South Pacific in 1787 and made themselves independent in that ocean. Each one of them wanted to be a king. Some of them fulfilled their dream, others were murdered by the islanders.

And one of the groups described by Enoch flew over the highlands of Kashmir, perceived the indescribable beauty of the landscape and sensed the ideal climatic conditions. A good place to live! But alas, 3000 years ago or whenever it was—I do not trust the biblical dating—there were no men in the Kashmir valley, no domestic servants. Being used to an aristocratic life, the gentlemen from another star could not imagine a day without servants, even in their worst nightmares. Rearing a domestic troop from a single pair of humans would take too long, they felt, so they decided to guide a tribe from Egypt to the Kashmir valley. That would be the land flowing with milk and honey. No sooner said than done. The mutineers led the Israelites out of Egypt to the Indian highlands! So they used columns of smoke and fire to show the way by night. Without these signals the goal could not have been reached. Marches through deserts are worse than wrong turns in a maze. The 'gods' would have to help. Wherever it was necessary, they intervened in battles so that their future domestics would arrive at their destination unharmed and victorious.

Those are just thoughts that came to me on the long journey. But I also thought about something else.

In order to reach Kashmir the Pir Panjal mountains have to be crossed. At the lowest point at which they can be passed, they are still 2510 m high. Today this pass is pierced by the Banihal Tunnel at a height of 2180 m. The fact that the Kashmir valley was uninhabited thousands of years ago can presumably be ascribed to this mountain barrier.

If we spin the colourful thread further, the Israelites now

had their own land which they could cultivate for themselves and their 'Lord'. Then as now the Israelites, now the Israelis, were and are an industrious obedient and intelligent people, obviously the reason why the mutineers brought this highly cultivated tribe into the country. With its help, temples, palaces and gardens soon came into being. The Kashmir valley became the promised land, a paradise.

These admittedly bold speculations have a snag. According to biblical exegeses King Solomon (*c*. 965–926) had a temple built in Jerusalem. Did King Solomon, like his predecessor David, not belong to the group which was piloted to the Kashmir valley? Did Solomon spend some time in Kashmir and some time in Palestine? No one can be in two places at once. Not even Solomon!

The *Kebra Nagast* is the oldest Ethiopian traditional scripture. In Chapters 30, 52, 58, 59 and 94 it tells at length about a 'heavenly car' which King Solomon inherited from his forefathers and used zealously.*

'But the King . . . and all those who obeyed his word, flew on the wagon without pain or suffering, and without sweat or exhaustion, and travelled in one day a distance which (usually) took three months to traverse.'[2]

From Jerusalem to Srinagar it is barely 4000 km as the crow flies. On foot this distance would take more than three months to cover. Given a day's march of 20 km, one could cover 600 km in a month and 1800 km in three months. And the land route is infinitely longer than the distance as the crow flies. But that is just the distance Solomon is supposed to have covered in one day in his flying machine, according to *Kebra Nagast*.

If the king had been in the air only 12 out of the 24 hours his craft would have had a speed of 150 km per hour. If we assume that he flew only eight hours a day, his heavenly car would have had an average speed of 225 km per hour, not the speed of jet planes, but fast enough to go back and forth between Jerusalem and Srinagar several times a month.

Supposing King Solomon had made an interim landing about half way between Kashmir and Israel, there should presumably be indications of such a landing in present-day Iran. Heavenly air machines, not an everyday sight in those

* The story of the heavenly vehicle is described in detail in *Signs of the Gods*.

days, could not have started and landed without being spotted by the inhabitants.

In fact the sugarloaf mountain Takht-i-Suleiman, Throne of Solomon, like the one near Srinagar, is located in northwest Iran at a height of 2200 m. On the *Iranian* Throne of Solomon there was a Sassanid fire temple in which fire and water were worshipped. Fire and water? They do not like each other. When they meet, steam arises. Was Solomon's flying machine driven by steam? Was the technique of the steam engine known, in the form in which it was first discovered by the Frenchman Denis Papin (1647–1712)? Did they worship fire and water because of this wonder? Oddly enough the neighbouring mountain is called Zendan-i-Suleiman which means 'Prison of Solomon'. Perhaps the pilot went off course and made a forced landing there.

Quite apart from any bold flights of imagination, the fact remains that there are two mountains called after Solomon one in Iran and one near Srinagar. There were temples consecrated to Solomon on both of them. The edifice in Iran no longer exists, but the temple near Srinagar is still in use, although it has been rebuilt many times. Incidentally, my assumption explains why Solomon had to fetch architects and master builders from Lebanon to build the temple at Jerusalem. His own people were working in the valley of Kashmir.

It is obvious that these hypotheses, which will take many of my readers' breath away, are connected with my extraterrestrials. It is not clear what they can have to do with Jesus who lived 1000 years later. Until I had hard facts to handle, I let my thoughts dwell on the matter.

The sect of the Essenes on the Dead Sea, who were bound by the Mosaic law, knew that at least one Israelite tribe lived in distant Kashmir.[3] They knew old writings from Solomon's reign and his Asiatic connections. Perhaps there was still contact in Jesus' day between the Essenes and their fellow countrymen who had gone to Kashmir. So these are my assumptions about how and why Jesus might have come to Kashmir.

Jesus was nailed to the cross at noon on a Friday. The Sabbath, the seventh day of the week, begins at midnight on Friday. It is the day of rest, of sanctification and spiritual renewal. The Roman occupying forces were intelligent enough to respect this religious law. Consequently no one who was punished could continue to hang on the cross on the Sabbath. Contrary to general opinion the Roman punishment of crucifixion was not inevitably a death sentence, but rather a barbarous form of torture which strong and healthy bodies, controlled by a stubborn will, could survive.

The Bible tells us that a Roman legionary pierced Jesus in the side with a spear and that blood and water flowed from the wound. That means that Jesus was not dead. Joseph and Nicodemus, in the presence of some women, including the mother of Jesus, were allowed to take the Master down from the cross. The men allowed the Roman soldiers to go on thinking that the Lord was dead, covered the martyred body with cloths and treated the wounds with salves and herbs in a secret place, perhaps the monastery of the Essenes, who had some outstanding doctors. That is the only way in which the following biblical text becomes intelligible: 'Why do you seek the living among the dead?', the question two men asked the women at the tomb (Luke 24.1).

John the Evangelist does not mention the resurrection and the statements of Matthew, Mark and Luke are contradictory. The biblical account relates that Jesus showed himself to his disciples after being taken from the cross and that he even allowed Doubting Thomas to touch the wounds in his hands and feet.

The Romans heard the news that Jesus was alive and began to look for him. As a well-known figure Jesus dared not show himself in public, a difficult task, for all the territory around present-day Israel was occupied by the Romans—Egypt to the south, Lebanon and Turkey in the north, and Europe to the west. There was only one suitable direction to flee in—eastwards! Were the Essenes in action again with their fifth column? Did they advise Jesus to fly in the direction of Kashmir because they could assure him that he would meet fellow countrymen there?

The Romans installed Saul as a persecutor because they knew that as a trained officer he hunted the Christians down. Saul, the crafty fox, realised that Jesus would have to go via Damascus in an easterly direction to escape persecution. Outside Damascus Jesus made Saul blind. 'Saul, Saul, why doest thou persecute me?' (Acts 9.4.) In conversation Jesus managed to convince the Romans that he was no longer dangerous to them and they could let him go on his way.

After this encounter Saul changed his name to Paul. He turned into a missionary to the heathens, in other words he was the first non-believer won over to Christianity by Jesus himself. Now Paul preached the doctrine of Jesus by which all are equal before God, a political programme of an explosive nature, because it was liable to misinterpretation. Paul's missionary journeys were punctuated by revolts by slaves—reason for the first post-Christian emperors to persecute the youthful Christian community in a bloodthirsty fashion. The Roman Saul/Paul was finally crucified head downwards, payment for his treason in the eyes of the Romans.

Was Christ's mother Mary unable to stand the rigours of the journey? Did she die a few kilometres west of present-day Rawalpindi in Pakistan? In any case the chapel *Mai Mari*, 'Last Resting Place of Mother Mary', still exists there today.

If we follow Indian traditions, Jesus continued on his way to Kashmir. He had escaped from his Roman persecutors. He would certainly have been given a friendly reception in Kashmir by the exiled community living according to the strict precepts of the Essenes. He would have married and died at a great age, venerated both by simple men and mighty rulers.

These thoughts put together from my reading and various pointers, though they contained many question marks, kept me going until I could follow up visible tracks.

Professor Dr F. M. Hassnain, with whom I had exchanged several letters in which I had told him of my forthcoming visit, was waiting for me on the terrace of the Hotel Oberoi, a former maharajah's palace. He is in government service and as Head of Archives not only looks after present-day state papers, but also documents from the past. I hoped that he would help to clarify my daring conjectures. Now he sat next to me under a sunshade. All was peace around us. Our view of an Eden-like park and the waters of Srinagar sparkling in the sunlight formed the ideal background for a quiet conversation. Only as the days went by was I to realise the respect felt for this amiable scholar by the highbrows of the city. Chance had led me to a really well-informed man.

When I began to talk about Jesus' possible sojourn in Kashmir and pointed out that the story of the existence of

Jesus' tomb was not enough for genuine conviction, Professor Hassnain obviously felt my scepticism was asking too much.

'The chain of proof has no gaps in it. It can stand up before any court!'

'Thank you, Professor, I am anxious to hear it.'

'I assume,' lectured Hassnain, 'that you have noticed during your drive through our country how similar the population of Kashmir is to the inhabitants of historical Palestine. These similarities are not confined to appearance and language, or even to religious rituals. You can recognise the similarities in ancient temple buildings, which all look like miniatures of the temple in Jerusalem. You saw the Throne of Solomon mountain and the Garden of Solomon barely 15 km from here. The mountains mentioned in Deuteronomy that you seek in vain in Palestine are here in Kashmir and, honoured sir, the tomb of Moses is also here in our country. No, believe me, when Jesus made his way here, he wasn't looking for some vague destination, but *the land of his fathers*!'

'How did Jesus know about this country?'

Professor Hassnain looked at me and took a drink of iced tea with lemon.

'There are several possibilities. Perhaps he knew about it from ancient writings in the Essene monastery. If there were no written references, there were oral traditions, after all it was not long after the Exodus. And there is one underestimated possibility. You know that Western Christian scholars cannot fill the gap in Jesus' life between the ages of 12 and 13. So we must ask whether Jesus had not been in our country from his boyhood.'

As the professor was pleading for accuracy, I asked 'There is an enormous distance of 4000 km as the crow flies between Jerusalem and Srinagar. How did Jesus cover it?'

The professor grinned and answered after lighting one of his super-king-size cigarettes:

'My dear fellow, think of the Canadian settlers in our century. They crossed from the east to the west coast—700 km—without railways, airplanes or cars. On foot, with families and household in the simplest of covered wagons. Given a day's march of only 15 km the distance from Palestine to Kashmir could be covered in a year and in biblical times the

people were definitely much better walkers than we are today.'

He argues well, this professor, I thought, but I persisted.

'Is there anything tangible to measure or photograph?'

The question obviously startled Hassnain; he sat up stiffly in his chair.

'We have the tomb of Jesus, mentioned in documents for more than 1900 years. The inscription reads: "Here lies the famous prophet Yuz-Asaf, called Yusu, prophet of the children of Israel." I should tell you that Yuz-Asaf and Yusu are identical with the name of Jesus. They are the local transliterations.'

The next day Professor Hassnain took us to a narrow alley which is in perpetual gloom. It is called 'A Prophet Will Come'. Our goal is Rauzabal Khanyar, a building combining elements of church and mosque. Unauthorised as we were, we would not have been allowed to enter without Professor Hassnain. He is known and respected and anyone accompanying him profits by his authority.

We all took our shoes off and said a prayer along with the custodian and his family. I admit that I felt uneasy. It was an uncanny thought that I might be close to the bones of the genuine Jesus.

The room is rather dark. A cross with lighted candles rests on beams. In the centre stands a delicately carved shrine protected by a lattice of narrow strips of wood. Incense sticks glowed in a bowl on the floor.

It is not only a place of pilgrimage for Christians, for Hindus and Moslems venerate the burial site, too. Although they look on Muhammad as the highest prophet of god, Jesus means much to them as an eloquent prophet and exemplary man.

At one point, which could not be entered, I saw footprints in the stone floor. 'What is that?' I whispered.

'Those are Jesus' footprints,' said the custodian, mumbling a prayer, lowering his head and folding his hands across his chest as pilgrims to Christian holy places do.

'May I touch the stone?' I asked. Without interrupting his prayer, the guide nodded with monkish meekness. Measuring

Rauzabal Khanyar, the place of pilgrimage, lies in a gloomy alley.

with my outspread hand, I estimated the prints to be equal to a size 12 foot. I felt depressions and unevennesses in the prints. The marks of wounds? That is what they claim here.

In a whisper I asked Professor Hassnain if I might be allowed to go into the tomb. My request would probably have been firmly refused, if Dr Aziz Kashmiri, author of the book *Jesus in Kashmir*, had not joined our group as agreed. He supported my request.

The shrine was opened. I said a short prayer to please those who were watching me. I got my camera ready and went inside through a small lattice door. Looking back on it I have to admit that I was annoyed for some inexplicable reason. At the time, I remember, I was forced to concentrate on complicated shots. The flashlight blazed. Sacrilege? I thought of the Jesus of my schooldays who, so we were taught, understood all kinds of human behaviour. I believe that he would also have understanding for my curiosity. I fished the compass from the breast pocket of my bush jacket. The stones of the tomb were aligned in a west–east direction.

I took photos with various objectives. I kept busy because I was disappointed. Does this tomb, this stoneclad burial place, offer conclusions about what is hidden in it? Is everything that is claimed about it simply a chimera? These stone slabs must be raised, the real grave must be opened. We would not have genuine proof until bones with wound marks in hands and feet were revealed. Perhaps the funerary adjuncts would also provide information.

One might also imagine that, in the case of such a famous figure as Jesus, a scroll with details of his life might have been laid in his last resting place. The exact time of his death could be dated from the smallest piece of bone.

'Professor, why is the grave not investigated so that assumptions would become facts?'

Hassnain explained that he had been trying to achieve this for years, but without success. The highest circles were afraid of offending the religious susceptibilities of Christians, Moslems and Hindus. He winked at me.

'Write about it! Your books are read and discussed everywhere. Besides it would be a great success if scholars from all over the world could obtain permission to open the grave from the highest Indian authorities!'

'Even an X-ray examination of the grave could supply important evidence,' I said, 'without disturbing the bones or the mummy or whatever is hidden down there.'

'Perhaps,' said Hassnain resignedly.

On our way back to the Hotel Oberoi I made it abundantly clear to the professor that this tomb could not convince anyone of the correctness of the assumption that Jesus had been in Kashmir, grown old there and been buried in Srinagar.

Hassnain looked at the teeming mass of humanity in the street and said, 'I freely admit that, but think of the documents!'

'Which documents?'

'Tomorrow I will show you two inscriptions on the Throne of Solomon mountain. One says: 'In this time the prophet Yusu preached.' The date reckoned by the Gregorian calendar is AD 54. The second inscription says: 'He is Jesus, the prophet of the children of Israel."'

'Could not one of Jesus' disciples have visited Kashmir in 54 to give rise to the inscriptions. The presence of Jesus was not needed for that.'

'Come to the library tomorrow. There I'll show you the Sanskrit book *Bhabishya Maha Purana*. It dates to AD 115. On pages 465 and 466 in verses 17 to 32 a meeting between Jesus and the ruler of Kashmir is described. I am asked about it so often by Western visitors that I always carry a transcript of it in my pocket. I can dictate the text on to your tape machine if you like.'

If I liked: Now I have a tape spoken in English in my archives. This is what Professor Hassnain read to me:

> During the reign of Raya Shalevahin—that was AD 78—the monarch had himself carried over the cool hills of Kashmir. There the king saw a happy person in white linen sitting on the grass, surrounded by many listeners. Shalevahin asked the stranger who he was. The man in the white robe answered in a calm and cheerful voice: 'I was born of a virgin. I am the preacher of the Mlacha religion of the true principles.'
>
> The king asked: 'What kind of religion is that?'
>
> 'Omaharay (great lord), I wandered and preached in the land of Mlacha (geographical Palestine) and taught the

truth and preached against the destruction of traditions. I appeared there and they called me Masih (Messiah). They did not like my teaching, rejected the traditions and judged me. I suffered much at their hands.'

When the king wanted to hear more about the religion which was unknown to him, the man in white linen answered: 'The religion is love, truth and purity of heart, and that is what I was called Messiah for.'

An exciting text!

After we had said goodbye outside the Oberoi, I sat out on the balcony for an hour in the early evening by the light of a storm lantern. In one great panorama I saw the river Jhelum which runs through Srinagar and on the slopes the temples from the Hindu period, the fourteenth- and fifteenth-century palaces and mosques. After an exciting day I regained my calm, reflected on what I had heard and played the tape over and over again.

According to this Sanskrit tradition from the year AD 115, Jesus-Masih answered the king: 'I was born of a *young woman*, I taught the truth and preached against destruction of the traditions . . . *they rejected the traditions and judged me* . . .'

The evangelists also tell us that Jesus was born of a virgin—a young woman. We know that Jesus preached the genuine doctrine of the tradition since the Dead Sea Scrolls[4] were found in the caves near Qumran in 1947. They give vital information about the beginning of the era which dates from the birth of Jesus. In AD 66 the Essenes put their most valuable scriptures in clay vessels and hid them in the caves above Qumran. Found by chance, the caves on the Dead Sea saw the start of a real thriller.[5]

Some scrolls went half-way round the world by routes varying from black to grey; they were put under the microscope in universities and monasteries and gold, too, played a part in the sensational find . . . before the unique documents, which transformed the theological world picture, came into the safe hands of Professors André Dupont-Sommer and Millar Burrows.

These finds prove definitively that Jesus took most of his teachings from the Essenes, for example, the Sermon on the

Mount, the core of his doctrine, and the battle of the 'Sons of Light' against the 'Sons of Darkness'.

Philo of Alexandria, who lived *c.* 25 BC to AD 50, wrote of the Essenes in his treatise *Quod Omnia Probus Liber Sit*[6]:

> Nor has Palestinian Syria, which is inhabited by a significant number of the very numerous Jewish people, been unfruitful in the cultivation of virtues. Some of the Jews, more than 4000 in number, are known as Essenes; in my opinion this name . . . is connected with the word 'holiness', for in fact they are men who are especially devoted to the service of God . . . They hoard neither silver nor gold, nor do they acquire large estates . . . but provide only the necessities of life . . . they reject everything that could arouse envy among them . . . They do not possess a single slave, on the contrary they are all free and help each other mutually . . . a thousand examples testify to their love of God . . .

The Jewish historian and general Flavius Josephus (AD 37–97) wrote as follows about the Essene community in his *History of the Jewish War*:[7]

> For there are three philosophical sects among the Jews: the followers of the first which are the Pharisees, of the second the Sadducees, and the third sect, which pretends to a greater discipline, are called Essenes . . . They neglect wedlock, but choose out other people's children while they are pliable and fit for learning, and esteem them to be of their kindred, and form them according to their own manners . . . But the management and habit of their bodies is such as children use . . . A priest says grace before meat . . . the same priest . . . says grace after meat . . . They also take great pains in studying the writings of the ancients . . . They condemn the miseries of life, and are above pain, by the generosity of their mind . . . For their doctrine is this, that bodies are corruptible, and that the matter they are made of is not permanent; but that the souls are immortal . . .

This psychogram of a community fits in with what we know of Jesus the loner. As a boy born of a virgin, was his education entrusted to the Essenes? Was the Mosaic law that there is only one God so firmly implanted in him that as a man he despised Roman polytheism and became a rebel? Did he learn from the Essenes to endure and overcome pain and martyrdom on the cross by spiritual strength? Ought we to dismiss it as coincidence when ancient Sanskrit texts say that the Masih-Messiah told the king that he was born of a maiden and had 'preached the truth against the destruction of the traditions' which was the Essenes' programme?

I saw the trail that led from Srinagar 2000 years back to the time of Jesus and yet further back in time to the gods and the mutineers. If in the future I say with conviction that the tomb of Jesus might be located in Srinagar, I know that Asiatic legends will only bring a forbearing smile to the faces of Western theologians. But they should combine to explain the Indian legend of Jesus! Is that an improper challenge, a heresy? May we not investigate the tomb of Jesus in Kashmir just because the resurrection should preclude the idea of there being any grave? Is it blasphemy?

The question should be answered for the sake of the ultimate Christian truth. If the bones of Jesus are really at that place of pilgrimage, Rauzabal Khanyar, that does not alter his noble teachings. We must be pessimistic as St Paul was in I Corinthians, 15.16–17: 'For if the dead are not raised, then Christ has not been raised. If Christ has not been raised, your faith is futile and you are still in your sins.'

Professor Hassnain showed us the ruins of the temple of Parhaspur, a scene of total destruction for kilometres around.

The terraced steps of the original complex are clearly recognisable. They immediately reminded me of the stone-dressing and building methods of blocks fitted into and over each other in Inca temples in South America, for example above Cuzco in Peru. Just like there, the masses of stone are sawn out of the rock without apparent effort, here as there, there seems to have been no transport problem. Here, as there, one is forcibly given the impression of an explosive destruction, an annihilation that cannot be attributed to the passage of thousands of years. A look at the wilderness, like the daily television shots after bombardments of war areas, forces one to think the chaos could not have been created without an explosion on the Hiroshima scale. If you look

Pyramids reminiscent of the Maya pyramids in the Central American jungle stand in the centre of Parhaspur. Were the same master builders at work?

around from the centre of the original complex, you notice that the thousands and thousands of broken stones are located about the same distance from the centre.

I am as familiar with the stories of the gods and their terrible weapons as I am with my 'one times' table. So to me there is nothing absurd about the idea of destruction from the air.

'Flying machines in old Indian Sanskrit texts.'

Professor Dr Dileep Kumar Kanjilal gave a brilliant lecture with this title to the Sixth Congress of the Ancient Astronaut Society in Munich in 1979.[8] Kanjilal is a professor at the Calcutta Sanskrit College and therefore a leading scholar in that tongue.

Kanjilal's statements, which I can quote with his kind permission, confirm my hypothesis that the 'mutineers' described in action by Enoch still possessed technical apparatuses and simple flying machines when the mother spaceship had been relaunched. The rebel angels, the beings from heaven, had intercourse with the daughters of men and begot children. They were called the 'sons of God' and certainly no longer had the *original* knowledge of the mutineers, who had belonged to the first space team and had grown up on a distant planet. The extraterrestrials' technical appliances disintegrated, rusted and got lost during the first centuries after the landing. The children produced by the 'mutineers' and their grandchildren grew up on earth. No one had the knowledge necessary to repair defective apparatuses. Nevertheless, thanks to the technical tradition of processes, the know-how of their forefathers, they were still able to build simple flying machines which gave them immeasurable superiority over their contemporaries.

My ears are open to any other explanation of the processes described in the old Sanskrit texts. They are by no standards obscure secret scriptures. The documents quoted by Professor Kanjilal can be seen in any large Sanskrit library and read, too, if you understand Sanskrit. The message from our Sanskrit scholar in Calcutta is so 'dangerous' for scholars stuck in the same old groove that they—without weapons to defend old points of view—can only ignore or mock it. They have no arguments against the traditions. I quote from Professor Kanjilal's lecture:

> There is a tendency to represent the arrival of extraterrestrial gods and their sexual traffic with terrestrial women, which frequently had consequences, as the discovery of the Vedic texts (the oldest religious literature of the Aryan Indians) and the *Mahabharata* (the Indian national epic).
>
> But if we follow the history of idolatry in India we come across two important works, the *Kausitaki* and the *Satapatha Brahmana,* dating from about 500 BC and telling us about images of the gods. Text and illustrations show forcefully that the gods were originally corporeal beings. But how, and this question must be faced, did these gods reach the earth through the atmosphere?
>
> The *Yajurveda* quite clearly tells of a flying machine, which was used by the *Asvins* (two heavenly twins). The *Vimana* is simply a synonym for flying machine. It occurs in the *Yajurveda,* the *Ramayana*, the *Mahabharata,* the *Bhagatava Purana,* as well as in classical Indian literature. Accurately translated the word *Yantra* means 'mechanical apparatus' and is found widely in Sanskrit literature.[9]
>
> At least 20 passages in the *Rigveda* (1028 hymns to the gods) refer exclusively to the flying vehicle of the *Asvins.*

This flying machine is represented as three-storeyed, triangular and three-wheeled. It could carry at least three passengers. According to tradition the machine was made of gold, silver and iron, and had two wings. With this flying machine the *Asvins* saved King Bhujyu who was in distress at sea.

Every Sanskrit scholar knows the *Vaimanika Sastra*, a collection of sketches the core of which is attributed to Bharadvajy the Wise around the fourth century BC. The writings in the *Vaimanika Sastra* were rediscovered in India in 1875. The text deals with the size and the most important parts of the various flying machines. We learn how they steered, what special precautions had to be taken on long flights, how the machines could be protected against violent storms and lightning, how to make a forced landing and even how to switch the drive to solar energy to make the fuel go further. Bharadvajy the Wise refers to no fewer than 70 authorities and ten experts of Indian air travel in antiquity!

The description of these machines in old Indian texts are amazingly precise. The difficulty we are faced with today is basically that the texts mention various metals and alloys which we cannot translate. We do not know what our ancestors understood by them. In the *Amaranganasutradhara* five flying machines were originally built for the gods Brahma, Vishnu, Yama, Kuvera and Indra. Later there were some additions. Four main types of flying *Vimanas* are described: *Rukma, Sundara, Tripura* and *Sakuna*. The *Rukma* were conical in shape and dyed gold, whereas the *Sundata* were like rockets and had a silver sheen. The *Tripura* were three-storeyed and the *Sakuna* looked like birds. There were 113 subdivisions of these four main types that differed only in minor details. The position and functioning of the solar energy collectors are described in the *Vaimanika Sastra*. It says that eight tubes had to be made out of a special glass absorbing the sun's rays. A whole series of details are listed, some of which we do not understand. The *Amaranganasutradhara* even explains the drive, the controls and the fuel for the flying machines. It says that quicksilver and *'Rasa'* were used. Unfortunately we do not yet know what *'Rasa'* was.

These extracts from the Book of Enoch and ancient Indian tradition may explain what is still considered a mystery today. The ruined site of Parhaspur on which I stood might have been the scene of 'divine' air battles.

In 1979 a book by David W. Davenport, an Englishman born in India, was published in Italy. Its title was *2000 AC Distruzione Atomica*, Atomic Destruction 2000 BC.

Davenport claimed to have proof that Mohenjo Daro, one of the oldest sites in the history of human civilisation and one of my destinations, had been destroyed by an atomic bomb. Mohenjo Daro is 350 km north of Karachi in present-day Pakistan, to the west of Sukkur on the Indus. Davenport shows that the ruined site known as the place of death by archaeologists was not formed by gradual decay.

Originally Mohenjo Daro, which is more than 4000 years old, lay on two islands in the Indus. Within a radius of 1.5 km Davenport demonstrates three different degrees of devastation which spread from the centre outwards. Enormous heat unleashed total destruction at the centre. Thousands of lumps, christened 'black stones' by archaeologists, turned out to be fragments of clay vessels which had melted into each other in the extreme heat. The possibility of a volcanic eruption is excluded because there is no hardened lava or volcanic ash in or near Mohenjo Daro. Davenport assumed that the brief intensive heat reached 2000 °C. It made the ceramic vessels melt.

The author says that in the suburbs of Mohenjo Daro skeletons of people lying flat on the ground, often hand in hand, were found, as if the living had been suddenly overcome by an unexpected catastrophe.

In spite of the interdisciplinary possibilities, archaeology works solely by traditional methods in Mohenjo Daro. They ought to use the former, for it would produce results. If flying machines and a nuclear explosion as the cause of the ruins are excluded out of hand, there can be no research by enlarged teams with physicists, chemists, metallurgists, etc.

The ruined site of Parhaspur is too extensive for the site of a temple. Indian traditions mention destruction from the air.

Kashmir and Bolivia are 1800 km apart as the crow flies, yet this slab is dressed like the slabs at Puma Punku.

At many places in Kashmir one stumbles across mysterious dressed stones, as at Sacsayhuaman above Cuzco! No one can explain such coincidences thousands of years ago.

As this iron curtain so often falls on sites that are important in the history of mankind, I cannot help feeling that surprising facts endangering existing ways of thinking might and should be discovered. A nuclear explosion 4000 years ago does not fit into the scenario? After reading Davenport's book, Monhenjo Daro fascinated me even more, as what I had learnt so far seemed to be only half the truth.

Before continuing my journey to the Indus valley, I had to visit my publisher Ajitt Dutt in Calcutta.

He and his family were waiting for me at the airport. His cries of delight on receiving the portable typewriter were combined with a torrential account of how they had expected me two days ago and had had to send home several thousand people who had come to hear me lecture.

Much as I would have liked to see Calcutta, India's largest city with more than 3.5 million inhabitants and an area of 425 sq km, I hardly set foot outside my hotel room. Journalists struggled for the door handle, radio reporters shoved microphones at me. I refused a television interview when I heard that there were only 2000 sets in the city. The television age has only just begun here.

The second day passed like the first. What I said the day before was on the front page of the newspapers next to topical political news and photos of Indira Ghandi. (I recognised it from my photograph.) What were they writing about me? I cannot read Bengali script, but it looked as if I was in clover.

An EvD reception committee appeared at midday with two archaeologists, the director of a museum and several university lecturers. As I had already been taught I placed my hands on my breast in an attitude of prayer and bowed. I was told that everything had been well prepared.

What I experienced in Calcutta that evening was more riotous than anything in my worst nightmares. When we drove up to the museum in the reception committee's car about six o'clock, I saw crowds being held back by the police. Was this in my honour? The police towed me into the inside courtyard. A cordon cleared an alley through which I was squeezed into the hall, a large hall with steps, galleries and wide window-sills. Every inch, one could say, was plastered with people. The air was hot, humid and stuffy. Four massive chairs, into one of which I was pushed, stood in front of a screen. A lady anthropologist, an archaeologist and the museum director praised me in such eulogistic terms that I felt terribly embarrassed. With my watch on the lectern, I stood for a minute without being able to speak through the din. Willi was somewhere in the crowd wearing a bright red shirt so that I could seek him out when I wanted a new slide on the projector. I realised at once that I was going to give an abbreviated version of my lecture. Nevertheless, my vocal chords gave out three times. That had never happened to me before; it must have been due to the stifling air.

A wild tumult broke out when I finished. Thousands thronged to meet me. Until that moment, I did not know how one could be so frightened of people. I was pressed against the wall by autograph hunters, but I could not move my hands. Some distance away I saw Willi who was trying to fight his way to me. The pressure of the throng put me on the floor. With my last ounce of strength I crawled into a corner to reach the protection of two walls. Suddenly I saw the police swinging batons. They laid in with a will, but it did not seem to bother the unrestrained mob. It was an unpleasant scene to have to witness. Was there no window through which I could escape? They all had iron bars. Then the police beat a path through to the car. We got in. Exhausted, bathed in sweat, bedraggled . . . and fairly happy all the same.

The whole of next day I was feeling rather afraid of the second evening lecture at the university. With 240,000 students (!) Calcutta has the oldest and largest university in India. I was told that the lecture would take place in the auditorium for nuclear physics, which was the biggest on the campus, and that the public would be mainly academic.

It did not turn out very academically. Things began when I could not get out of the car because it was besieged by students. Once again the police roughly cleared the way. The students did not mind; they shouted in chorus: Long live Däniken! Can you imagine?

The auditorium was packed to overflowing. I spoke for two hours. You could have heard a pin drop. The volume of the applause at the end was indescribable.

I sensed a wave of sympathy among the faculty leaders. Professors were ready to help me with their specialised knowledge. Sanskrit scholars said they could supply me with a wealth of material from India. They were as good as their word. One scholar assured me that the theories in my books were realities to Hindus that he had always waited for. What I wrote was confirmation of the thoughts of the simple man.

A shy lanky student handed me a book bound in pink. 'That's for you.' I quickly read the title, *Vymaanika-Shaastra Aeronautics,* by Maharishi Bharadwaaja.[10] I asked politely what the book was about. The student smiled.

'It is an extremely old collection of texts that will interest you.' He disappeared into the crowd.

Back at the hotel I opened my present and was afraid I would have to go back to school to learn Sanskrit, when to my delight I found English translations of the texts starting in the middle of the book. My night's rest was done for.

Ten sections dealt with uncannily topical themes such as pilot training, flight paths, the individual parts of flying machines, as well as clothing for pilots and passengers, and the food recommended for long flights.

There was much technical detail: the metals used, heat-absorbing metals and their melting point, the propulsion units and various types of flying machines.

If I had not known that I was looking at Sanskrit texts thousands of years old, I would have taken the book for a manual for trainee pilots. There was a check list with 32 instructions to pilots which the man in charge of an aircraft had to know before he could fly the machine. Among them were secrets such as how to 'jump' with the flying machine, how to fly in a zig-zag, how the pilot can see on all sides and hear distant noises. There were also instructions about the use of the machines in battle. How an enemy manoeuvre could be recognized in time, how to spot the direction of hostile attacks and then prevent them.

The information about the metals used in construction name three sorts, *somala, soundaalika* and *mourthwika.* If they were mixed in the right proportions, the result was 16 kinds of heat-absorbing metals with names like *ushnambhara, ushnapaa, raajaamlatrit*, etc., which I did not understand. And presumably the translators had not identified them either, or they would have been in English.

The texts also explained how to clean metals, the acids such as lemon or apple to be used and the correct mixture, the right oils to work with and the correct temperature for them.

Seven types of engine are described with the special functions for which they are suited and the altitudes at which they work best. The catalogue is not short of data about the size of the machines, which had storeys, nor of their suitability for various purposes. I recommend the texts mentioned here to those who doubt the existence of flying machines in antiquity. The mindless cry that there were no such things would have to fall silent in shame.

The book that came into my hands from the student by chance should be compulsory reading for aeronautical and aerospace engineers and constructors. Perhaps they will discover solutions to projects they are sweating over in the Sanskrit texts. Perhaps they will soon be able to take out patents! Copyright in technology so many thousands of years old no longer exists. But first of all our would-be-clever scientists must decide to take old texts for what they are—descriptions of what once were realities.

When I flew back to Srinagar, all I had seen of Calcutta was my hotel room, the museum, the university and streets teeming with people. But my publisher Ajitt Dutt was very happy.

We profited by our previous experiences and left Srinagar at about 4 a.m. At that time the caravans of pedestrians are still camping by the roadside. We drove 100 km, then the natives and the nocturnal sleepers, cows, camels, dogs and goats awoke and buses and lorries roared along, as rashly as tanks into battle. After the great awakening we only covered 40 km an hour and took a good eight hours for the 350 km to Jammu.

Jammu, capital of the state of Jammu-Kashmir, was once the winter residence of the north Indian maharajahs. Today officials from Srinagar winter in the pleasant climate at 403 m above sea level. It is difficult to pick out particular characteristics in Indian cities. They all overflow with people, they are all bogged down with unregulated traffic, they all have the same filth and they are all dominated by skinny cows.

On the level road leading to Amritsar we wanted to make up for lost time by pressing on fast in order to see the famous 'Golden Temple', the supreme sanctuary of the Sikhs, a religious community with 8 million adherents. Founded by gurus in the sixteenth century, the town also has the 'Pool of Immortality', the literal translations of Amritsar. How can a town bear the promise of immortality in its name? Something unfathomable must have happened here, for under the gold-clad dome of a building there is also a 'Throne of Immortality'. Today the religious guardians of the Sikhs reside under the dome.

At that moment our sturdy Range Rover proved that it was not immortal. There was a blowout in the left rear wheel. Just at high noon. The road was baking. No shadow, not a cloud in the sky. We burrowed under the mountain of luggage for a spare tyre; we wanted to get it over quickly. When I let the jack down, the newly changed wheel spread out alarmingly. We had forgotten to replace the air let out for the car's transport by air. The foot pump over which we sweated did not inflate the tyre; it must have been overworked at Karachi airport. Hell! At a pace a snail could have followed we crawled on to the next filling station. 'Do you have air?' I asked, but English is only understood by the upper classes.

At such moments one has recourse to a pantomime of signs, just like the first men. I demonstrated pumping movements, puffed out my cheeks and blew hissing air through my lips. No, he had no air, the attendant explained using comical gestures. Air is not normally provided at Indian service stations. Roasted by the sun, we dawdled on to Lahore. Night was already beginning to fall. In a workshop a nine-year-old boy inflated the tyre and repaired the damaged tube in a flash.

The road from Lahore to Sukkur via Multan was marked on the map by a red line, which meant that it should be asphalted. From Lahore to Multan the red line lived up to its promise, afterwards it was terrible. I asked a policeman the shortest way to Sukkur.

Asians are sympathetic. If they cannot wrap up a distressing piece of news in polite words, mourning crape descends over their features. What the policeman had to tell us tallied with his mournful expression. At a distance of only 32 km from Multan the Indus flows past the village of Muzaffargarh. Contrary to the seasonal norm, the heavens had opened their sluices; the weather had gone crazy. Although we had sunned ourselves in Srinagar, here the water was absolutely pouring down. Further south on the other side of the Indus it was already impossible to reach Mohenjo Daro. After the policeman, who spoke tolerable English, had consulted the locals, he advised us to drive further south via the dam of Alipur.

One can only accept the forces of nature humbly; it is no good getting angry about them. So we drove towards Alipur. The dam was already under water. The floods were washing over the bridges on the two arms of the Indus. However, we were advised to drive 320 km northwards where the dam near Dera Ismail Khan was still open. A gigantic detour, but what could we do?

For a long time the speedometer had shown more than the 320 km announced. The road became narrower and finally turned into a muddy country lane. There was no sign of the dam. In a nameless village we heard that the dam of Dera Ismail Khan, too, had been taken over by the Indus hours ago, so we had to make haste. All we had to do was go back southwards for 140 km where the Taunsa dam was still intact and open to traffic according to the latest news.

The Taunsa dam is a large structure with concrete carriageways. Tanks could roll over it, but unfortunately the builders had forgotten the access roads.

Six o'clock in the evening. We had been on the road for 16 hours and hoped that now it would be plain sailing all the way to Sukkur. Hope springs eternal in the human breast, but...After I had overtaken a mass of lorries and buses, we came to a river. The road ended somewhere in the mud. What was our cross-country car with four-wheel drive and a winch for? Now I wanted to find out what technology could do.

Willi got out, wearing knee-high wellingtons and waded ahead of the car like a sailor on a rolling deck through the bubbling yellow soup so that I could check the level of the water against his long legs. I drove after him at walking pace and felt slippery mud under the wheels. I prayed that the car would not stop. After minutes that seemed like hours, I was over the river. Eureka! I had found the other saving shore. What was it Archimedes discovered when he shouted Eureka? I think it was the law of specific gravity. If he had been here, he would have shouted Eureka two or three times.

Although it was night, we wanted to continue. We were stopped at the first crossroads and told that all roads to Sukkur were closed as the bridges were flooded. That news sapped all the energy from brain and body and we drove slowly to the haven of Dera Ghazi Khan. Near roadside fires people were selling fruit and vegetables by the light of oil lamps, but against all the rules of salesmanship they looked at us in a most unfriendly, almost hostile manner and were reluctant to give information.

A young man of untrustworthy appearance speaking mangled English recommended the Shezan hotel as the best in town. The Shezan was filthy and bug-ridden with an unappetising coffee bar and an interior courtyard with a water-pump that had not spouted a drop of water for years. A Pakistani who spoke English fluently and kept himself apart from the other men whispered that we ought to be careful. Many travellers had been robbed here and the authorities were powerless because the people stuck together like the Mafia. I asked to be allowed to park the Range Rover in the courtyard. Dog-tired and still in our filthy clothes we collapsed on to the dirty bedstead.

We awoke from an uneasy sleep. The rattle of chains and the sound of a voice came from the courtyard. By the light of their glaring carbide lamp we watched four men inspecting our car and obviously not because they were curious about Western technology.

We went down, stood with our backs to the wall, looking braver than we felt, and glared at the men challengingly. My flashlight formed a bulge in my lightweight jacket so that it looked as if I was ready to draw a revolver. Willi was next to me with his arms crossed, holding in his right hand a canister of teargas which we had brought with us on a prophetic impulse. Figures whom we had not seen before emerged from the darkness. They spoke to the four men, and pointed to the bulge under my jacket and to Willi's spray. The gang withdrew. We left immediately because we suspected that reinforcements would be coming. It was a short night.

It was not surprising that the road to Sukkur was impassable. The roads here are built in a primaeval way. Ox carts bring large stones which Pakistanis hammer into chips. At random they distribute the chips as a foundation, without any binding material. Naturally the tar they pour over it in a thin stream does not stop the Indus from sweeping the surface away every year. Aid from developed countries could really be useful here if it provided instruction in road-making, but not with modern machines, for that would only put the poor locals out of work.

Christopher, the patron saint of travellers, withheld his blessing. We had our second puncture in the middle of the water. The brown Indus broth was up to the hubcap. As St Christopher blesses, but does not help, we plunged into the clinging mud with the jack. Why isn't there a button inside the car to set a hydraulic pump in motion? In every aircraft life jackets are inflated automatically after being connected to a valve. Why do jacks never raise the vehicle high enough? Why do car manufacturers imagine that punctures always happen on firm ground? As they only drive their cars on testing grounds, they have no idea that tyres can lose air anywhere. If I was a technician, I know how someone could have a guaranteed million-dollar business—even after the zip-fastener—by making a jack that could be used in every situation.

In Sukkur which we finally reached after taking many wrong turnings an officer in the Pakistani army told us that it was impossible to drive on southwards. The whole area was flooded and it would be weeks before the water subsided and the roads were repaired. Mohenjo Daro, the place of death, did not want us. We left the sinister inaccessible site to our left.

Tepe Yahya, the excavated site, the circular Sassanid city of Ardashir Khurrah and the caves near Kermanshah were still on our list of destinations. So on to Iran . . .

The officer who I asked if the road from Sukkur to Quetta and from there to Iran was passable looked at me uncomprehendingly.

'Where do you want to go?'

'To Iran.'

'Haven't you read the papers?'

I suddenly realised that I had not seen a newspaper since my arrival in Karachi. Our programme took up every moment of our time.

'Haven't you heard any news?'

The officer did not understand. How could foreigners listen to news in a language they did not know?

He said with military precision: 'All frontier posts with Iran are closed. A revolution has taken place. Follow me, please.'

We followed him to his simple office on the roadside. Having served under the British in the past, he still read *The Times*. He opened a drawer and handed us a bundle of old copies.

'There, have a look.'

DEMONSTRATIONS AGAINST THE SHAH IN SHIRAZ.

SHAH'S DEPARTURE FOLLOWED BY HEAVY CLASHES.

AYATOLLAH KHOMEINI ANNOUNCES HIS RETURN.

TROOPS OCCUPY TEHRAN AIRPORT.

SOLDIERS FIRE ON DEMONSTRATORS.

TRIUMPHAL WELCOME FOR KHOMEINI IN TEHRAN.

CIVIL WAR IN IRAN. CAPITAL IN THE HANDS OF THE REBELS.

ATTACK ON US EMBASSY.

REVOLUTION IN IRAN. ALL FRONTIERS CLOSED.

Headlines from *The Times*. The latest paper contained the information the office had given us and was dated 20 February.

After the forces of nature the superior forces of politics! We had to give up. So back to the port at Karachi which we knew only too well. Our baldhead grinned at us. He seemed to enjoy doing so.

'Do you know what we're missing?' asked Willi, after we had sat in stunned silence for hours.

I pondered. 'Luck!' I said.

'No, the four days after our arrival in Karachi and our three days' wasted driving in the rain.'

A week sooner and we should have been in Iran but we should have driven into the revolution which, so we read, showed all the signs of xenophobia.

'No,' I said, 'we were lucky really . . . and we will be back again.'

No longer in a hurry, owing to the forces beyond our control, we loaded our Range Rover on board a ship in the port of Karachi. With the help of our well-known baldhead everything went smoothly. At the end of April we received a letter in Switzerland. We could collect our car from the customs at Venice.

6 Twilight of the Gods

'Don't let your minds be cluttered up, with the prevailing doctrine.'

Alexander Fleming (1881–1955)
to his students.

It's a terrible thing. So many nice amiable people speak to me on my journeys, offering me—in this case at least—helpful hints and often their visiting cards. When I am back home again and sort out these souvenirs, I sometimes find that some of them are missing. I dislike this because I am an orderly person and like to drop people a line or two of thanks.

This time I hope that the man in his fifties wearing a dark blue suit who spoke to me in Chicago will read this book and know that I am grateful to him for putting me on an important trail.

In the foyer of the hotel in which the Fifth World Congress of the Ancient Astronaut Society* took place in 1978, the man approached and gave me two aerial photographs, which he had taken from a copy of the *National Geographic Magazine* from the thirties. As the organ of the National Geographic Society, Washington DC, this magazine has appeared monthly since 1888.

I looked at the panorama of a hilly almost primaeval landscape, traversed by furrows. Presumably it was in some sort of foothill for the ground had scars scored by mountain streams full of pebbles and it also lay in a hot part of the earth, as was easy to see. The area had no vegetation, not a tree or a shrub. The photograph at once reminded me of the spurs of the South American cordilleras, the mountain chain in the west of South America which stretches to Tierra del Fuego.

'Do you know it?' asked the man, who was watching me closely.

'I've never seen it!' I answered.

* The Ancient Astronaut Society is a non-profit membership society which discusses my theories. The address of the English-language section is 1921 St John's Avenue, Highland Park, Illinois 60035, USA.

'What do you make of this trail?' he asked, pointing to the dark band which led over hill and dale. Naturally I could see the dark hatching which led over hills and gorges from the distant background of the picture to the foreground, standing out clearly from the natural slopes.

My Chicago well-wisher had another surprise. He pressed a second photo into my hand, an enlargement of part of the first. It showed the same trail, but hundreds of small holes were punched in it, as regularly as if a knobbly rolling-pin had been pressed into the ground. I took the normal width of mountain streams as a criterion and estimated the strip to be about 15 m wide. I was electrified by these aerial photos.

'What is it?' I asked my well-dressed friend.

'Gods have travelled along it in some kind of vehicle,' he answered, as if he knew all about it. 'Look. It must have been a fantastic vehicle. Can you think of a modern method of locomotion that would leave such marks in the rock or could travel at all at these heights? Just look how the trail goes up the mountains and down into the gorges. That is no product of modern . . .'

'Do you know where it is?'

The gentleman said that unfortunately he could not give the precise place; the photos were taken from a series about Peru, but the text accompanying the photos did not mention the locality. He left me with the two photos and disappeared with a 'God bless you' into the crowd of guests who turn the foyer of every American hotel into a railway station.

Back home in my study I thumbed through a hundred books on Peru, feeling sure at first that I would come across the sensational photos. But they did not appear. I found illustrations, taken from many angles, of the famous Inca wall which runs for 60 km, from the coast near Paramonga to the Peruvian mountains, flanked to left and right by 14 fortresses. The only feature the Inca wall had in common with the dark dark band in the two photos was the way they both crept over hills and valleys like prehistoric snakes.

This photo appeared in the well-known *National Geographic Magazine* in the thirties.

One thing I was not looking for was the Inca wall. But what could this dark band be? Was it rows of ancient graves? Or had a freak of nature caused this accurate and unusual pattern. Was it a sophisticated protective wall? Was it the remains of ancient plantations? The question nagged at me. I must go there, but where?

With its 1,285,216 sq km, Peru is very large, especially if one is looking for a relatively small area in impassable terrain. Letters flew from my Swiss retreat to my friends in Peru. Every letter contained copies of the two aerial photographs and asked the same question: Tell me where it is. For weeks the answers were depressing. I no longer wanted to open the letters. When I had almost given up, my secretary put an opened letter on my desk.

It came from Omar Chioini Carranza, a colonel in the air force. I knew that this friend of mine was recognised as a first-class aviator and amateur archaeologist. For some years, commissioned by the Air Ministry, he had been involved in the building of an Aviation Museum in Lima, the capital. Colonel Chioini had circulated my photos among his friends and Peruvian archaeologists. He wrote that one of the archaeologists knew the location of the pockmarked strip. It was in the north of Peru in the spurs of the Andes, north-east of the town of Trujillo, the centre of remains of ancient Indian cultures. I must come out. He would be glad to organise the journey to the region; all I had to do was advise him in advance of my date of arrival in Lima. I chose 15 August 1980 for the beginning of the expedition.

As I would be in the region I wanted first to visit El Baul, a small town in Guatemala to which my friend Dr Gene Phillips had drawn my attention. Extremely interesting and quite neglected statues of the gods are to be found there. It is only a step from Guatemala City to Lima by jet plane.

Sitting at my desk with my flight plan all worked out, I had no idea what awaited me in my search for the dark band in Peru.

Having learnt from experience, I tried to rent a cross-

I could not find the remarkable pockmarked band in any of the books about Peru. What was it? Who laid it out?

country vehicle in Guatemala City airport. Why car rental firms can only offer you flashy limousines suitable for good asphalt roads I fail to understand. In Central and South American countries cross-country vehicles are the only sensible means of locomotion, but there aren't any. The pretty Guatemalan girl at the desk asked where El Baul was.

'Near Likkin, which is close to San José on the Pacific Ocean,' I said, for I had done my homework.

The charming lady showed her toothpaste-ad teeth.

'You don't need a cross-country car there. The roads are in perfect condition.'

If a man with brown teeth had made such a promise, I would not have fallen for it. On the pretty lady's recommendation, I accepted a big American Dodge for 28 quetzal a day plus 11 cents a kilometre. The quetzal is the currency of the country and one quetzal is worth one US dollar.

Outside the city a four-lane motorway leads with a great many curves into the deeper lying region in the direction of Escuintla. Apparently my Guatemalan beauty had not been lying. It started like a tourist trip, but the joyride ended after only 20 km, outside Escuintla. Dripping jungle steamed on both sides of the road. Buses and lorries stuck close together and sent out sooty plumes of noxious exhaust gas. Overtaking was out of the question. As far as the eye could see there was a queue of stinking monsters crawling round the hairpin bends at a snail's pace. The only thing that impressed me about Escuintla, a miserable dump, were potholes as deep as wells. What must axles and shock-absorbers suffer under heavy loads? I should not have fallen for the smiling assurance that I did not need anything except the Dodge.

The road forked. The main road led westwards to the Mexican border, my route went south along the CA9 to San José. It was only partially asphalted and the Dodge creaked into and over potholes as deep as a bathtub and groaned over lumps of stone when they were too close together to drive round. On my right I was accompanied by a stream about two metres wide that would undoubtedly overflow the road if there was heavy rain. But it wasn't raining, at least not on that day.

The speedometer showed 49 km for the journey from

Escuintla to San José, covered in the record time of three hours! Oh that smile!

Shaken and jolted, with the five hours' difference in time still making themselves felt, I drove 10 km from San José to the modern holiday town of Likkin to have a good sleep. I wanted to be in peak condition for next day's drive to El Baul. The madonna of the airport was still smiling at me when I fell asleep.

A lot can happen overnight, both pleasant and unpleasant. When I pulled back the curtains in the morning, the sky was full of heavy clouds. Looking on the bright side, I thought that at least the sun would not turn the Dodge into an oven. In the jungle, clouds of this massive kind sometimes threaten without breaking. One can even escape them in a good cross-country vehicle.

I had just reached the route, when the heavens opened their sluices with a deluge of such proportions that they might have been trying to fill ten lines in the *Guinness Book of Records*. It was no first time for me; I have known heavy tropical rain before, but what happened on this 12 August exceeded all my previous experiences.

The stream that had been on my right the day before now grumbled on my left and rose menacingly until it overflowed the road, sweeping along uprooted trees, stones and small animals. Only suicides or greenhorns unused to the jungle would continue in these conditions. I stopped, took the tow-rope out of the boot, already up to my knees in water, and tied it round a massive mahogany tree.

During my disagreeable paddle in the yellowish-brown broth I saw the smile of the seductive Guatemalan like a mene tekel on the surface of the water. If only I had a cross-country car! Their axles are higher; they allow the water to flow unhindered between the wheels and the engine is better protected against water and dust. The brown soup frothed in front of the Dodge as if it were the bow of a ship. I took off my shoes and jeans, piling the luggage as high as possible on the rear seat and on the ledge under the rear window, for the stream had long since forced its way into the car.

I always take a NASA insulation cover, a present from Houston, with me for use in emergencies. Today I used it to wrap up the engine as best I could. It was unpleasant in the roaring stream. It swept along the highly poisonous *barbamarilla*, a local snake. I disliked it intensely, but in spite of several encounters I came out unscathed. The Dodge pulled at the towrope like a bucking bronco.

I crouched on the roof and wondered fleetingly why I kept on exposing myself to such adventures. I sent heartfelt wishes to my wife and daughter in our beloved home in idyllic Switzerland.

After two hours the deluge ended as suddenly as it had started. Presumably the angels had emptied all the celestial swimming pools and switched on the sun again. Suffocating vapours rose over the jungle as if from a mediaeval wash-house. The birds twittered and crowed proudly as if they had closed the sluicegates.

A cowboy wearing a rig-out decorated with silver and a black sombrero rode up to my car as it lay at anchor to inform me that the banks of the stream had collapsed in many places and the road was damaged. He advised me to take care if I was driving on. That had already occurred to me without his horse-borne information service.

Three hours elapsed before the water subsided a little. The road was still under dark water that hid the potential dangers. I took the protective covering off the engine and got it to go after a few false starts, a bit of luck I tried to preserve by driving fast through the spray. The engine was ceaselessly baptised from below. My intention of getting away from the scene quickly and avoiding the swarms of mosquitoes which had simultaneously declared my body their feeding ground failed. A victim of the deluge, I pushed and pulled my car out of the mud, often with the help of farmers. Thirty-eight km beyond San José the level of the road rose above the bed of the stream. The gods had set me a severe test before the encounter with El Baul, for they knew that they have an attraction to offer that is worth a lot of trouble.

El Baul is a little hamlet a few kilometres from Santa Lucia Cotzumalguapa. You find its attraction in a wooden shelter with no sides and open to wind and weather, next to a sugar-cane factory. The stone sculptures, my goal, were found by chance some years ago when the jungle was being cleared and then installed here.

Archaeologists have classified the star attraction as 'El

'Monument No. 27' is to be found under a wooden shelter in the village of El Baul.

Baul monument No. 27'. It has at least been given a catalogue number. Let us take a look at it.

'Monument No. 27' is a stele 2.54 m high and 1.47 m wide. The stone sculpture is dominated by a figure standing with arms akimbo, rather self-confidently it seemed to me. It wears what look like boxing gloves and the hands hold balls the size of tennis balls. On its feet the figure wears boots which reach to the knees and have trousers like knickerbockers tucked into them. A broad belt separates the trousers from the close-fitting upper part. To that extent the figure could be dressed in the fashion of its day, but the helmet enclosing its head is amazing. Like a modern diving suit, it ends on the shoulders in broad bulges. A tube leads from the back of the helmet to a small tank-like chest, a container. The helmet leaves a peephole free for the eyes protected as if with a transparent disc. Behind it you can make out an eye with an eyebrow, the beginning of a nose and part of the nose.

Now the stone object becomes even more remarkable. As

The 2.54 m tall figure, with arms akimbo, wears 'boxing gloves' and holds 'tennis balls'.

a direct extension of the nose, but outside the helmet, the stonemason has modelled an animal snout, possibly a jaguar's. The figure's breath emerges from the snarling jaws, as if it was being forced out. It has two bands round its neck, one of which ends on the breast in a small square chest, the other in a round object, perhaps an amulet.

This helmet wearer must have been somebody important, for a small figure crouches fearfully at his feet on the ground. It, too, wears boxing gloves and holds a tennis ball which it offers to the mighty one. To complete the relief, a broad rectangle at the foot of the stele contains six indefinable goblins. In the view of the archaeologists the relief is supposed to represent a scene from the traditional deadly dangerous Mayan ball game and the victor wears the mask of an ape, a jaguar or perhaps an opossum, for then the tube from helmet to tank would simply be the little creature's tail and the 'air' from the mouth would symbolise water. The opossum is an aquatic animal.

Which is the more fantastic, to make out an opossum on the stele or to see parts of a clearly recognisable technique? How blind must one have become by blinkered study to 'believe' that an opossum, ape or jaguar dips its tail over its shoulder into a container on its back?

Unfortunately one cannot find the first bold 'discoverer' who explained the recognisable stylised breath as the symbol of water. He must have been smart, this interpreter of images, for his rumination was acclaimed and put in the textbooks and once something is in them, it is declared taboo by scholarly opinion. I did not find a single word explaining what the tank meant. An animal accessory? Scientific belief does not need an explanation. One has to believe. Basta: enough.

The idea of the Mayan ball game would be an attempt at an explanation, were it not for the properties which, apart from the balls, are unnecessary and even a hindrance in a ball game. Even the Maya would hardly play in trousers and boots, and tight-fitting overalls.

I agree with Sir Alexander Fleming and refuse to clutter up my brain with the prevailing dogma. My interpretation is as follows.

Two extraterrestrial beings, 'gods', had a fight; the vanquished god offers the victor his weapon and begs for mercy. Or, only the large figure represents a divinity and a kneeling ruler or priest is begging for the favour of the mighty alien. The dominating figure is the victor, who is dressed differently from the earthly one; he protects himself from bacteria and viruses on what to him is an alien planet with hermetically sealed clothing. Earth-born locals did not need this protection; they were immune to the native bacteria and causes of infectious diseases. That also explains the closed-circuit breathing apparatus. The alien draws filtered air into his helmet from the tank through a tube.

The Indians around El Baul still worship this stele as the representation of a great alien god. Until a few years ago they lit candles at the figure's feet. The Indians of Guatemala are Maya, descendants of those Maya who built the grandiose temples and pyramids. According to the ancient Maya beliefs matter had a soul, like the stele of El Baul, which contains *mana*.

A creature with an elephant's head on a human body greets us from a temple wall on Monte Alban in Mexico.

The animal-like snout outside the helmet is irritating. My critics will remind me loudly that extraterrestrials did not have animal muzzles and besides they would not carve sculptures and leave them behind.

For the umpteenth time I must state that no extraterrestrial had a hand in the work here! The stonemason who perpetuated a 'god' with helmet, overalls and technical accoutrements did not know what he was portraying. He saw this strange figure, this apparition from the cosmos. It impressed him and he portrayed it as he perceived it, in complete technical ignorance. I am convinced that all the ancient sculptors were led along this path. An aircraft becomes a bird, an excavator a fabulous animal, a laser beam lightning in the god's hand, a helmet an absurd-looking mask.

On a temple wall on Monte Alban in Mexico the visitor is greeted by a being with an elephant's head on a human body. Trousers flutter over the feet, which are shod, and its hands are controlling some apparatus. I can safely assume that no man ever had an elephant's head around which a wreath of rays flickered.

Monte Alban, capital and religious centre of the Zapoteks, and its complexes were dated to 600–100 BC. How did the Zapoteks know about elephants at that time? Sacrosanct science says that they only existed in Africa or Asia. If I am told—and nothing is too silly to be advanced—that elephants and mammoths made their way to America via the Bering Straits 12,000 to 15,000 years ago, then Monte Alban must be dated synchronously to 12,000 BC. One cannot have it both ways—100BC *and* elephants! Take it easy. There were no elephants. As elephant reliefs are in fact exhibited on the walls at Monte Alban the stonemasons depicted something that was unknown to them.

Yet I have read, I swear it, that Egypt's Pharaoh Rameses III (1195–1164 BC) sent a fleet to Mexico and in that way elephant pictures arrived across the high seas. Good heavens! Rameses' elephants in Mexico! There are also archaeologists who are unable even to see elephants in the Central American depictions of trunks. They see an extinct species of bird.[2] Birds with trunks, that's not bad! These gentlemen should buy themselves spectacles!

I harbour the suspicion that the beings with trunks are neither elephants nor birds. In the Anthropological Museum of Mexico City I stood in front of a massive kneeling figure with a broad flat skull and eyes set wide apart. A trunk, which disappears into a strange swelling on the chest, protrudes from the middle of the skull. Anyone who defines this monster as an elephant must accept an extraterrestrial import. Elephants on our earth look quite different.

Between the pyramids at Tikal, in Guatemala, there is a large stone in the grass that has been exposed to the ravages of thousands of years. The once precise contours have been worn away by wind and weather. But if you take a close look, the outlines of a figure are still discernible. It, too, carried a tank on its back or chest. You can still make out a cog wheel from which a trunk, or more likely a tube, leads to the top of the torso. Strange?

It is said that the Maya did not possess the wheel. This unproved assumption results from the observation that no

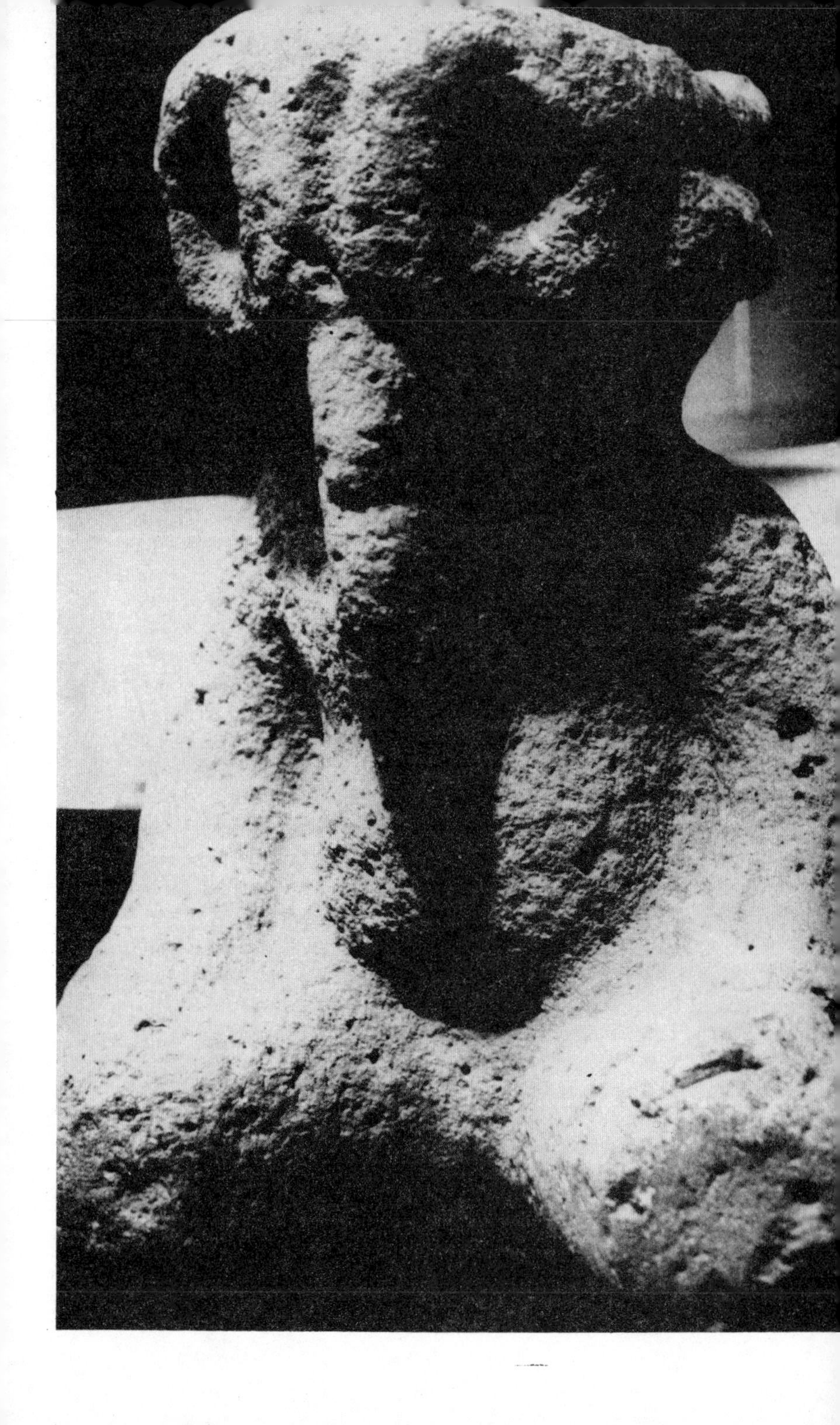

carts are portrayed in Maya temples or on Maya steles. What an unceremonious method of misunderstanding and underrating peoples, cultures and civilisations! Contrary to scholastic opinion, I dare to suggest that there are no reliefs of carts or wagons to be found because their representation was forbidden.

My industrious friend Dr Gene Phillips photographed two perfect cog wheels perpetuated in stone in the Maya ruins at Copan, Honduras. Equidistant spokes lead from the hub to the rim, the exterior of which is marked with the broad teeth of a cog wheel.

As this truly sensational find can never be accepted as a cog wheel, I look forward gleefully to the evening when some terribly clever TV professor peers out of the long-suffering screen to tell us that it represents the teeth of the rain god, the stone teeth of the patron saint of maize farmers or a high priest's bundle of bootlaces. 'The frontiers between arrogance and ignorance are fluid,' said Alfred Polgar.

The restored ruins of Copan are a treasury of finds for anyone who keeps his eyes open. The Sunday archaeologist, Dr Gene Phillips, a lawyer from Chicago, has his eyes open, as befits his profession. Between the ruins of a temple wall, he spotted and photographed two busts which do not fit into any scenario, and therefore have not found the shelter of a museum. The busts, without abdomens, wear a broad bib which the wearer originally pulled over his head through the hole in the middle and let it hang down over his shoulders. A rectangle 50 cm long and 20 cm wide dangles from this bib. Once again there are the outlines of a chest. With bent arms and hands almost clenched, the timeworn figure is working some no longer existent levers which obviously lay at chest height.

Depictions of technology have been observed so frequently that we cannot dismiss them lightly. Often it is simply a question of what kind of technique was handed down in stone. Some 200 m from the busts, in a small museum in the middle of the ruins of Copan, stands a stone bust with a

This kneeling figure with the broad flat skull is housed in the Anthropological Museum of Mexico City. An elephant? Don't make me laugh!

These sculptures exhibiting two perfect cog wheels stand in the Maya ruins of Copan. Spokes run from the hub to the rim, the exterior of which clearly shows the teeth of the cog wheel.

perfectly preserved head, not as charming as the Venus de Milo, but lacking arms, like her. A kind of small concertina is suspended by braces; it has a porthole-like eye in the middle with two crosspieces inside it. Maya archaeologists say they are glyphs, i.e. characters. That does not solve the matter. One would be equally entitled to assume that the object was a morse lamp, of the kind used on ships, or even a small motor. In fact, the Austrian physicist Friedrich Egger, excited by this 'glyph', constructed a highly practical small rotary piston motor which was granted a patent. One really ought not to have one's eyes blinkered by dogmas.

I turned to some Indian boys who had been haunting me for a long time, gaping at my cameras and me, the stranger who had stood so long and so thoughtfully in front of the

A lump of stone crouches between pyramids in Tikal, Guatemala. In spite of heavy weathering there are signs of a cog wheel in the middle, with a tube-like connection leading from it. The stone itself shows its tremendous age.

Also in Copan! The bust, without the lower body, wears an apron which was pulled over the head. The bent fingers of the damaged figure are working some kind of apparatus.

mysterious stele. I asked them, 'What is that?' I pointed to the helmet and the tank.

'*El astronauta!*' answered the oldest, as if it was the most natural explanation in the world. I smirked.

'And why does the astronaut wear boxing gloves and hold balls in his hands?'

'Can't you see that it is a god?' The lad looked at me in astonishment and his dark brown eyes grew even darker. 'It is a god and god is always *un misterio*!' Yes, the boy was right, he is a mystery.

I wished with all my heart that these children would preserve their artless way of looking at things, even when Western development agencies have the mistaken idea that they can make the Indians happier by studies at foreign universities or in high schools in their own country. They lose

This figure is in the small museum at Copan. It holds a remarkable object like a concertina, presumably a product of a past technology.

their identity as soon as they are taken out of their own mental world. They may bring the revolution, but the happiness of a simple existence is irrevocably destroyed.

As agreed, I sat in the hall of the Sheraton in Lima on 15 August waiting for Colonel Omar Chioini. He came through the swing doors punctually on the stroke of twelve as befitting an officer. Unchanged during the years I had known him, a gentleman of perhaps 60, with hair streaked with grey, a neatly trimmed moustache, heavy dark eyebrows and wrinkles caused by laughter round his eyes. As he stood before me in a dark-grey mohair suit, white shirt and dark blue tie, you would have taken him for a banker from Wall Street or the City of London rather than an air force officer.

Our greetings were hearty, with the obligatory South American backslapping and embracing, but thank heavens without the repugnant exchange of kisses which is the Kremlin men's ritual.

We sat at a marble-topped table and ordered the national drink, a pisco sour. Pisco is a grape spirit mainly distilled around the little town of Pisco on the Pacific coast. Lemon juice, sugar and white of egg are shaken in a cocktail shaker. A milky green drink becomes the preferred astringent end-product through the addition of a little Angostura bitters.

'Everything is ready,' said the colonel after we had exchanged some private news. 'A Land Rover will be ready at 6 a.m. tomorrow; if all goes well, you can be back in four days. My friend Frederico Falconi, an expert archaeologist, will accompany you. He knows *la muralla* very well . . .'

'*La muralla* means wall, doesn't it?' I realised there was a mistake; I sensed the great difference.

'Of course,' said Chioini. 'Naturally you want to see it.'

Although I was used to trouble, the error irritated me, but it did not get me down. Only too often I had had to explain in detail what I was interested in in foreign countries, even after the most careful travel preparations. Colonel and archaeologist assumed that I wanted to see the world-famous great wall of Peru. Take it easy, Erich, I say to myself quietly at moments like these. I took the two *National Geographic* photos from my Swissair travel bag and showed the dark band full of holes running up hill and down dale.

'*Amigo*, *that*'s what I want to see. I know the wall already.'

The colonel twirled his moustache for a second, bit his lips in confusion, apologised for the mistake and went to the telephone booth next to the reception desk. Shortly afterwards he returned with the message that he had cancelled the Land Rover and put off the archaeologist. He had also tried to get hold of the architect Carlos Milla, but had been told by his wife that Carlos was unavailable over the weekend and could not be phoned until Monday. The colonel said that Milla knew every archaeological oddity in Peru. He was friendly not only with official archaeologists, but also with the unofficial grave robbers and fences. If anyone could give me the information it was Carlos Milla.

I had not the slightest desire to wait in Lima. I knew the city with its important museums from earlier visits. I had been in the 350-year-old cathedral with its precious, carved choir stalls, considered to be the most beautiful in America. The building was consecrated in 1624 and Francisco Pizarro, the Spanish conqueror of Peru, laid the foundation stone. Numerous earthquakes and architectural taste changing with each reconstruction have made the cathedral into a calendar of art history, in which one can distinguish Gothic, Baroque and Classical elements. I admired the splendid houses from the colonial period with their spacious inside courtyards and their art treasures carved out of fine jungle woods or hammered and chiselled from iron. In the centre I know the Plaza de Armes where Francisco Pizarro drew the plan of the city on the ground with his sword in AD 1535. No, the busy city of 1½ million inhabitants would get on my nerves if I had nothing to do but wait. Colonel Chioini realised this and offered to drive me through the delightful countryside of his homeland.

'I'm going to fly to La Paz!' I said dryly.

'You know it as well as you know Lima. What do you want in La Paz?'

'I want to visit the ruins of Puma Punku,' I explained and could see from Chioini's face the Puma Punku might have been Timbuctoo as far as he was concerned.

'Aha,' was all he said. 'When shall we meet again?'

'In a week's time, I suggest, on the 22nd at the same time in the same place. OK?'

The colonel toasted me with the rest of his pisco sour.

'OK, Erich!'

The next norming I flew from Lima at 7.30 in a Lloyd Boliviana plane and landed in La Paz at 10.30.

Once again the wrangling over a cross-country vehicle began. Here, too, the rental firms can only offer small European cars or petrol-gobbling American limousines. They are all battered and have been repaired on countless occasions—wrecks that should be scrapped.

In Bolivia a car that works is an unattainable treasure, as rare as owning one's own house. If you see a gleaming car gliding silently past in La Paz, by far Bolivia's largest city with nearly 400,000 inhabitants, you can be sure that a diplomat from the capital Sucre is out sightseeing.

I chose a 1969 Volkswagen with 264,000 km on the speedometer, which had presumably been 'adjusted' several times. The dead straight unasphalted roads on the treeless plateau 4000 m above sea level were familiar to me from previous years. By Swiss standards you only have to go over a hill, but the Bolivians call it a mountain pass. My VW began to falter on the steepest stretch. In the thin oxygen-starved air the pistons shook in their cylinders and no longer transmitted the full force of their explosions to the driving shaft. A tried and true trick came to my aid. I made a U-turn and put the car into reverse. In this way my sturdy VW covered the few hundred metres to the top, but it was a fiendish bit of driving, constantly crowded from behind by fast buses covered in clouds of dust. On either side of the carriageway lurked packs of wild dogs, wolfish mongrels. The locals call them *los perdidos*, the lost ones. Half-starved and mangy, they would turn any animal-lover's stomach. The *perdidos* band together, hunting and uttering bloodcurdling howls; at night they are even dangerous to man.

The Indians of the plain are just as poor as the dogs. They

This relief, surrounded by railings, lies on a hill near Tiahuanaco. It is called the 'Writing Desk' in archaeological literature. 155 × 162 × 52 cm in stone—a strange writing desk!

Accurate rectangles, right-angled ledges and sharply demarcated mouldings imply a technical matrix which had a counterpart.

drive a few goats or sheep over long distances to poor grazing grounds, crouching by the roadside with glassy eyes. Here, as in the jam-packed buses on the streets of La Paz, they chew the leaves of the coca shrub, which is native to the Andes. Cocaine is the main alkaloid in the coca leaves, which taste bitter and temporarily numb the nerves of the tongue. The bushes with their delicate leaves and yellowish clusters of flowers are cultivated in plantations. The first travellers in the Andes related that chewing coca leaves gave the natives strength. But in fact medicine has discovered that eating, chewing, or sniffing large quantities of cocaine over a long period leads, via the central nervous system, to mental derangement after an original feeling of well-being. On sale abundantly at the lowest prices in the tiniest market, this narcotic enables the Indians to tolerate their apparently hopeless poverty. If you speak to one of them, he has to summon himself back to reality from his dream world before he can answer.

After two and a half hours I passed the little village of Tiahuanaco with its controversial ruins about which so much has been written, some of it by me. To the left of the main road a narrow lane leads south-east over the closed-down overgrown railway line from La Paz to Lake Titicaca. There stands a grass-covered hill surrounded by a wire fence. In specialist literature the little hill is described as a 'pyramid', although there is nothing pyramidal about it.

At the foot of the hill lies a monolith as if it had been hurled there by a giant. The Swiss travel-writer Johann Jakob von Tschudi[3] saw it in 1869 and wrote this:

> On the way to Puma Punka we found in a field a strange monolith 155 cm high by 162 cm wide; it is 52 cm thick at the base and 45 cm thick at the top. It has two rows of compartments. The lower row has two large compartments with two smaller rectangular ones one above the other in the middle, the upper row has four rectangular compartments separated from the lower one by simple mouldings. The monolith is known as *El Escritorio*, the Writing Desk.

The christening of this carefully dressed lump of andesite

was presumably undertaken by a scholar who was reminded of his own writing desk with its compartments and drawers. So far there is nothing in the literature to suggest what we are to make of this artistic work or what purpose it served. It was certainly not a writing desk.

There can be no doubt that it was made according to plan. Accurate rectangles of different sizes, with right-angled ledges terminating in a point, with sharply drawn mouldings and faultlessly carved gradations. This matrix had a companion piece with fitted into it firmly and exactly, to the millimetre, without joints. Such work is not carried out without a plan. But a plan means taking measurements and presupposes a knowledge of writing.

At the top of the hill you can see the mystery of the Andes, Puma Punku, a stone structure of incredible power, variety and precision. Its purpose has never been understood nor has it been adequately appraised in any *modern* work known to me. In the latest large general work about South America[4] Puma Punku is dismissed in these few lines:

> In the south-west corner of Tiahuanaco stands the great pyramid called Puma Punku. Two areas of different heights form its upper platform which is reached up several steps. A temple probably stood on one of the platforms, the entrance to which consisted of three portals executed in the style of the Gate of the Sun.

That is miserly, as if the Berlin Philharmonic were to play the 16 upward beats of the 'Eroica' to represent the whole work. Let us devote our full attention to Puma Punku!

The descendants of the Spanish conquerors brought the first news to the old world. In the middle of the sixteenth century Pedro de Cieca[5] described Puma Punku as a unique site with 'gigantic statues and a vast terrace. No one has seen the uncanny place other than in ruins.'

His fellow countryman Antonio de Castro y del Castillo, who was Bishop of La Paz in 1651, wrote:

> And although it was formerly assumed that the ruins were the work of the Inca, as a fortress for their wars, it has now been realised that they are structures from before the

> Flood . . . For if it had been a work of the Inca in a plain without water, and set so deeply into the ground, not even the Spaniards could have constructed such a wonderful building or one so beautiful. What I marvel at are those stones that fit one another so accurately . . .[6]

In the first half of the nineteenth century the French palaeontologist Alcide Charles Victor d'Orbigny (1802–57) travelled through South America. Describing Puma Punku,[7] he wrote about monumental gates which stood on horizontal stone platforms. He says that one of the complete platforms was 40 m long. Today there are no such connected slabs to be seen; they have collapsed, shattered and eaten by the teeth of time. But what remains is monumental enough to leave us awestruck.

As a 'collector' of ancient buildings it is hard to impress me, but Puma Punku, this grandiose panorama from another age, left me speechless. Massive lumps of granite, andesite and diorite, the grey-green plutonic rock of enormous hardness and resistance, lie about in a confusing chaos that still allows you to sense their original arrangement. The monoliths, which are simply astonishing, are dressed, cut and polished with such precision that they might have been delivered from a workshop with ultramodern machines, hard steel milling tools and drills. Extremely accurate grooves 6 mm wide and 12 mm deep run along diorite monoliths over 5 m long as if drawn by a ruler. The monsters were connected with their counterparts by mortises. Metal clamps united the stone monsters into a structure which eludes imaginative reconstruction today.

The Dresden archaeologist Max Uhle (1856–1944) is looked on as the 'father of Peruvian archaeology', indeed, he is called the 'second discoverer of Peru'.[8] At the Royal Zoological, Anthropological and Ethnological Museum Uhle

Puma Punku . . . the real mystery of the Andes! Your very first look makes you marvel at the force and precision of the dressed stones.

In 1651 the Bishop of La Paz wrote that the structure must have originated before the Flood. We must not contradict the venerable gentleman!

got to know the geologist and travelling scholar Alphons Stübel (1834–1904), who had already published a three-volume work about archaeological excavations in Peru. After some years of joint research Uhle and Stübel edited the standard work *Die Ruinenstätten von Tiahuanaco im Hochland des alten Peru.* It is 58 cm high, 38 cm wide, weighs 10 kg and contains detailed drawings of Puma Punka, and data that are accurate to the millimetre and have not been improved on to this day. The sketches accompanying my text are taken from the work published in Leipzig in 1892.

The two scholars were fascinated by Puma Punku. Faced with the incomprehensible complex, they decided to take accurate measurements and sketches of the layout home with them. It is conceivable that they were not driven merely by scientific zeal, but by the worry that otherwise their account of the mystery of the Andes would not be believed. The on-the-spot impressions were too powerful. Stübel noted:

> The most remarkable feature of the ruins of Puma Punku is formed by the still extant 'platforms' and the whole or broken blocks lying scattered between them which exhibit extraordinary diversity in their shape, size and workmanship. There are platform-like stones, symmetrically dressed lava stones, others with small gate-like excisions, stones with depressions like basins, stones with ornaments like crosses, with small niches and thick or quite thin embossed mouldings, as well as countless other shapes. With the exception of the three main platforms, which run in a straight line, the present state of the ruins is extremely disordered. The three so-called main platforms run in a north–south direction. They cover an area 43 m long and some 7 m wide.[9]

Max Uhle had to stand by and watch a unit of the Bolivian

In the first half of the nineteenth century the archaeologist d'Orbigny reckoned that the stone platforms still had a total length of 40 m. They are shattered today . . .

. . . but even a photo taken in 1980 makes us puzzle over the tremendous power of the stone masses and the wonderful work done by the stonemasons.

army organise practise shoots at the statues. If the builders of Puma Punku had not planned their complex for eternity, only a mass of rubble or not even that would have been left.

Puma Punku means Gate of the Lion. Today there is no sign of a gate, for the Spaniards and after them the Indians broke up many of the stones and took away whatever they could carry or drag. But even if Spaniards, Indians and the whole Bolivian army had combined in a communal robbery, they could not have altered the position of the gigantic dressed platforms. Could it be done today?

In 1964, for example, Abu Simbel was sawn into sections, numbered and put together again 60 m above its former site close to the Nile, using the massed technology of Western industry. Nothing of that kind has been attempted at Puma Punku. So far, we still do not know how deep the andesite and diorite blocks and platforms stick into the ground. So far excavators have not been able to lift the biggest blocks, thank heavens. If they were transportable, they would be exploded and disappear as cheap long-lasting building material in the walls of pompous office blocks or stores, or at best reconstructed by diligent archaeologists in the very places where they do not belong. Nevertheless, the terrain, as Siegfried Huber[10] writes, gives one the impression of a busy building site:

> The area gives one the impression of a stonemason's workplace; the masters and apprentices have just left for their teabreak to return immediately to work with hammer and chisel. A vast mount of skilfully dressed and polished material, platforms, blocks, millstones, fragments of friezes, stone seats and doors seem to be waiting for transport.

If you see what is anchored in the ground at Puma Punku, the method of transport to and from the sites remains a mystery. Alcide d'Orbigny relates that he saw the main platforms, now divided into three, still in one piece over 40 m long. A block of stone 40 m long and 7 m wide buried to an unknown depth has the volume of an eleven-storey house. The raw mass must have been much more voluminous, because it had to be fashioned and dressed first. In places where stone is worked, chips are left behind. There is no stone debris at Puma Punku.

To sum up: the stone masses weighing many thousand tons must have been transported over the treeless plateau by human muscular strength in the absence of modern lorries and cranes. Anyone who says lightheartedly that it was all feasible should remember that one thousand tons equals one million kilograms and that many thousand tons were moved at Puma Punku! Were the celebrated wooden rollers pushed under these stone monsters as well? Only people who talk about colour like blind men could risk that theory. Wooden rollers would have been crushed and split. If transport columns had managed to get the burden from some site to the slopes and just one tropical rainstorm had fallen, the stones would have vanished like raisins in a cake, sunk in the morass. The transport was effected somehow, otherwise there would be no stone platforms and monoliths at Puma Punku. How? This is the mystery without a convincing solution.

The precision of the works is as mysterious as their transport.

Example 1:

We have a rectangular block 2.78 m long and 1.57 m wide, with an average height of 88 cm. The block has six main surfaces: top, bottom and four sides. The six surfaces are divided into small and large surfaces, with each surface on a different plane. To explain: on the lateral surface B surfaces (1) to (7) are 1 cm higher or deeper than their neighbour. Surfaces (6) and (7) are separated by a ledge of 5 cm that narrows to a cornice 4 cm thick. The narrow moulding (8) running dead straight between surfaces C and D is only 2 cm wide. The block is wedge-shaped. The rear part (in Figure 1) is thicker than the front.

Nowadays such precision work—if there was a stonemason to take it on—would be executed with the help of milling tools and high-speed drills cooled by air, water or artificial ice. The work was made particularly difficult because it had to be carried out on diorite, a stone as hard as granite. The prize question: what tools did the Puma Punku stonemason use?

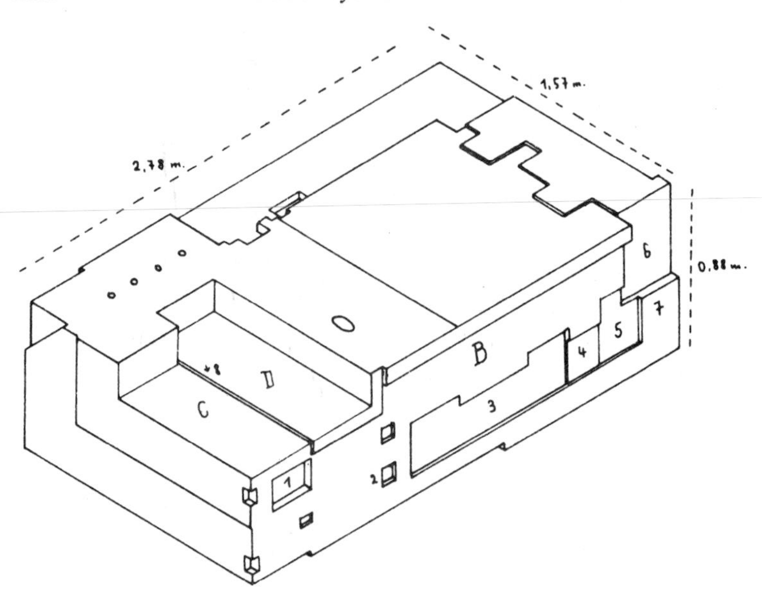

There is no better survey, of Puma Punku than the book by Uhle and Stübel. This sketch to accompany Example 1 shows the brilliant construction in detail.

Example 2:

The block consists of andesite lava; it is 1 m high and 1 m wide at its broadest point. I have marked the main visible surfaces A, B, C and D. Between the surfaces B and C two niches have been cut out, one above the other, and small rectangles, 8 mm deep have been cut into their rear walls. These small depressions are reminiscent of a carbine breech which fitted into its counterpart.

Easier said than done. Apart from the two elements fitting into each other, an apparatus was necessary to allow them to fit without the stone mouldings splintering during opening or closing. Wooden rollers or the arm of a lever would not have been adequate to allow blocks weighing tons to slam to like safe doors. The process presumably took place on the heights, not after the blocks were lying on the ground. Given the complicated difference in height between the various planes, with rectangles, squares, ledges and mouldings, it was not enough to lower the block on ropes from a wooden appliance into the piece lying on the ground. Rotatory move-

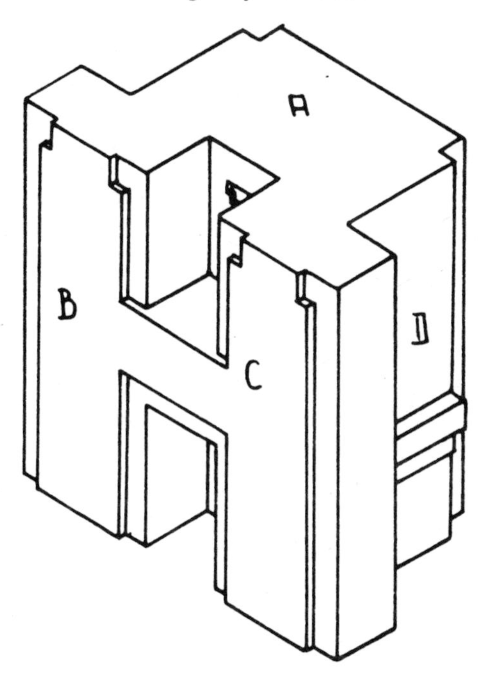

This architect's drawing shows the articulation of a block of andesite lava.

ments would be needed so that blocks of this size could be led into the spaces. Nowadays pre-cast concrete elements are less complicated and comparatively more primitive than the handicraft technique used at Puma Punku. If that is what it was . . .

Example 3:

A diorite block rises 1.1 m high from the yellowish-brown ground, surprisingly enough barely touched by the ravages of the millennia. A groove 3 mm wide and 2.5 mm deep runs from the front of the blocks 8.5 cm before the polished surface. Tiny holes 1.5 mm deep have been drilled in it 4 cm apart, as if made with a diamond drill. Such precision could not have been achieved with stone or wooden tools, or a drill of the hardest animal bone.

Example 4:

A large rectangle with a depth of 2.5 mm is let into an andesite block measuring 7.81 m by 5.07 m. There was no

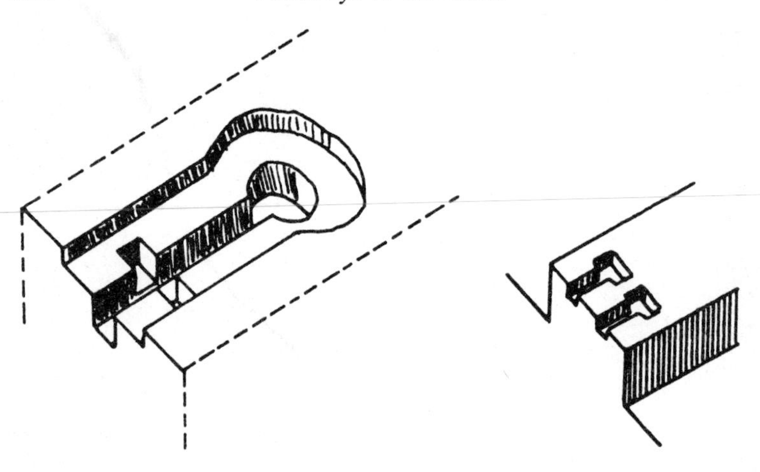

These small excisions on the rear side of the stone are reminiscent of the very latest carbine breech.

botched work here, no damaged places smeared over with mortar or cement. It is a masterpiece of the stonemason's art. This indentation also exhibits the openings used to fit the platforms together.

Example 5:

The builders of Puma Punku were not only familiar with rectangular work, they also knew the straight edge and the circle. I saw and photographed circles 26 cm in diameter cut out of the stone.

I look on Puma Punku as proof of some of my most important claims in connection with the buildings of antiquity.

The Aymara, a pre-Inca tribe who are supposed to have worked here on the plateau, could not have been responsible, for the technique employed goes far beyond the knowledge and abilities attributed to pre-Inca tribes.

This work was carried out according to a plan. The overall planning was based on geometrical measurements.

Barely touched by the teeth of the millennia, this 1.1 m high diorite block stands in the yellowish-brown earth. A groove only millimetres deep with small holes in it every 4 cm runs down its outer face.

A large rectangle is sunk 2.5 cm into this andesite block measuring 7.81 × 5.07 m.

The execution of details testifies to an advanced technology.

As regards the transport of the stone masses, the builders must have known their weights and taken stability and hardness of the material into account.

Planning on this scale implies knowledge of *writing*. There were so many positions to be considered, calculated and fixed that even the cranky 'memory culture' of Stonehenge does not get us any further.

The possibility that a genius, a once-in-a-millennium architect, flexed his muscles here can be excluded. Given so many building sites with the attendant transport, stone dressing, instructions to the masons, etc., even a genius would have crumbled, quite apart from the fact that, if done by human powers, the topping-out ceremony could not have been celebrated in one man's lifetime, or even in several generations.

Result:

As planning is obvious, we must credit the builders with knowledge of writing. But, and there the archaeologists and ethnologists are wonderfully unanimous, the Aymara had no writing. Which means their exclusion as the builders!

There can be no building plan without detailed drawings. They existed at Puma Punku. Even the archaeologists speak of 'copper clamps' with which the blocks were supposed to have been held together. Copper is a weak material. It is only 3 on the Mohs scale of hardness, as opposed to iron with 4.5. Copper could not chain together slabs weighing tons. Johann Jakob Tschudi[4] already had something to say about this:

> Even more astonishing than the transport of these enormous masses of stone is the perfect technical execution of the stonemason's work, especially when we think that the ancient Indian artisans had no iron tools and that the alloys of copper and tin known to them were much too weak to dress granite successfully. It is still a puzzle how

Archaeologists say that the blocks were held together with copper clamps. Copper is far too weak a metal for these stone masses!

Knowing that the ancient Indian craftsmen had no heavy iron tools, the traveller Tschudi was amazed by the transport and dressing of the colossi.

they managed it, but the most feasible view is that the final polishing of the stone was effected with fine stone dust or plants containing silica.

Tschudi's astonishment reveals that already in the last century there was a desperate search for a plausible solution to the Puma Punku mystery. The final polishing of the outer surfaces might have been possible using stone dust and plants containing silica, but they could not have been used to scour grooves millimetres wide and squares with accurate right-angles in hard stone!

Today we know that the granite found at Puma Punku was formerly quarried at Cerro de Skapia near Zepita in present-day Peru, a good 60 km from the complex. Sixty kilometres is no distance. Not on level carefully maintained roads, but here it is a seemingly endless route leading over mountains and rivers.

The formula is simple.

Planning + arithmetic + geometry + transport + hard

Puma Punku, 1980! One gets the impression that the confusion was caused by an earthquake or an explosion. A subject for tourists!

metal tools = a technology that was presumably beyond the men of those days.

Indian tradition says that Puma Punku 'was built by the gods in a single long night'.[11] No men had a hand in it and the gods, who could fly, destroyed their own work by lifting it into the air, turning it over and letting it fall.

Today it still looks as it might have done after such an act of violence. Can we not take the simple mythological tradition seriously? Why should we be ashamed to admit that in the rarefied air of this grandiose 4000 m high landscape there is a magnificent achievement which we cannot explain?

'What is man? Certainly not what he takes himself for—the crown of creation!' wrote the poet Wilhelm Raabe (1831–1910).

For three days I plodded through the ruins, measuring individual items, photographing and dictating keywords into my pocket machine. Twice daily, around 11 a.m. and 2 p.m., a Crillon Tours bus deposited some 50 camera-draped tour-

'You must stop measuring at once!' an Indian shouted. Why?

ists on the site. They included many Americans. Some of them whispered to each other. Then they recognised me and asked me to pose in a group photograph or give them my autograph. On the last day the two o'clock bus had just off-loaded its passengers at the village church of Tiahuanaco, when two sour-looking Indians appeared in dark-green ponchos, their *chullos*, and woollen peaked caps pulled down over their ears.

'Stop measuring at once!' one Indian ordered.

'Why, señores?' I asked.

'Foreigners are forbidden to undertake excavations without written permission from the University of La Paz.'

I could understand that. For a moment I thought of telling them that the Universidad Boliviana, General José Ballivian, Trinidad, had conferred an honorary doctorate on me on 12 February 1975, but I let it go. At the time, when I heard the news, I was suspicious of this honour. Honorary doctorates are often conferred when endowments have been made and I had not given the university a penny. Not until the Bolivian Ministry of Education, the Ministry of Foreign Affairs and the German Embassy confirmed that it was genuine did I thank them for the honour. This was the first time I could put it to good use, but I did not. I was pleased by the Indians' vigilance. Where should we be if every tourist or Sunday archaeologist was to put a souvenir in his rucksack? I said, 'You're right, but I'm not digging. I'm not touching anything; I'm only taking a few measurements. Is that allowed?'

'No, Señor von Däniken. We have been ordered to stop your activities.'

So they were addressing me by name? Who knew me in this desolate landscape? I had not given interviews to any papers. Who knew that I was here? They confiscated my tape-measure and would not let me out of their sight, but I was allowed to take photographs. Who disliked me tackling Puma Punku? Was someone afraid of the fresh streams of visitors who would be drawn there by my report, as actually happened at Tiahuanaco?

In the evening, in the bar on the 25th storey of the Sheraton skyscraper in La Paz, I was chatting with a young married couple from Munich over a drink. She was studying ethnology, he was a qualified lawyer. They had crossed Lake Titicaca by hydroplane from Peru. They had both read my books and both were disappointed by what they had seen during the day. They queried my descriptions. The lady said to me, 'We saw the ruins of Sacsayhuaman above Cuzco, but with the best will in the world we could not find anything extraterrestrial of the kind you describe.'

The lawyer added drily: 'The guidebook explains how the stones were dressed. You can still see the same sort of dressed stones in the streets of Cuzco today!'

The same old song, the eternal error! Even the crew who shot my film *Memories of the Future* at Sacsayhuaman did not find the ruins *I* describe, for they did not bother to. Even when I look at the masses of enticing holiday cruises to South America I can imagine some of the participants knowing my books and being disappointed, like the couple from Munich. Apropos of the boom in cruises to South America, I shall describe the route that leads to *my* ruins.

'Ladies and gentlemen, in the morning—it doesn't have to be at the crack of dawn—take a taxi to the ruins of Sacsayhuaman. Get the driver to drive another 1.5 km up the mountain on the old road to Pisac and stop just before the first left-hand curve. Pay off the driver, even if he screams

Above the fortress of Sacsayhuaman lies a labyrinth of rocks that does not merit the term 'ruins' in the normal sense.

and gesticulates. He will try to persuade you that he will wait for you. That only means extra expense.

'Now look down the mountain in the direction of the Inca fortress. Climb the small height with fissured rocks that lies 200 m above you to your right, just next to the roadside. You reach a labyrinth of rocks that does not merit the description "ruins" in the ordinary sense. Indefinable masses of stone lie about, large and small stone blocks, the unrecognisable remnants of some historic buildings. You soon get the impression that at some time a structure built with the latest technological refinement was totally destroyed here.

'Via clefts and grottoes you clamber to the platforms. Astonishingly and unexpectedly you stand before beautifully cut stone monsters. Ladies and gentlemen, take a good look at these polished concrete walls that look as if they had been taken out of their wooden mould only yesterday. You are wrong! It's not concrete, but granite!

'If you have lost the ability to be amazed, that important

Strange rock formations can be found on the mountainsides to the left of the road.

faculty will easily return to you here. Grottoes stand on their heads as if shaken by some primaeval force, tunnel entrances are telescoped and their formerly straight courses interrupted. Look closely; nothing has been put together with mortar or some other binding agent, there is no trace of depressions for metal clamps of the kind to be found at Puma Punku. No, up here, above the fortress of Sacsayhuaman, the tourist goal, everything seems to have come "from one casting". Edges are right-angled, fresh surprises await you behind every colossus.

'If you have already gone on the tourist excursion to the Inca fortress, you will note that the real sensation of Cuzco, the genuine prehistoric mystery, lies up here, behind and above the mountainsides of Sacsayhuaman. Seldom visited. And more or less ignored.

'Keep your eyes open! These stone masses are only one mosaic stone in an inexplicable jigsaw puzzle. Discover the large and small cliff formations on the mountainsides to the left of the road. No one disturbs or warns you here, so march confidently over the rough meadows and dry fields, climb

Angled edges, cave-like depressions, stone wedges—as if made of wax.

fearlessly over the fences. No Indian farmer has ever stopped me. They are all polite and if necessary a couple of soles (the local currency) works wonders.

'After a couple of hours spent wandering in the past, you will realise that nearly all the cliffs have been dressed. No itinerant archaeological priest will be able to convince you that mother nature conjured up the right-angled edges in the cliff, with their surfaces so carefully polished, set the gigantic "stone seats" in the landscape just for fun, hammered the stone showcases, created the steps which run from ceiling to floor. The fact that they are standing "on their heads" is the final proof that the gigantic labyrinth was once violently shaken and rotated on its axis. No one can use the steps as they exist today. If we turn them over, they provide a first class ascent to the "dress-circle" and even higher.

Steps run from the floor to the ceiling—proof that everything here was turned upside down at some time.

Rock faces bow toward each other; clean-cut angles run along the mouldings.

'A look behind the scenes at the Inca fortress! Turn your backs on the much-photographed walls. At the same height lie monolithic rocks which have been dressed and have no conceivable purpose. As you see them today they make no sense. You will see nothing, absolutely nothing, that can be fitted into an acceptable scenario. No arrangement, no walls fitted together, no piled-up monoliths. Blank rock faces bow to each other, clear-cut surfaces end in topsy-turvy steps leading to the ceiling.

'Once you have seen all that and taken another look at my descriptions and photographs when you get home, you will be glad you did not simply take the well-trodden tourist path!'

I will quickly run over what you cannot find in my books on your return home.

The relevant literature asserts that the rock called Lacco or Kenko Grande with its niches, chambers and tunnel entrances was a holy place, the niches being thrones of the dead, and that everything belonged to the magical kingdom of the underworld. It is brazenly asserted that the order (disorder!) to be seen today was presented by the builders in the same form.

Garcilaso de la Vega[11] remarked as early as 1720 that the stone field today known as Chingana Grande, the Great Labyrinth, was dragged towards Sacsayhuaman by 20,000 workers, but got out of hand and in falling buried 3000 men. Today archaeologists[12] take a different view: 'The stone was never meant for Sacsayhuaman. Indeed it was never transported, it was always lain where it now lies.'

Scholars make the builders into fools, imagining them to be so stupid or mad as to have cut steps in the rock that run from top to bottom, steps that could never have been used at any period. According to this curious interpretation, they cut out niches with sloping surfaces on which no one could even lay a bouquet of flowers in honour of the gods of the underworld, not to mention a statue in honour of the holy place. The poor fools laboriously polished surfaces and hollowed out depressions that were completely useless.

For those who miss the boat to South America and so cannot check my descriptions, I present three photographs which were taken in the summer of 1980 a few hundred metres from the Inca fortress. For those who are going to visit Sacsayhuaman, I shall resume my role of guide.

'Ladies and gentlemen, please stand by the right-hand third of the fortress wall facing the fortress. Immediately behind you there are clefts in the ground. Climb down into them, there is no danger. You are transported into an extremely mysterious rocky landscape. In front of you lie stone monuments 3.5 m high, with overhanging cornices. Just at the corner you will find broad stepped bands perfectly cut out of the rock. The rock leans slightly forwards; in some places it touches the opposite walls. Please look closely. It is not a composite structure. It is one solid mass of rock. The rough undressed natural rock only begins above the dressed surfaces. The dressed stones could never have served any purpose in the form you see them now. Linger a while in the chamber of mysteries. I wager that you will soon realise that the dressed stones once stood further up the mountain and fell into their present chaotic positions owing to a natural event, say an earthquake, or deliberately owing to an explosion.'

The whole leads to the same conclusion as at Puma Punku. The verifiable technology used up here above the Inca fortress was more advanced, more titanic and more grandiose than that with which the cyclopean Inca walls of Sacsayhuaman were constructed. Since the Inca walls existed when the Spaniards conquered the country and nothing has been added since, the dressed rocks to which I constantly refer are older than the Inca fortress. As at Puma Punku, there must have been planning, ergo some kind of writing was known. The monumental structure was bigger than anything the Inca and their forefathers were in a position to build.

Where the same master builders at work here as at Puma Punku? Need I mention that here, too, mythology relates that the gods destroyed their work themselves, once they recognised the ingratitude of the men they had created?

After I had explained their mistake, the married couple from Munich promised to visit Cuzco again. While I was writing this chapter, a postcard arrived with greetings and thanks and comment, 'That was never the work of simple Indians! Why doesn't someone speak about it?'

I do speak about it. Continually. As I do here. Recommended for checking.

My conversation with Colonel Chioini and the architect Carlos Milla began in Lima on 22 August, the Friday agreed on, with an unpleasant bit of horse-trading. Milla was a polite man; he spoke only when spoken to. He had rough hands which indicated that he was prepared to roll up his sleeves and help his workers, if necessary.

'You know what I'm looking for,' I began without preliminaries. 'Please show me on the map where I can find the pockmarked bands.'

Carlos Milla was taken aback by my blunt question.

'Si si, señor, I know to a metre where it is, I can draw it in on a Peruvian cadastral map.'

'Please do so,' I urged him.

The architect closed his eyes, opened them and looked for

These are three photos of the same rock complex, a few hundred metres from the tourist attraction. Taken in 1980. Here one learns how to wonder again; one senses the mystery of the remote past on our earth.

help from the colonel who was nervously drumming on the marble-topped table. He was obviously embarrassed and said in English, 'I believe he wants money.'

The expedition was not going to founder because of that. I have long since been used to paying for information. As discreetly as possible—I still don't enjoy bribery—I pushed a green fifty-dollar bill up to his glass of pisco sour.

'Please, where is it?'

Carlos Milla disregarded the money. He wanted more. He said that he had incurred expenses in obtaining the information and in addition he was prepared to accompany us for what it cost him to leave his practice.

'What will it cost?' I asked.

'Six hundred dollars for three days, plus 225 dollars for the Land Rover which I'll provide!' said the architect who was obviously not bashful about figures. I hate being done, besides it occurred to me that this businesslike character might suddenly ask for extra cash on the journey. Given the information that the mysterious band with the holes existed, we would have to find it without Carlos Milla.

'You needn't come with us. I'll pay you 200 dollars!'

I looked at him expectantly and slowly put the documents on the table into my briefcase. I wanted him to know that it was my final offer. Colonel Chioini spoke firmly to his acquaintance, he found the bargaining as painful as I did. Carlos Milla closed his eyes again, a good trick to puzzle the potential buyer, and opened them when he realised that 200 dollars cash was better than nothing.

In a hurt voice he explained, 'Your band with the holes in extends much further over mountains and valleys than the old *National Geographic* photos show. The most suitable spot for you is 2 km past the village of Humay in the Pisco valley. Drive to the Hacienda Montesierpe. Behind the hacienda there is a strip of cultivated land 300 m wide. Immediately above it on the barren hills you can see your strip with the holes.'

If correct, it was a useful piece of information. On the map the Pisco valley runs at right-angles to the Panamericana, one of the dream roads of the world. I paid over the 200 dollars and promised Carlos Milla future business if I wanted to track down other mysterious places in Peru. If anyone is interested, the address of the topographical expert is: Architect Carlos Milla, Avenida Salaverry 674, Lima.

Immediately after the conversation, I telephoned my acquaintance, Professor Dr Janvier Cabrera, in Ica, which is only 70 km from Pisco. Perhaps he knew the Hacienda Montesierpe, perhaps he would like to come with us. Cabrera, an unorthodox anthropologist, agreed on the spot. We arranged to meet the next day at 1700 hours in the Museum of Ica.

The journey in a rented Datsun took a good four hours. For 40 km outside Lima the Panamericana is built like a genuine motorway, then it narrows to a single lane which runs along the coast, but mostly through desert. Although the coastal strip down to Pisco on the Pacific lies in a geographical zone which allows luxuriant vegetation to flourish in other parts, that is not the case here. The cold water of the Humboldt current cools the hot atmosphere heated by the sun so that one must count on fog both morning and evening. But because the fog is dried out in higher, hot layers of air, there are hardly any precipitations. Long stretches of the dream road show the result. You see dunes, fields covered with pebbles and the uprooted trunks of plants like thistles drying out on the sand of the desert. The locals form them into letters on hillsides, like gigantic advertising slogans.

The scenery changes abruptly: luxuriant valleys with cotton fields and fruit—and sugar-cane plantations on both sides of the road. By the roadside Indians sell fruit, vegetables and of course pisco, their favourite spirit, and wine in fat-bellied bottles. No sooner are you used to seeing such cases of fertility, when there is a harsh cut in the landscape film, and it continues with the absolute desolation of the desert, the whole region a kaleidoscope of sea, mist, uninhabited desert and strips of fertile land.

Buses dash along at excessive speeds carrying tourists to Nazca. The tourists doze, thanks to the indispensable air-conditioning. A good sweat would be more beneficial, but people demand this cursed comfort.

I am waiting for Professor Cabrera.

Skulls taken from ancient graves around Ica stare out from the museum's showcases. They are deformed. The deforma-

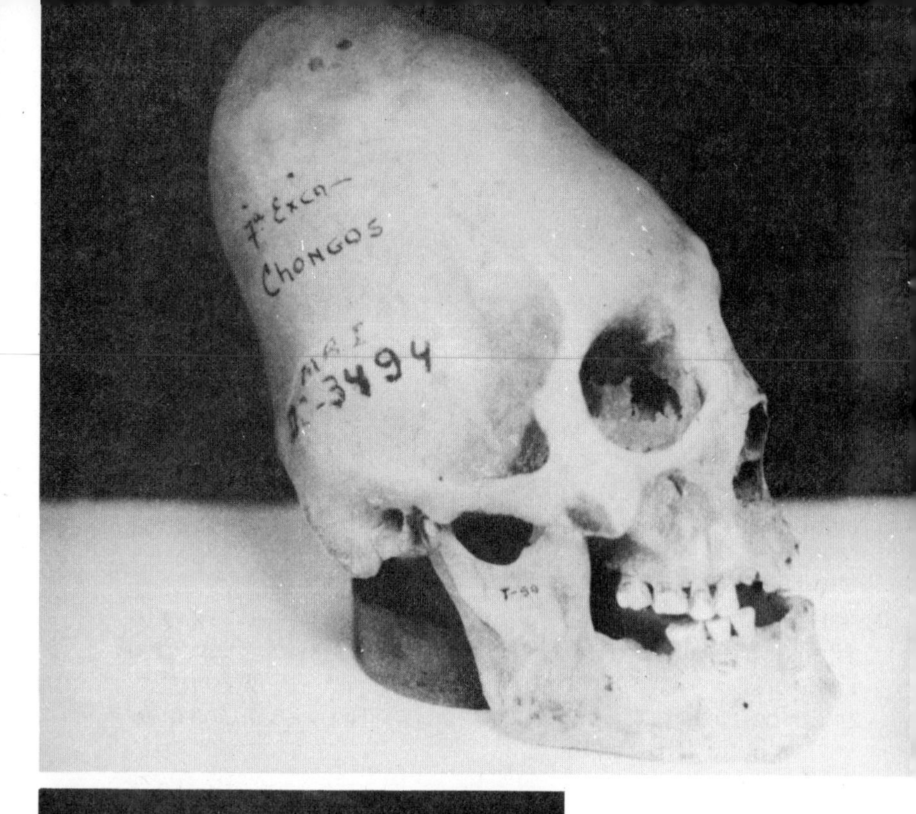
Chongos
3494

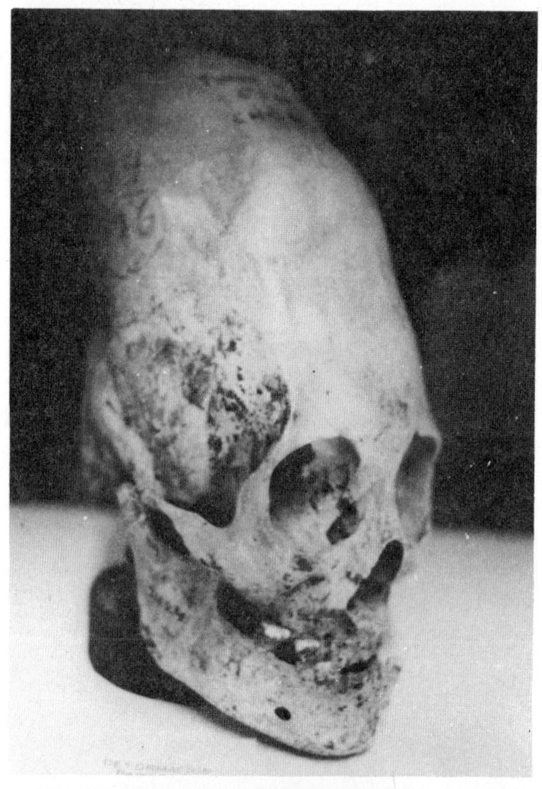

tions begin at the temples, then arch back upwards from the temples like the body of a hornet. The back part of the head often has three times the volume of a normal skull.

In erudite tomes I find this explanation of the monsters.

Inca priests selected boys at a very tender age and put their still malleable little heads between padded boards. Cords were pulled through hinges and slowly and steadily reduced the space between the boards. Some children must have suffered indescribable torments in the process, otherwise we should not have these deformed adult skulls.

The sight of these monstrous heads, which might have come from the Gothic novel *Frankenstein* by Mary Shelley (1797–1851), spurred me to ask questions.

Why did this agonising ritual take place?

How did men get the idea of deforming children's skulls? Skulls of this kind are no Peruvian or South American speciality. They are found among the Maya in Central America, in the north-west of the USA among the flathead Indians, as well as in ancient Egypt.[13]

The various peoples seem to have been copying something.

Is it true—after all, no one was there—that the deformed were chosen to become future priests and high priests? Why? Did children have to be misshapen so that their adult skulls would resemble those of the ancient gods? Did man once meet intelligent beings who inspired respect and strive to resemble them, externally at least? Were the priests using a barbarous trick to conjure up the omnipotence attributed to the vanished figures with these highly individual head masks? Did the priests mean these oversize skulls to show that they were different from the common people and formed an elite? Possibly, for their rituals are supposed to have taken place in secret. If these unpleasant relics of a brutal past were confined to the territory of a *single* people, special religious reasons might lie behind the custom, but they are found in widely separated regions on different continents. Was skull deformation practised to imitate the heads of alien beings seen

I photographed these deformed skulls in the Museum of Ica. Have they anything to tell us?

by men when they visited the earth? Were deformed skulls intended to salvage something of the aura of the powerful masters in a distant future—at least visually? If only one of these questions could be answered affirmatively, these skulls could provide significant indications of the appearance of the extraterrestrials who blessed our forefathers with their presence in the very very distant past.

Professor Cabrera ended my meditations with warm torrential greetings in the best South American style. We drank a pisco sour and I showed him the photos of the hole-ridden band which ran through his homeland. He did not know it and was rather dubious when I assured him that it ran over hill and dale barely 100 km from Ica.

'In the Pisco valley? I know it well; I've flown over it many times. I know the Hacienda Montesierpe, too. But I've never seen this remarkable band,' Cabrera admitted.

He was still sceptical the next morning when we drove along the Panamericana to Pisco. Every time I drive through Pisco, my stomach rebels. Pisco stinks; I do not know any other town that sends up such noisome smells. A large fishing fleet is anchored in the harbour. The factories nearby are not manufacturing attar of roses, but malodorous fish manure. The 'aroma' of Pisco, a cloud of fish oil, also lingers loathsomely over the coast road. It reminded me of my childhood when my mother used to dose me with big spoonfuls of cod liver oil, because of the vitamins which children need for growth. Children are better off today; they swallow pleasant-tasting vitamin tablets. Hens are fed horrifying amounts of fish manure with the result that eggs and chicken meat taste fishy. In other parts of our humane world the idea of battery hens spoils my appetite for the chickens I once loved to eat, here the fish-hen smell did the trick.

It was a marvellous day with blue skies that raised my hopes of success. Four kilometres north of Pisco a rough road leads into the Pisco valley to Humay, then up into the high Andes to Castrovirreyna and Huancavelica. In the fields which are irrigated, fruit and vegetables thrive. The abrupt transition from desert to cultivated landscape and vice versa is consistently irritating. Rocky hills and sand dunes flanked the tortuous narrow road.

After 31 km we passed through the town of Humay and in

North of Pisco a dirt road leads into the Pisco valley and then upwards into the high Andes.

five minutes we reached the Hacienda Montesierpe. We drove into the courtyard, which had seen better days. The former seignorial house had been turned into cottages. There was also a church, the roof of which had fallen in, and small statues with their heads lying in the mud. Paintings fluttered from the walls of the big house and the church. After the first land reform under the then socialist military government, when the owners were driven out, everything of any value went to rack and ruin. Only the most essential things were repaired. The Indians are as badly off as before the revolution. An unjust regime was overthrown, another one of the same calibre assumed power and the sufferer was the little man.

Brown-skinned children with large dark eyes crowded round us, wearing dresses and trousers that were too large or too small. They were ragged and pitifully dirty. The revolution promised a new paradise. Nothing has changed. Once again all that happened was a transfer of power.

Professor Cabrera went into the house and I followed him.

He showed my photos to a fat woman who was seated at a spinning-wheel. Next to her there was a huge pile of oranges above which tattered brightly coloured shirts were drying on clothes lines.

Cabrera and the woman fired salvoes of words at each other that my limited Spanish could not follow. He came back and said that the matron did not know it and had never seen anything like it. I remember Carlos Milla, the architect, and his claim that I would find my goal only 300 m from this hacienda. Surely the lady, who had certainly never left the place in her life, ought to have known about it.

A broken-down tractor rattled into the yard. Cabrera went straight to the two men and asked for information. I kept in the background, reading what was said and thought from their faces. At long last one of the two tractor drivers indicated that he knew something. With an infinitely tired gesture he pointed to the mountains behind the hacienda. Without waiting for Cabrera's news, I shouldered my cameras.

The cultivated land behind the hacienda is only a strip of 250 m. One after the other, we climbed the first hill on a narrow path and checked the countryside around us, but there was no sign of the band with the holes. We panted on. The sun was beating down and the air was oppressive.

We took a break and sat down. The light was glaring, the sun stood perpendicularly above us and there was hardly any shade. Nowadays I have problems with my eyes; they often hurt and cannot stand bright light. I sometimes think that it started this midday when I strained to find contours, points of reference and small hints in the blinding light. My eyes smarted then as they do today when I sit at my desk and write by the bright lamplight. Sometimes the lines blur and flicker like the slopes of the hills and the verges of the desert.

Did my eyes deceive me? In the shimmering iridescent air black stripes stood out on the other side of the valley, a black snake which clung to the hills. I said nothing, but took the tele-objective and checked my observation. It confirmed what I had seen with my bare eyes. Somewhere out of the distant haze the band crept over hill and dale to end in the area of cultivated land in the Pisco valley. In my mind I built up a further piture of the formation. An extension of it ought

Dark stripes stood out in the shimmering air. The band crawled towards us from the distance.

to lead in our direction. I handed the tele-objective to Cabrera and indicated the point he was to look at. He saw what I saw, I was sure of that.

We had to climb very steeply to get a better look. We panted. We clambered on to the ridge of the mountain. To our right and left there were nothing but arid valleys, scree, shimmering air and yet more scree which you could not take your eyes off. We stumbled. Then I stumbled into the first hole of the dark band . . .

I knew at once that this was it!

Professor Cabrera, the sceptic, scratched the back of his sweaty head, stared at the ground and said, 'Erich, we're here!'

The hole I stumbled over was one metre deep and one metre in diameter. Next to it there were a second, a third and fourth hole, a veritable band pierced with holes that unfolded into the distance as far as the eye could see. I looked up,

When I stood before the first hole in the ground, I knew that we had reached my goal.

followed the route taken by the holes and saw it disappear far above beyond the mountains.

Five hundred metres above the hacienda we stood by the foremost row of holes. All the holes were empty, except for a little crumbled scree. They were simply there, just as in my first impression from the old photos, like an exact pattern impressed into the earth by a rolling-pin. We followed the trail of holes upward, climbing the mountain like weary warriors, but secretly glad to have reached our goal.

Every time we went a little higher, the holes changed. More and more often they were surrounded by stones. Sometimes we saw little walls piled up around them. On the ridge of the mountain every hole was enclosed by a wall. In an endless line the holes clung to the sloping sides of a valley like a snakeskin. It looked as if Indian pioneers, acting on orders, had simultaneously dug into the ground, side by side on a band 24m wide. There was room for a man in each hole.

Had it been a defence installation? That was the first ques-

We followed the band as far as the eye could see. There was no end to it; it was simply swallowed up by the haze.

tion that suggested itself. It must have been a gigantic army with a wide, open flank over hills and valleys. That runs counter to any kind of rational strategy. The soldiers could not have harmed the attackers if they were cooped up in holes in the ground. The course taken by the bank also refutes the assumption of a defence installation. If it covered only the tops of hills and mountains it could have fulfilled a purpose. From above—if there was anything to defend up there—the attackers, fighting uphill, would have had to show themselves; they would have been within the field of vision. Major defence works such as the Inca wall in Peru and the famous Great Wall of China dominate mountain ridges. Logically. Mediaeval knights planted their castles on mountain tops from which any enemy in the valley was visible. None of that applies here, because the band with the holes often clings to the slopes in the valleys in gentle elegant curves. If the holes had been one-man bunkers for defenders, they would often have been lower down than the onrushing enemy army.

So what purpose did the hundreds and thousands of holes fulfil? Clay soil which would have made digging child's play never existed here; the ground was always stony hard and dry. But why had men undertaken such strenuous work?

We crouched in the holes next to each other. We looked up the mountain and down into the valleys, following the band into the distance where the harsh shimmering heat haze swallowed it up.

Was it a burial place? It would be the only one in the world, laid out over many, many kilometres, whose graves were never discovered. Burial places always exhibit something that points to their purpose—memorial stones, the remains of bleached bones and funerary gifts. There was nothing up here to point in that direction.

Did the holes mark the territorial boundaries of some monarch or state? Even to primitive minds the cost of digging the holes would have been colossal. Stones placed next to each other would have served the purpose. Would men have also put boundary demarcations on the steep sides of valleys? Even a dictator, who forced his subjects to carry out this work, would have accepted the course of a river as a boundary. But the band with holes frequently runs along such slopes, now straight, now curved, an unparalleled infrastructure. It was certainly not a boundary line. So what was it?

Were signs set up here to form a line of signals? Can we imagine that on dark nights—on the birthday of a king or a priest—hundreds of thousands of Indians cowered in the holes and lit torches on the word of command? A chain of lights illuminated by the brilliance of the streets of Las Vegas? Come now, they did not need holes in the ground for that; all the Indians had to do was stand in line.

Are we dealing here with signs for the gods, as on the plain of Nazca, only 180 km to the south as the crow flies? Has the band as astronomically determined alignment? So far that has not been investigated. The old photographs from the *National Geographic* are forgotten, the band of holes is unknown. It is not mentioned in a single book. I am not sure whether the old photos slumber in the archives. Will they be given catalogue numbers and properly filed so that one day they may inspire a young unblinkered archaeologist to inquire into the mystery of the Andes? I lack the means to finance the necessary research, but at least I have prepared the way for the unknown inquirer. He no longer has to waste time looking for the goal, he can follow the stretch that I have described.

Just before I left Ica, Professor Cabrera informed me that for centuries the natives have called the band *la avenida misteriosa de las picaduras de viruelas*, the mysterious avenue of the pockmarks.

The avenue really is mysterious. As I myself am uncertain what it is that runs over hill and dale in Peru as a sign of the past, I ask for suggested solutions. I shall eagerly read any hypothesis that reaches me at this address: CH-4532 Feldbrunnen SO, Baselstrasse 10, Switzerland.

Twilight of the gods?

Photographic Credits

Erich von Däniken: Page Nos. 22, 24, 48, 50 (bottom), 51, 53, 64, 71, 73, 85, 87, 88, 90, 91, 138, 140 (top), 152, 161, 162, 172, 182, 183, 203, 204, 206, 216, 220, 222, 229, 231, 232, 233, 236, 237, 238, 239, 240, 242 (top and bottom left), 246, 249, 251, 252, 253

Colour Plate Nos. 1, 2, 4, 11, 13, 14, 15, 16, 17, 19, 20, 21, 23, 24, 25, 29, 30, 31, 32, 33, 34, 35

Enrico Mercurio: Page Nos. 18, 28, 33, 50 (top), 208

Colour Plate Nos. 3, 6, 7, 8, 10, 18

Willi Dünnenberger: Page Nos. 40, 44, 49, 179, 190

Colour Plate Nos. 5, 9, 12, 22

Professor de Aguilar: Page Nos. 140 (middle and bottom)

Dr Gene Phillips, Ancient Astronaut Society: Page Nos. 210, 211, 212, 213

W. Siebenhaar: Page Nos. 234, 242 (bottom right)

Andreas Faber-Kaiser: Colour Plate Nos. 26, 27, 28

Wide World: Page Nos. 196, 198

Bibliography

1 Journey to the Kiribatis

1. Grimble, Arthur, *A Pattern of Islands,* London, 1970
2. Grimble, Rosemary, *Migrations, Myth and Magic from the Gilbert Islands,* London–Boston, 1972
3. Tentoa, Tewareka, *This is Kiribati,* Curriculum Development Unit Offset, Tarawa, 1979
4. *Kiribati—Aspects of History,* Ministry of Education, Training and Culture, Tarawa, 1979
5. Aitken, Robert T., 'Ethnology of Tubuai', *Bishop Museum Bulletin* No. 70, Honolulu, 1930
6. Buck, Peter H., *Vikings of the Pacific,* Chicago, 1972
7. Handy Craighill, E. S., 'The Native Culture in the Marquesas', *Bernice P. Bishop Museum Bulletin,* No. 9, Honolulu, 1923
8. Handy Craighill, E. S., 'Polynesian Religion', *Bernice P. Bishop Museum Bulletin,* No. 34, Honolulu, 1927
9. Andersen, Johannes C., *Myths and Legends of the Polynesians,* Vermont–Tokyo, 1969
10. *Bild der Völker,* Band I, Die Bewohner der Gilbert- und Ellice-Inseln, ed. Dr John Klammer, Wiesbaden, undated
11. Turbott, I. G., 'The Footprints of Tarawa', *Journal of the Polynesian Society,* extract from Vol. 58, No. 4, December 1949, Wellington, New Zealand

2 For Some Reason or Other

1. Geoffrey, B., *Faustkeil und Bronzeschwert,* Hamburg, 1957
2. Atkinson, R. J. C., *What is Stonehenge?,* Department of the Environment, Crown Copyright, 1980
3. Hawkins, Gerald S., *Stonehenge Decoded,* New York, 1965
4. Atkinson, R. J. C., 'Moonshine on Stonehenge', *Antiquity* Vol. XL, 1966
5. Hoyle, Fred, 'Speculations on Stonehenge', *Antiquity* Vol. XL, 1966
   Hoyle, Fred, *'From Stonehenge to Modern Cosmology',* San Francisco, 1972
6. Thom, Alexander, *Megalithic Sites in Britain,* Clarendon Press, 1967
   Thom, Alexander, 'Megalithic Astronomy', *The Journal of Navigation,* Vol. 30 No. 1, 1977
7. Paturi, Felix R., *Zeugen der Vorzeit,* Düsseldorf, 1976
8. Grimm, Rudolf, 'Geheimnisvolles Stonehenge', *Prager Volkszeitung,* 11 April 1980
   Grimm, Rudolf, 'Im Süden Englands steht ein "Computer" der Steinzeit', *Weser-Kurier,* 4 October 1979
9. Krupp, Edwin C., *In Search of Ancient Astronomies,* Chatto & Windus, London, 1980
10. Strempel, Edwin C., 'Das Steinerne Rätsel von Stonehenge', *PM-Magazin,* No. 2, 1980

11. SOFAER/ZINSER/SINCLAIR, 'A unique solar marking construct', *Science*, Vol. 206, 19 October 1979
12. CHADWICK, N., *The Celts*, London, 1970
13. ELIOT, Alexander and others, *Mythen der Welt*, Zürich, 1978
14. CAMP, L. S. de, *Citadels of History*, Souvenir Press, London, 1966
15. ROBINS, G. V., 'The Dragon Stirs', *Alpha*, London, July/August 1979
16. ROBINS, L. V., *The Rollright Stones and Their Folklore*, Guernsey, 1977
17. 'Archäometrie—Physiker schreiben die Geschichte neu', *Bild der Wissenschaft*, No. 7, 1978
18. TOPPER, Uwe, *Das Erbe der Giganten*, Olten, 1977
19. HOMET, Marcel F., *Nabel der Welt—Wiege der Menschheit*, Freiburg, 1976
20. BUCK, P. H., 'The Rangi Hiroa, Ethnology of Tongareva', *Bernice P. Bishop Museum Bulletin*, No. 92, Honolulu, 1932
21. WARWICK-TRUMP, *Lexikon der Archäologie*, Bd 1 and 2, Hamburg, 1975
22. BURL, Aubrey, *Rings of Stone*, Frances Lincoln/Weidenfeld & Nicolson, London, 1979
23. 'Our World of Mysteries', *Radio Times*, London, August 1980
24. CHARPENTIER, Louis, *Das Geheimnis der Basken*, Olten, 1977
25. WERNICK, Robert, *Steinerne Zeugen früher Kulturen*, Hamburg, 1977

General:
Lübbes Enzyklopädie der Archäologie, ed. Daniel-Rehork, Bergisch-Gladbach, 1980
ZANOT, Mario, *Die Welt ging dreimal unter*, Vienna, 1976
CLES-REDEN, Sybille von, *Die Spür der Zyklopen*, Cologne, 1960
BRUCE, Cathie, *The Pulse of the Universe*, Wellington, 1977
BORD, Volin and Janet, *Mysterious Britain*, London, 1974
RIESENFELD, A., *The Megalithic Culture of Melanesia*, Leyden, 1950

3 Mind: the Fundamental Basis of All Matter

1. ARBER, Werner, 'Wie die Schöpfung hier und jetzt weiterwirkt', *Basler Zeitung*, 21 June 1980
2. ILLIES, Joachim, 'König Wissenschaft, der neue Tyrann', *Die Welt*, 18 June 1980
3. THÜRKAUF, Max, 'Der Primat des Geistes', *Esotera*, February 1980
4. CHARGAFF, Erwin, 'Der Teufel steigt von der Wand', *Der Spiegel*, No. 39, 1980
5. CHARON, Jean E., *Der Geist der Materie*, Vienna-Hamburg, 1979
6. WILDER-SMITH, A. E., *Grundlage zu einer neuen Biologie*, Stuttgart, 1974
7. CHARON, Jean E., *Théorie de la relativité complexe*, Paris, 1977
8. TAYLOR, John G., *Black Holes: The End of the Universe?*, Souvenir Press, London, 1973
9. BREUER, Reinhard, 'Schwarzes Loch im Zentrum der Milchstrasse', *Bild der Wissenschaft*, November 1977
10. KIPPENHAHN, Rudolf, *100 Milliarden Sonnen*, Munich, 1980
11. GARANGER, José, *Sacred Stones and Rites of Ancient Tahiti*, Paris, 1979
12. ZIEHR, Wilhelm, *Hölle im Paradies*, Düsseldorf, 1980
13. AITKEN, Robert T., 'Ethnology of Tubuai', *Bishop Museum Bulletin*, No. 70, Honolulu, 1930
14. BIEDERMANN, Hans, 'Magnetische Dickbäuche in Guatemala', *Universum*, No. 3, 1980
15. ECKERT, Michael, 'Magnetsinn des Menschen?', *Süddeutsche Zeitung*, 23 October 1980

General:
FORD, Arthur, *Unknown but Known*, Psychic Press, London, 1969
DETHLEFSEN, Thorwald, *Das Leben nach dem Tode*, Munich, 1974
BERNSTEIN, Morey, *Protokoll einer Wiedergeburt*, Berne, 1973

4 Chasing Little Green Men (and Canards)

1. Gris, Henry, 'Is There a Dead Ship from Outer Space?', *Rand Daily Mail,* South Africa, 20 August 1979
2. 'Scientists Discover Damaged Alien Spacecraft Is in Orbit around Earth', *National Enquirer,* Lantana, Florida, August 1979
3. Extract from Henry Gris's taped interview with Professor Bozhich and others, EvD's archives
4. Bagby, John P., 'Terrestrial Satellites: Some Direct and Indirect Evidence', *Icarus,* No. 10, 1969
5. Letter from Professor Harry O. Ruppe to EvD, 10 January 1980
6. Letter from Jesco von Puttkamer, NASA, to EvD, 28 January 1980
7. Letter from Professor Frank D. Drake, Director of the National Astronomy and Ionosphere Centre, Arecibo, to EvD, 12 January 1980
8. Will, Wolfgang, 'Brachten "Bomben" aus dem Weltall das Leben auf die Erde?', *Die Welt,* 11 January 1980
9. Lahav, Ephraim, 'Kam Adam aus dem Weltall?', *Die Welt,* 25 June 1980
10. 'Kalte Dusche für die grünen Männchen', *Weltwoche-Magazin,* Zürich, 1980
11. Abarzua/Posselt, 'In Gräbern aus uralter Zeit: Tote von anderen Sternen', *Bild,* 29 April 1975
12. Chavez, Mauro, 'Seres de otro mundo en manta?', *Vistazo,* Mexico
13. 'Um psiquiatrano terreiro', *Gente,* 24 December 1979
14. 'El esqueleto de Panama', *Mundo Desconocido,* May 1979
15. Letter from the Swiss Embassy to EvD, 4 March 1980
16. Letter from the Swiss Embassy to EvD, 7 May 1980
17. Letter from the Swiss Embassy to EvD, 6 June 1980
18. Krassa, Peter, *Phantome des Schreckens—Die Herren in Schwarz manipulieren die Welt,* Vienna, 1980
19. 'Kannten die Inkas das Diamanten-Geheimnis?', *Bremer Nachrichten,* 5 June 1980
20. Möller, Gerd and Elfriede, *Peru,* Pforzheim, 1980
21. 'Archäologie um La Silla', *Sterne und Weltraum,* 1980/4

5 In the Promised Land?

1. Kautzsch, Emil, *Die Apokryphen und Pseudepigraphen des Alten Testaments,* Vol. II, Book of Enoch, Tübingen, 1900
2. *The Queen of Sheba and Her Only Son Menyelek* (*Kebra Nagast*), translated by Sir E. A. Wallis Budge, London, 1932
3. Stoll, Heinrich A., *Die Höhle am Toten Meer,* Hanau-Main, 1962
4. Dupont-Sommer, André, *Die Essenischen Schriften vom Toten Meer,* Paris, 1959
5. Burrows, Millar, *More Light on the Dead Sea Scrolls,* London, 1958
6. Philo, Judaeus Alexandrinus, *Works,* 12 vols., Loeb Classical Library, Heinemann, London, 1929
7. Josephus, Flavius, *Works,* 2 vols., Chatto & Windus, London, 1875
8. 'New Proofs of Preastronautics', Lectures at the Congress of the Ancient Astronaut Society, Munich, 1979, Rastatt, 1979
9. Davenport, David W., *2000 AC Distruzione Atomica,* Milan, 1979
10. Bharadwaaja, Maharishi, *Vymaanika-Shaastra Aeronautics,* translated into English and edited, printed and published by G. R. Josyer, Mysore, India, 1979

General:

Faber-Kaiser, Andreas, *Jesus Died in Kashmir—Jesus, Moses and the Ten Lost Tribes of Israel,* London, 1977

6 Twilight of the Gods

1. GREENE, Merle, *Maya Sculpture,* Berkeley, 1972
2. WUTHENAU, Alexander von, *Unexpected Faces in Ancient America*
3. TSCHUDI, Johann Jakob von, *Reisen durch Sudamerika,* Leipzig, 1869
4. ALCINO, José, *Die Kunst des alten Amerika,* Freiburg, 1979
5. CIECA DE LEÓN, Pedro, *La Cronica del Peru,* Antwerp, 1554
6. DE CASTRO/DEL CASTILLO, *Teatro Eclesiástico de las Iglesias de Peru y Nueva España,* Madrid, 1651
7. D'ORBIGNY, *Alcide, Voyage dans l'Amérique Méridionale,* Paris, 1844
8. STINGL, Miloslaw, *Die Inkas,* Düsseldorf, 1978
9. STÜBEL A. and UHLE, M., *Die Ruinenstätte von Tiahuanaco im Hochland des alten Peru,* Leipzig, 1892
10. HUBER, Siegfried, *Im Reich der Inka,* Olten, 1976
11. DE LA VEGA, Garcilaso, *Primera Parte de los Comentarios Reales,* Madrid, 1723, and *Historia General del Peru, Segunda Parte,* Madrid, 1722
12. UBBELOHDE-DÖRING, Heinrich, *Kulturen Alt-Perus,* Tübingen, 1966
13. DINGWALL, E. J., *Artificial Cranial Deformation,* London, 1931

General:

MÖLLER, Gerd and Elfriede, *Goldstadt-Reiseführer Peru,* Pforzheim, 1976

'Tiahuanaco oder die Schweigenden Steine', from 'Die letzten Geheimnisse unserer Welt', *Das Beste*

HELFRITZ, Hans, *Südamerika: Präkolumbianische Hochkulturen,* Cologne, undated

KENNEDY-SKIPTON, R., *Bild der Völker,* Band 5, Südamerike, Wiesbaden, undated

KUBLER, George, *The Art and Architecture of Ancient America,* Harmondsworth, 1962

Index

Abaiang Island 13, 32 *et seq.*, 41
Aguilar, Prof. Ramón de 135, 138–140
Air Nauru 17, 18, 20, 21, 66
Aitken, Robert 57
Amaranganasutradhara 181
Ancient Astronaut Society 15, 179, 195
Antebuka, village 62
Aomata 12
Arahurahu 111
Arber, Prof. Werner 101
Archaeoastronomy 78 *et seq.*
Ardashir Khurra 150
Arorae Island 47 *et seq.*, 61
Astronauts 37
Astronomers, Stone Age 77
Atkinson, Prof. 75 *et seq.*
Atolls 23, 41
Atu Ona Island 55
Aubrey Holes 74, 76, 77
Aubrey, John 74, 75
Auckland 17 *et seq.*
Auriaria light 36
Aveni, Anthony 78
Avinski, Dr Vladimir Ivanovich 78, 99
Azhazha, Dr Vladimir Georgeyvich 118

Bagby, John P. 119 *et seq.*, 122
Baiiri library 38
Bai Matoa 55
Bairiki, village 35 *et seq.*, 38
Baker, Robert E. 115
Banaba Island 22, 65
Biedermann, Dr Hans 113
Big Bang theory 105
Black body radiation 104 *et seq.*
Black holes 105–108
Black Stone 96
Bluestones 73 *et seq.*
Botosha, Dr Kamil 149
Bozhich, Prof. Sergei Petrovich 117 *et seq.*
Braun, Wernher von 111, 124
Breuer, Reinhard 106
Brownlee, Don E. 128
Burl, Aubrey 90
Burrows, Prof. Millar 176
Butler, Gil 34, 44, 47, 66
Bwere 25–33, 67

Cabrera, Prof. Dr Janvier 245, 249–250, 252, 255
Calcutta 80 *et seq.*
Cape Town 11, 52
Cardiff University Archaeology Department 75
Caroline Islands 26
Carranza, Colonel Omar Chioini 199, 214–217, 243, 244
Chang, Sherwood 127, 128

Chargaff, Prof. Erwin 102
Charles II, King 74
Charon, Jean E. 102, 104 *et seq.*, 109, 115
Charpentier, Louis 100
Chioini *see* Carranza
Clarke, Arthur C. 96–97
Collins, Mr 143
Conant, James Briant 125
Coral islands 13, 23
Cosmic system 109
Crick, Francis C. 110
Croiset, Gérard 110
Cuca, ruins 143 *et seq.*
Curie, Marie 58
Cybele 95

Davenport, David W. 183
Drake, Prof. Frank 124
Druidical temple 75
Druids 75
Dünnenberger, Willi 15, 49, 153
Dupont-Sommer, Prof. André 176

Eddington, Arthur 111
Eddy, John A. 78
Egger, Friedrich 211
Einstein, Albert 69, 104, 107, 109, 115
Ellice Islands 52
Elsässer, Prof. Hans 127
Enoch, the prophet 164 *et seq.*, 179
Equator 18, 21
Eritaia, Reverend 15, 25, 26
Etana 39
Ethnologists 39, 52, 57
Evolution theory 80, 90
Ezekiel, the prophet 9

Faber-Kaiser, Andreas 133 *et seq.*
Faraday, Michael 61
Feynman, Prof. Richard Phillips 107–108
Fiji Islands 14, 52
Fixed stars 14, 52
Flavius Josephus 177
Flying machines 179 *et seq.*, 186 *et seq.*

Genetic code 110–111
Geoffrey of Monmouth 83
Gilav, Prof. Emmanuel 128
Gilbert Islands 12, 14
Gods-astronauts theory 36
Grimble, Arthur 27, 36, 38

Hässig, Dr Rosina 57
Hassnain, Prof. Dr F. M. 170–175, 178
Hawaiian Islands 52, 56
Hawkins, Gerald 76, 78
Hegglin, Father 57
Helmholtz, Herman Ludwig Ferdinand von 127
Homet, Prof. Marcel 92
Hoyle, Sir Fred 77
Huber, Siegfried 224

Illies, Prof. Joachim 101
Incas 143, 197
Indonesia 27
Iran 150, 192–193
Ireland 70, 83, 96
Israelites 164

Jacob 93 *et seq.*, 98
James I, King 74
Jesus 168 *et seq.*, 176 *et seq.*

Jo, god of creation 56
Jones, Inigo 74

Kaaba 96
Kamoriki, Reverend 15 *et seq.*, 21, 23, 25, 29
Kanjilal, Prof. Dr Dileep Kumar 179
Karitoro 36, 37
Karongoa sun clan 27
Kashmir legend 163
Kashmir valley 162 *et seq.*, 175
Kausitaki 180
Kebra Nagast 167
Kei-Ani, Mount 55
Kippenhahn, Prof. Rudolf 108
Kiribati Islands 11–67
Krupp, Edwin C. 78 *et seq.*
Ky kau akahi, the god 56

Landing place of the gods 13
Lavoisier, Antoine Laurent 144
Le Paige, Gustavo 132–135
Life, first form of 28
Lockyer, Sir Joseph Norman 75

Magnetic fields 114–116
Mana 112–113
Maneaba 33, 47, 48
Maoris 54
Marae 111 *et seq.*
Matinaba 55
Maui, the god 55, 113
Maya steles 209
Maya temple 209
Megalithic structures 72, 80, 97
Megalithic yard 73, 78
Megaliths 69
Mercurio, Rico 16, 49
Merlin, the magician 82 *et seq.*
Micromondes 120
Micronesia 14, 27
Milla, Carlos 215, 243–244, 250
Mohenjo Daro 183–184
Molecular genetics 101
Monod, Jacques 130
Monolithic circles 74
Monoliths 42, 51, 67 *et seq.*, 111, 218 *et seq.*
Monte Alban 206
Mormons 28
Moses 163–164, 171
Muhammed, the prophet 96
Mythology 25 *et seq.*, 54

Nareau, the god 35 *et seq.*, 67
NASA 122, 124
Nauru 14, 18 *et seq.*
Nauru Phosphate Corporation 19
Nei Tewenei 36
Neolithic era 72, 82
New Guinea 35
New Zealand 15, 17, 52
Nirahi ni Karawa 39
Niutao Island 52

Observatory, Stone Age 77 *et seq.*
O'Keefe, Dr John 122
Otintai Hotel 21, 26, 29, 58

Panamericana 245
Papin, Denis 168
Paturi, Felix R. 78
Pembrokeshire 75
Pentagram 78
Peru 197 *et seq.*
Phillips, Dr Gene 199, 209
Photon drive 37
Photons 108
Pisco, valley 244, 245, 248, 250

Planck, Max 116
Polymers 128
Prehistoric era 69
Prehistoric seafarers 52
Pulsars 106
Puma Punku, ruins 218, 219, 221, 223–233, 237, 243
Puttkamer, Jesco von 122, 124
Pythagoras, theorem 74
Pythia 95, 98–99

Raiatea Island 111
Raivavae Island 55
Rauzabal Khanyar 178
Rigveda 180
Robins, Dr G. V. 84, 86–89
Roche limit 124
Ruppe, Prof. Dr Harry O. 122

Sacsayhuanan 235 *et seq.*
Sadducees 177
Salisbury 69, 70
Samoan Islands 39, 54, 56
Sänger, Prof. Eugen 37
Sanskrit 178; book 175; texts 178, 180 *et seq.*; tradition 176
Sassanids 150
Satapatha Brahmana 180
Satellites: artificial 120, 123, 127; geostationary 120; terrestrial 119
Scarborough, Reverend C. 11, 12, 14, 25, 32, 40, 43, 45, 48, 52, 63, 66
Schwarzschild, Karl 107
Schwarzschild radius 107
Scotland 69
Shaw, G. B. 116
Shlovski, Prof. J. S. 129 *et seq.*
Sikhs 188
Silicate 86
Sinai Desert 163
Skylab 163
Society Islands 55
Solar Energy 181
Solomon, King 167 *et seq.*
Solstices, summer and winter 73, 77, 81
Srinagar 167, 168, 176, 178
Stone circles: Ain es Zerka 92; Ajun-uns-Rass 92; Australian 92; Avebury 70, 74; Balquhain and Loanhead of Daviot 70; Brahmagiri 92; Brodgar and Stenness 67; Castlerigg 70; Cullerie and Sunhoney 70; Garynahine 69; Gilgal 92; Lios 70; Msoura 92; New Grange 70; Nioro du Rip 92; Old Keig 70; Portela de Mogos 92; Quebrada 92; Sillustani 92; Stanton Drew 70; Swinside 70; Temple Wood 70
Stonehenge 69, 70, 72 *et seq.*, 90, 99
Stone sculptures 203
Stübel, Alphons 223
Supernova 106

Ta'aroa, god of creation 55
Taboo circle 41
Taboo zones 57, 58
Tabuariki, the giant 65
Tabunia 13
Tagaloa, the god 56
Tamana Island 45
Tarawa Island 13, 14, 15, 16, 23, 45, 57 *et seq.*
Taylor, John 106
Te Aba-n-Anti 65
Tebanga, village 42

Te Bomatemaki 35
Te Bongi Ro, legend 55, 65
Te I-matang 12
Te Kananrabo 65
Technology, extraterrestrial 118, 230
Teeta 29–30, 34–35, 58–67
Tepe 24, 32
Tepe Yahya 150, 192
Thermoluminescence, analysis by 86 *et seq.*
Thom, Dr Alexander 75, 78, 79 *et seq.*, 99
Thürkauf, Prof. Max 102
Tiahuanaco 218, 234, 235
Tikal 207
Tinirau 54
Tonga Islands 54
Trilithons 77
Tuamotu Islands 52, 233
Tubuai Island 113

UFOs 125
Uhle, Max 221 *et seq.*
UN 129
Universe 35

Vaimanika Sastra 181
Velikovski, Immanuel 79
Vimana 181

Ward, Captain 15 *et seq.*
Watson, J. D. 110
Watt, Dr Robin 52–54
Wernick, Robert 100
Wilder-Smith, A. E. 102
Wolman, Prof. Yeheskel 128 *et seq.*

Yajurveda 180
Yuz Asaf (Yusu) 173, 175

Ziehr, Wilhelm 112
Zolotov, Prof. Alexei Vasilievich 119

Ancient Astronaut Society
World Headquarters
1921 St Johns Avenue
Highland Park
Illinois 60035
USA
Telephone: (312) 432-6230

Dear Reader,

Last but not least, may I introduce to you the Ancient Astronaut Society, abbreviated to AAS. It is a tax-exempt, non-profit membership society. It was founded in the USA in 1973. It now has members in more than 50 countries.

The Society's objective is the collection, exchange and publication of evidence tending to support and confirm the following theories:

The earth received a visit from outer space in prehistoric times . . . (or)
The present technical civilisation on our planet is not the first . . . (or)
A combination of both theories.

Membership of the AAS is open to everybody. A newsletter for members is published in English and German every two months. The AAS takes part in the organisation of expeditions and study journeys to archaeological and other sites of importance for the proof of the theory. A world congress takes place every year. Previous congresses were held in Chicago (1974), Zürich (1975), Crikvenica, Yugoslavia (1976), Rio de Janeiro (1977), Chicago (1978), Munich (1979), Auckland, New Zealand (1980), Vienna (1982).

Please write directly to the Society for membership information and a free copy of the Society's newsletter *Ancient Skies*.

Most sincerely,
Erich von Däniken

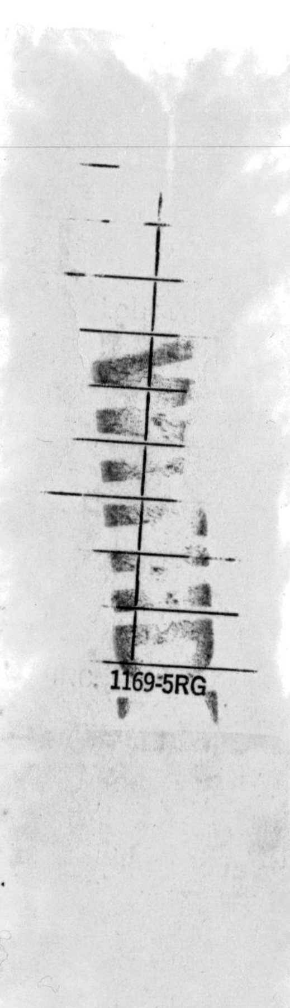